Riding the Indian Tiger

RIDING THE INDIAN TIGER

UNDERSTANDING INDIA—THE WORLD'S FASTEST GROWING MARKET

William Nobrega
Ashish Sinha

WILEY
wiley.com

Times Group Books

Riding the Indian Tiger
Understanding India—The World's Fastest Growing Market

Authorised reprint by Wiley India Pvt. Ltd., 4435-36/7, Ansari Road, Daryaganj, New Delhi-110002.

Marketed and distributed exclusively in India by

Times Group Books
(A division of Bennett, Coleman and Company Limited)
Times Annexe, Express Building 9-10
Bahadur Shah Zafar Marg, New Delhi - 110002

Published by John Wiley & Sons, Inc., Hoboken, New Jersey.

Reprint: 2009

Printed at: *Delhi Press, New Delhi*

ISBN : 978-81-265-2043-5

CONTENTS

PREFACE

This book is about the new India, not the old. Economically, India has not mattered much for the past 40 years or so. It has long been a travel destination, but from a business perspective, who cares if you have a billion customers with no money to spend! But now that the world has witnessed the economic rise of China and sees India on a similar path, and Indian entrepreneurs are making bold moves on the global stage, the "new India" is on everyone's radar.

The international media and business community are beginning to take notice, but unfortunately, much that has been written recently has either focused on political issues, such as Hindu nationalism, or social issues, like rural poverty, or the sorry state of the Indian infrastructure. What the media has overlooked is the important ways the infrastructure is improving and what that means for business. What about India's capital markets and a rising middle class? How will those factors impact business opportunities? And what about India's democratic institutions, which we believe will give the country a long-term advantage over China's authoritarian model?

We wrote this book to give businesspeople and other interested readers an exciting look at "new India." If you are a business executive, investment banker, investor, or entrepreneur, and you think that the third largest economy in the world might translate into opportunity, then you should read this book. If you are a politician, student, or academic, and you think that the world's largest democracy might be worth taking a closer look at, then you should read this book. If you are a citizen of the planet Earth and you are curious to know how the world's fastest-growing market and second most populous nation will impact your life—this book is for you.

INTRODUCTION

THE HISTORY OF INDIA IN EIGHT PAGES

FROM COLONIALISM TO SOCIALISM TO VIBRANT CAPITALISM

Imagine living in a country in which it took 10 years to receive permission to buy a car, 8 years to receive permission to buy a motorcycle, or 11 years to get a license for a phone line for your apartment. A country where a license was required to purchase three bags of cement or two gallons of milk. Now imagine that as a citizen of that country you wanted to travel abroad and the only restriction placed on your travel was the fact that you were only permitted to exchange $200 in foreign currency during any 24-month period (not exactly enough for an around-the-world cruise!) A country where licenses became more valuable than the underlying commodity or service that they were meant to authorize; a country whose government failed to provide clean drinking water or basic sanitation for more than half of the population! No, I'm not taking about the Soviet Union or some other eastern European communist dictatorship. This was India in 1987, 20 short years ago. It was a country in which the government had shackled the economy and the creativity of the people. To understand how and why this level of government interference and control emerged in the world's most populous democracy—and to fully understand how far the country has come since—requires a short journey through India's history.

On a hot day in July, 1497, the Portuguese explorer Vasco da Gama, a ruthless profiteer by almost any standard, left Lisbon with four ships on a quest to find a sea route to India. At the time, India was one of the wealthiest countries in the world, the source of valuable commodities, including spices, semiprecious stones, silks, and other exotic goods that could be sold at great profit in Europe. With a crew of 170 men, ten of whom were convicted killers whose death sentences had been commuted for what was a suicidally dangerous mission, da Gama sailed around the Cape of Good Hope and arrived in India on May 20th, 1498, 11 months later. He was hardly prepared for his first encounter with India, failing to understand that he would be dealing with a sophisticated culture that controlled considerable wealth. As a result, he had failed to bring the gold, silver and other valued material that successful trade would require. Departing India with a limited cargo of spices, his business venture was not looking good. By the time he returned to Lisbon in 1499 he had lost 116 members of his original crew from disease, malnutrition, and murder. The small quantity of spices that he returned with was sold for a profit of 3000 percent—however, by all accounts the trip was still considered to be a disaster.

Despite this, the king of Portugal organized a second expedition, with thirteen ships under the command of Pedro Alvarez Cabral. After veering off course and accidentally discovering Brazil, Cabral continued on to India. Although he carried gold and other valuable trade goods, Cabral was unable to do business with the local Calicut merchants; He and his men were finally driven out of the city after local Muslims rioted and killed many of his men. Cabral had greater success at another Indian city, Cochin, and returned to Portugal with a very valuable cargo of spices. The Portuguese had successfully opened up a new trade route to India, and the implications of their actions would carry well into the twentieth century. The enclave of Goa, on the west coast of India, was annexed by Portugal in 1510, and remained in Portuguese control until it was retaken by force by the Indian government in 1961. Even today, the Indian government still honors the soldiers that fought in that short battle with Western colonizers.

Not to be outdone by the Portuguese, England's Queen Elizabeth, under pressure from the powerful British mercantile establishment, created the East India Trading Company on December 31, 1600. Twelve years later, four British galleons defeated the Portuguese at the naval battle of Swally, gaining the good graces of the Indian Mughal Emperor Jahangir in the process. Jahangir was a flamboyant ruler who was quite popular with his subjects. Fortunately for the British, he was also an alcoholic, and the story is that he signed over trading concessions to the British during one of his many drinking binges.

By the mid-1600s, the East India Company had established trading posts and factories in major Indian cities, including Bombay, Calcutta, and Madras. In 1670, King Charles II granted the company incredibly broad powers to acquire territory, raise an army, mint its own money, and exercise legal jurisdiction over areas under its control. By the end of the seventeenth century the foundation for the British colonization of India had been laid. (Recently, in a final symbol of the *end* of British colonialism, a wealthy Indian businessman bought the name, title, and crest of the East India Company so that he could create a distinctly Indian line of high-end clothing, furnishings, and accessories!)

While the British wanted to expand mercantile trade with their colonies they also had a desire to impart the British way of life, believing that they were following in the tradition of the Roman empire. Some of the loftier concepts they wanted to integrate into the social fabric of the country included private property, the rule of law, Western education, and the liberty of the individual. Unfortunately for India, the British gave very little attention to these nobler aspects of colonization during the first 150 years of rule. Instead, they focused on profits and power. This they did with great success. Many historical economists believe that India accounted for 25 percent of the world's GDP in 1800.

At the turn of the nineteenth century, Governor General Lord Wellesley took the "profits and power" mantra to a new level and began expanding British dominence in India on a large scale. He defeated Tipu Sultan, annexed Mysore in southern India, and removed all French influence from the subcontinent. In the mid-nineteenth century, Governor-General Lord Dalhousie continued this expansion of British power, defeating the Sikhs in the Anglo-Sikh wars and annexing Punjab. He also justified the takeover of small princely states such as Satara, Sambalpur, Jhansi, and Nagpur under the guise of the doctrine of "lapse," which permitted the British to annex any princely state whose ruler had died without a male heir.

For the Indian people this was the last straw. Having tasted enough of the British "civilizing influence," soldiers of the British Indian Army, known as Sepoys, mutinied in Meerut, a fort 80 kilometers northeast of Delhi, on May 10, 1857. The war raged for over a year, with numerous instances of heroism and compassion on the part of the Indian soldiers. In fact, on several occasions Indian soldiers escorted British noncombatants to safety. The British did not share the same sense of chivalry, often bayoneting the inhabitants of entire villages on vague accusations of collaboration. Indian prisoners were strapped to British cannons and blown to bits during countless summary executions. Even veterans of the British military were shocked by the level of ruthlessness displayed by British troops.

On July 8th, 1858, after a year of vicious combat, the Indian forces were finally defeated and a peace treaty was signed, ending the war. British rule would last for another ninety years but the die was cast. What the British sought to deride as a mere "Sepoy mutiny" is now viewed by India as its First War of Independence, when people from all walks of life, irrespective of their caste, creed, religion, or language, rose against British rule. The 150th anniversary of the war was recently celebrated throughout India with elaborate commemorations.

The British were shaken by the war and the tenacity of their Indian opponents, and immediately began introducing reforms they hoped would reduce resentment to their rule. The new British viceroy to India stopped land grabs, decreed religious tolerance, and admitted Indians into civil service. British reforms now began in earnest, with the establishment of a judicial system that transformed Hindu law into a form of English case law and that ensured property rights for the individual and provided protection of the individual. Western-style education was aggressively developed, with the belief that it would help enable the efficient administration of India by a local educated elite, loyal to the dictates of the British Crown.

The British pushed the development of a laissez-faire economy that was based on the free circulation of capital, productive enterprise, and large-scale production. They made large-scale investments in infrastructure, leading to the development of what would become the second largest rail system in the world. The rail lines stimulated the growth of local industrial development, which laid the foundation for capitalist enterprise and the growth of an Indian business class. By the end of the First World War the British had moved toward the development of self-governing institutions with freely elected individuals in all departments of the Indian government. Significantly, there was also a free press—a cornerstone of any modern democracy. Evidence of British rule is everywhere in India, with parts of Mumbai reminiscent of an English town—replete with a university, government buildings, and a library. Even the old-style British club remains—but it's now home to India's entrepreneurs.

The aggressive pace of reforms and the development of modern democratic institutions only fueled the Indian public's desire for independence. Under Jawaharlal Nehru and Mahatma Gandhi the freedom movement gained momentum, and calls for independence from Great Britain grew louder. The outbreak of World War II did nothing to dampen Indian aspirations for independence, and in August 1942 the Quit India Resolution was passed by the Bombay session of the All India Congress.

Among Indian patriots were many who did not share Gandhi's philosophy of nonviolent resistance. Chandra Bose, twice president of the Indian National Congress, came to the conclusion that the British would never quit India voluntarily, and argued for war against the British colonizers. "If people slap you once, slap them twice." In many ways Bose was much more representative of India than Gandhi—tough, independent, and willing to fight against incredible odds—traits that are clearly evident in India today. During World War II the British placed him under house arrest. With the help of his brother and a fast car he escaped and made a daring journey to safety in Japan. His harrowing story included British assassination attempts and a transfer in the Pacific Ocean from a German U-boat to a Japanese submarine. Bose eventually created the Indian National Army (INA), with the sole aim of ending British colonial rule.

At the peak of its strength the INA had over 85,000 soldiers and the only female combat brigade ever fielded in Asia. The INA fought hard in the forests of Assam, Bengal, and Burma, but, owing to disrupted logistics, a lack of training, and inadequate arms and supplies, they ultimately failed in their effort. However, Bose's heroic actions energized a new generation of Indians. By August 14, 1947, the British had seen the writing on the wall, and independence was granted to India. India, the largest democracy the world had ever seen, stood in stark contrast to her neighbor to the north, China. The rule of law, private property, religious freedom, a free press, individual liberty, and a respect for education, although elitist in nature, offered enormous potential for a country and economy that had been exploited by British rule.

Flush with independence, Indian leaders still appeared intent on snatching defeat from the jaws of victory. Choosing to follow Gandhi and his disdain for modernization and the values it upheld, the government leadership decided to follow a village-centric model of self-sufficiency. The result was one step forward for independence and two steps backward for the future of India. However, it was the first prime minister of India, Jawaharlal Nehru, who put the final nail in the coffin of India's economic growth, modernization, and global competitiveness for the next 40 years. Nehru, who had received the finest British education available at the time, was a socialist and a fan of Joseph Stalin. His belief, shared by many leading economists of the time, was that the government should drive industrialization and control the economy. This approach culminated in the infamous "License Raj" and created the basis for an economy that grew at a snail's pace. It also stifled innovation and the entrepreneurial spirit and kept hundreds of millions of Indians in a state of abject poverty. At the height of its lunacy the "license regime" required permits for just about anything, until the licenses became more important than the underlying products or services that they permitted.

While his economic and agricultural policies were an unmitigated disaster, Nehru was more successful helping to create world-class institutes, including the Indian Institute of Management and the Indian Institute of Technology. These have been instrumental in creating a generation of talented professors, engineers, and entrepreneurs who have been the frontrunners of India's economic revolution. Many of them have also played leading roles in the United States in Silicon Valley.

It is worthwhile to note that at roughly the same time in history, China was going through a much more brutal type of economic and social engineering. Chairman Mao Tse-Dong took the Chinese people through the Cultural Revolution, which decimated almost every aspect of Chinese society and economy and resulted in the deaths of an estimated 30 million people from malnutrition and forced labor.

By 1991, after years of centralized economic planning, India stood on the brink of bankruptcy. Dramatic increases in the price of oil, caused by the Gulf War, wiped out its limited foreign currency reserves, driving the country further into despair. That sense of desperation helped drive the economic reforms that continue to gather momentum today.

From an historical perspective, the pain of British colonization and the subsequent agony of economic mismanagement by the early post-colonial Indian government only served to strengthen the depth and breadth of the Indian democracy. In 1991, over 57 percent of the 600 million registered voters voted in the general election, compared to just 49 percent of the eligible population that voted in the 2004 United States presidential election. Of all the Indian voters that cast their ballots, over 50 percent were women. By UN standards, India's elections are some of the most transparent in the world, and electoral fraud is minimal—and unlike the United States, no recent national election has been contested.

This brings us to the end of our story—or rather, the beginning. The Indian people have only recently been released from the economic shackles and social experiments that previously stifled the vibrant economic entrepreneurial spirit that is at the heart of India. You happen to be at a unique time and place in history—able to witness and perhaps participate in one of the greatest economic expansions that the world has ever seen.

RIDING THE INDIAN TIGER

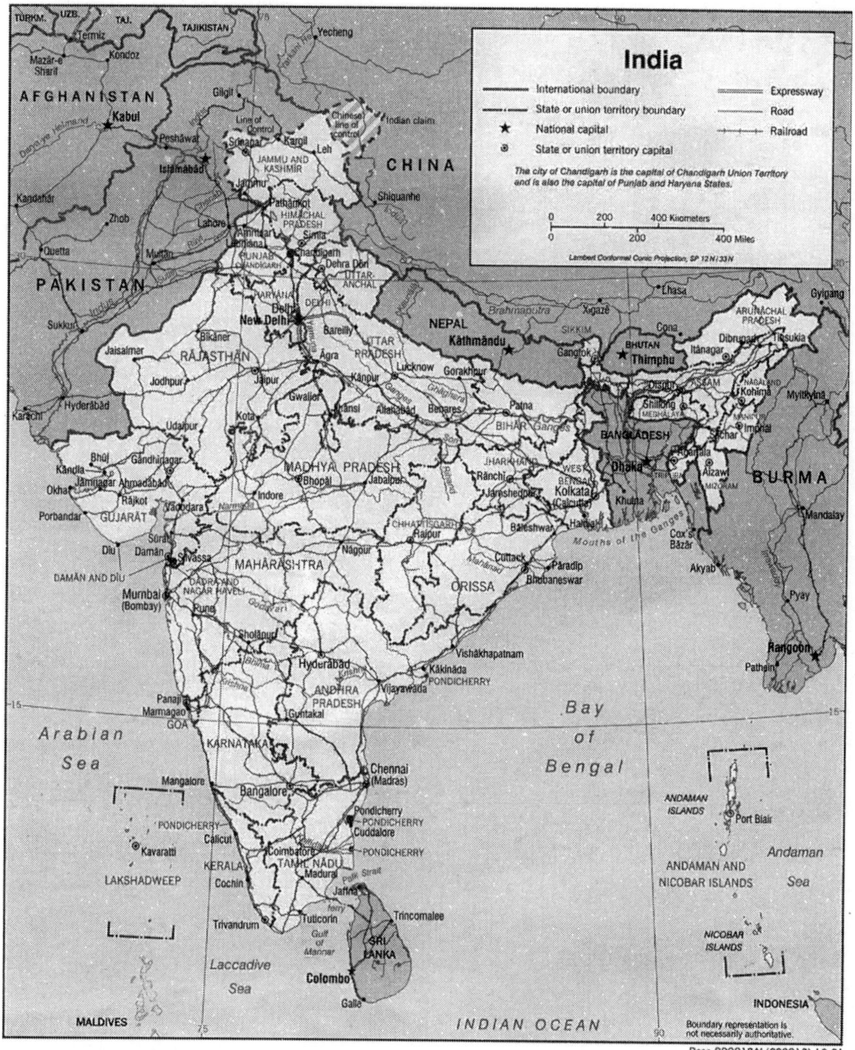

Base 802812AI (C00213) 10-01

Map of India

1

The Largest Market the World Has Ever Seen

Bombay Stock Exchange

So far as I am able to judge, nothing has been left undone, either by man or nature, to make India the most extraordinary country that the sun visits on his rounds. Nothing seems to have been forgotten, nothing overlooked.

Mark Twain

The world's largest truck manufacturer, the largest manufacturer of motorcycles in the world, the country with the most FDA-approved drug companies outside the United States, the largest number of Fortune 500 R&D centers outside the United States, the third-largest stock exchange in the world in terms of volume (Figure 1.1), the second-largest producer of sugarcane (got ethanol?), the largest producer of milk and fruits, the third-largest producer of cotton, and that's just the beginning. Here are a few more statistics to overwhelm you, before it's all put in context:

India is home to the world's fifth-largest coal reserves and the third-largest bauxite reserves. It is the fourth-largest steel producer in the world, the sixth-largest aluminum producer, and the third-largest manufacturer of CDs and DVDs. Indians purchase six million cell phones per month. There are 40 million Internet users, projected to grow to 200 million by 2015. The middle class comprises more than 60 million people today and is expected to exceed 583 million people by 2025. Seven hundred million Indians own property and 100 million households have bank accounts today. Eighty million Indians hold secondary degrees and India is home to the largest number of engineering graduates in the world.

Now for the context. India is a complex and growing country and is on its way to becoming a world economic power. Despite the accomplishments listed here, most Indian business leaders and many of the more progressive politicians are painfully aware of the fact that India has a long way to go before the country can become what they would like it to be. The country is in a transition period between "Old India" and "New India." You can never be sure which you will find.

There is a common perception that India has a lopsided economy built on information technology and business process outsourcing, but that is changing rapidly as national and multinational firms scramble to meet the demands of a rapidly growing middle class. The rapid expansion of India's manufacturing base is, in turn, creating millions of skilled and semiskilled jobs for a very young working-age population.

FIRST IMPRESSIONS CAN BE MISLEADING

When I first visited the country—in late 2001—my first impressions were mixed, starting from the moment my American doctor prescribed antimalaria medications for my trip. "You're kidding!" I responded, when I read the prescription. "No," he replied, "I am not. Malaria is widespread on the Indian subcontinent. By the way, you're going to need a series of vaccinations." Now I was beginning to get a bit nervous. Wasn't I traveling to the fourth-largest economy in the world, home to some of the leading outsourcing and technology firms? Wasn't Bangalore supposed to be like Silicon Valley? This was beginning to sound more like a safari, with mosquito netting and a rifle for tigers.

I arrived in New Delhi after spending what seemed like an eternity on a flight out of Chicago. The New Delhi airport was nondescript and long overdue for a major renovation. There seemed to be an islandlike attitude among the security staff and airport personnel that gave me the feeling that I was somewhere in the Bahamas. I finally located my car—only to find my driver fast asleep behind the steering wheel. It took me several minutes to revive him. After navigating out of the parking lot—which required numerous parked cars to be physically pushed out of the way, we made it to the highway. There I enjoyed a forty-minute ride down potholed streets while my driver played chicken with motorized scooters and the occasional cow.

The next morning I was standing at a crowded intersection in the heart of the city when I noticed a pack of monkeys moving steadily toward me. These weren't the cute little spider monkeys that your kids would giggle at while spending a relaxed Sunday at the local zoo. These were more like baboons; in fact, it seemed to be a gang of ill-tempered baboons, and they were coming my way. I looked around to see if anything else was amiss but my fellow pedestrians seemed uninterested. Later, as I headed back to the safety of my hotel, I found myself repeating over and over, "fourth-largest economy in the world, fourth-largest economy in the world." That was 7 years ago.

By now, a local court has ordered the monkeys to leave the city—although it is still unclear if they will comply. When you fly into New Delhi you will still not be impressed by the airport; it is a mess. But by 2010 the airport will have been completely renovated, boasting a passenger capacity that will rival Chicago-O'Hare, with futuristic terminals that would make any architect proud. This is the New India, partly here, partly under construction.

AN ECONOMIC TOUR THROUGH INDIA

It is often said that the only thing Indians have in common is their national currency, the rupee, and their geographic borders, stretching approximately 2,500 miles from north to south and about the same distance from east to west (Figure 1.2). There are 28 states, four major ethnic groups, 16 official languages, hundreds of local dialects, and every religion known to man—calling the country complex would be an understatement. But if you had the luxury of time and money you might be able to get a more complete picture by taking a journey through each of India's states. We've done that in this section, giving you a high-altitude statistical survey of each state and major city in the country. You may want to skim over this section unless you're interested in a particular region or state, but a quick look at some of the numbers will give you a sense of the key roles that agriculture, manufacturing, IT, and tourism play in the Indian economy. The main theme of this chapter—why we think India is developing the world's largest market, and why it will eventually be larger than the China market, follows this economic tour.

Jammu and Kashmir

Our economic tour of India starts in the far north of the country, in the state of Jammu and Kashmir, home to the awe-inspiring Himalayan mountain range, which includes Mt. Everest and other 7,000-meter peaks. This mountain range stands like a sentinel on India's northern border, providing climatic influences and an abundant supply of fresh water for the country. India's northern neighbors, Pakistan, Afghanistan, Tajikistan, and China also border this region, an area that resembles the Colorado Rockies. Muslims account for 80 percent of the state's population, with significant minorities coming from the Hindu, Buddhist, and Sikh religions. The economy depends on farming, animal husbandry, and a nascent manufacturing and transportation sector. Kashmir is problematic in that it is a contested area between India and Pakistan and has been the victim of several border wars. A few years back many analysts believed that Kashmir would be the scene of the world's first nuclear conflict. Tensions have eased between the two countries in recent years, but the fate of Kashmir is yet to be decided, and until a final agreement is reached between Pakistan and India it will remain a sensitive issue.

Northern India in many ways resembles the delta region of the Mississippi River valley, with a vast river system traversing the region, and like the delta it is rich in agriculture, known to many as the "Granary of India," producing 60 percent of India's wheat and 40 percent of its rice. The problem is that between 30 to 40 percent of all of India's produce is lost in the supply chain as a result of spoilage, loss, and so on. For those of you looking into the future, this differential represents a big economic opportunity. An interesting side note is the fact that India has a total arable land area of 162 million hectares—25 percent more arable land than China. Now can you imagine what will happen when India gets its supply-chain act together? Exports of every type of agricultural product will explode. Over time, this is going to translate into a real advantage.

Reliance Industries, India's top conglomerate, is already working on the problem of 30 to 40 percent spoilage in India's produce supply chain. The company has recently launched a new retail chain called Reliance Fresh supermarket stores. Recognizing the inefficiencies in the produce supply chain, Reliance decided to create a retail operation that cuts out the middleman. By negotiating long-term contracts directly with farmers and modernizing the supply chain with refrigerated warehouses, trucks, bar coding, and other supply-chain management tools, the company will be able to provide fresh produce and other farm products to India's rapidly growing middle class at prices up to 30 percent lower than traditional markets. Averaging between 2,500 to 4,000 square feet in size, the air-conditioned Reliance Fresh stores are a radical departure from the mom-and-pop outlets or open-air stalls that currently represent the bulk of India's retail outlets. Reliance plans to expand its supermarket chain to 70 cities within the next 24 months, with over 4,000 stores in more than 1,500 cities planned by 2012. And, the company expects to hire and train 500,000 people during the same period. That's significant, considering the fact that India's retail sector, currently dominated by over 15 million mom-and-pop stores, is currently valued at over $200 billion per year and growing at an annual rate of more than 25 percent.

Punjab and Uttar Pradesh

The north of India is also home to the states of Punjab and Uttar Pradesh (UP), two centers of cultural, religious, and economic power. The Himalayan foothills to the north of Punjab help define the state and the people that live there, with many of the famed Gurkha soldiers of the British army having been recruited from this area. The Gurkhas, tough characters by any standard, have most recently been deployed in Iraq. This area also has a lot of potatoes; Frito-Lay, a subsidiary of PepsiCo, recognized that fact and built a processing plant here in 1996. They entered into the first long-term contract agreements with local farmers, an approach that is being replicated by Wal-Mart as well as it moves into India's retail arena. As you continue to travel through this region you cannot help but notice, as evidenced by ancient landmarks, that at 5,000 years old Punjab and Uttar Pradesh is also the oldest living civilization. Known to many as the Indus Valley and the birthplace of Buddhism, it is a good place to relax after you have completed your first few business deals in India.

The towns of Kullu, Manali, McLeod Ganj, and Dharamsal have become famous tourist destinations because of the influence of Tibetan exiles in setting up monasteries, temples, and schools following their relocation from Tibet in the mid-1960s. Consequently, its thriving hospitality industry and the class of hoteliers are responsible for this region having one of the highest per capita rates in the nation, a fact not overlooked by leading hotel chains like The Four Seasons and Hilton. Currently, India has an estimated shortfall of over 200,000 hotel rooms, and hotel operators like Starwood, Four Seasons, Sheraton, Hillwood, Accor, Trump, and Marriott are all rapidly developing new properties. The lack of hotel accommodations will become painfully clear to you when you try to book your reservations. Getting a room is hard enough—and the rates you will pay will make New York City look like a bargain!

Not surprisingly, this region is also India's wealthiest, with the majority of its revenue generated from wheat, fruits, vegetables, and sugarcane. India is the second-largest producer of sugarcane in the world, and that's important, considering the fact that sugarcane is the ideal crop for the production of ethanol, a vital element of the struggle against global warming. That point has not been overlooked by the GMR Corporation, which has built two state-of-the-art ethanol production facilities here. These two plants have a combined annual production capacity of 16 million gallons of ethanol, and the company has plans to build three more plants of similar size over the next 2 years. With its current sugarcane production levels, India will have the ability to produce over 350,000 barrels of ethanol per day, a staggering number when you consider that the United States only produces 194,000 barrels of ethanol a day. India's proximity to Japan will also create a very attractive export market opportunity for ethanol as Japan moves aggressively to implement the Kyoto Protocol.

The first important city to consider is Ludhiana, which serves as the industrial hub of Punjab and which had a total export market that surpassed US$120 million in 2006. With continued GDP and trade growth, Ludhiana's exports are expected to climb to over US$500 million by 2012. India is the largest producer of motorcycles in the world, and this region is the headquarters of the country's leading motorcycle companies—Avon Bicycles, Hero cycles, and Eastman Industries. It is also the home to over 6,000 textile companies—an industry that had been shackled by poor economic policies of the past but is now poised to become a global competitor. When you consider the fact that India has a middle class that exceeds 60 million and a large, very young population that is highly fashion conscious, you begin to get a sense of the size of that country's fashion apparel market!

This area is also considered to have the best infrastructure in India, with an extensive network of roads, rail, air, and river transportation. Good infrastructure is still a rarity in India, but that is rapidly changing, as an estimated US$60 billion dollars a year (US$180 billion dollars in local terms) of annual investments are being invested to modernize the infrastructure.

Haryana

A little further to the south is the state of Haryana, close to the capital city of New Delhi. It is an agrarian state that has developed a rapidly growing economy. Like its parent, Punjab, Haryana grows significant amounts of wheat and rice, which has made it the second-largest contributor to the country's central pool of food grains. Dairy farming is also an essential part of the economy, as India is the largest producer of milk in the world. The problem again is the supply chain—almost none of the dairy products produced in India are pasteurized or cold stored, which leads to an incredible amount of lost revenues. Of course, if you look at the glass as being half full, it also provides a major opportunity for new business opportunities (take note Kraft Foods, Land O'Lakes, and Dannon!)

Over one thousand medium and large companies, with capital investments topping US$4.4 billion, have been established in the cities of Gurgaon, Panchkula, and Faridabad, all of which lie in close proximity to New Delhi, the capital of India. There are more than 80,000 small-scale automotive, truck, and motorcycle support industries in the state. Numerous manufacturing entities, including Maruti, Escorts, Hero Honda, Alcatel, Sony, Whirlpool India, and Bharti Telecom have made Gurgaon home. Bharti Telecom is one of the companies that is capturing the growth of the middle class. Working through three individual business units—mobile services, broadband and telephone services, and enterprise services—the company has captured a significant amount of the revenues being created from the sale of six million cell phones per month. The company, established in 1995, is a public limited company and is headquartered in New Delhi. It was founded by Sunil Mittal, the same individual who has entered into a joint venture with Wal-Mart. The mobile services business unit offers mobile services throughout India across 23 telecom circles. By 2006 the company had more than twenty million customers, a market cap of more than US$30 billion, and an annual growth rate of more than 80 percent! If that many people have cell phones, what other products and services will they need next?

Gurgaon has seen the emergence of an active information technology industry in recent years, with firms like IBM, Hewitt Associates, Dell, Convergys, and NIIT setting up back offices or contact centers there. Besides a strong manufacturing and service sector growth, Haryana also possesses a strong agrarian economy, which involves 70 percent of the state's population.

India's most prominent real estate development firm, DLF Group, has taken the lead in turning agrarian Gurgaon into a home for tens of thousands of foreign and Indian professionals. This is a growing trend in India, as developers attempt to create modern cities in what were, until recently, sleepy backwaters. It is a trend worth noting, since these class-B and C cities will soon become major commercial centers.

Founded in the mid-1970s, the DLF Group is India's leading real estate developer (based on the size of their holdings). It has six divisions: residential, commercial, retail, hotels, infrastructure, and townships. The company has made a name for itself in its design and planning of massive office parks, master-planned communities, and leisure facilities. Currently, its flagship project—DLF City, a township encompassing 3,000 acres—is Asia's largest private township, with schools, health care, hospitality, and shopping facilities, amounting to a total investment of US$15 billion.

And then there is the capital city of New Delhi, with a population of 14.1 million. It's not the largest city in India, but it boasts the most tree cover of any large city in the world—and of course, it's home to the ill-tempered monkeys that I mentioned earlier. But New Delhi is known for more than monkeys and tree cover—it is also India's capital city and a center for commerce, with a per capita income that is nearly three times the national average. The city is also home to the Delhi metro, a light rail system (completed on time and within budget), and a new highway system that will be completed by 2009.

Uttar Pradesh

As you continue your journey across India you will pass through Uttar Pradesh (UP), the most populous subnational entity in the world. It has the largest urban area and population and is possibly the state with the largest number of million-plus cities. Only five nations have higher populations than UP—the People's Republic of China, the United States, Indonesia, and Brazil. It has the second-largest economy in India, after Maharashtra. Uttar Pradesh is a very fertile agricultural area and a major contributor of grain, livestock, and dairy. National and international tourists are attracted to UP, with huge numbers flocking to Agra and the holy cities of Varanasi, Ayodhya, and Matura. Uttar Pradesh recently (2007) held state elections that saw an unlikely coalition of voters emerge, as the poorest and the wealthiest members of Indian society came together to elect the new (and first female) governor of the state.

Uttarakhand

Formed from the hill districts of Uttar Pradesh, the state of Uttarakhand was created in 2000; it lies along a stretch of the Himalayas that contains Hinduism's most sacred pilgrimage destinations. Uttarakhand is comprised mostly of Rajputs, a martial caste of Hindus who claim to be descended from the warrior dynasty of Kshatriyas—the principal military order of the Vedic society.

Madhya Pradesh

The state of Madhya Pradesh, affectionately referred to as the "Heart of India," is located south of New Delhi. Its powerful Narmada River, by tradition, separates northern from southern India. The state provides India with 70 percent of its soy production, and since India is the fourth-largest producer of soybeans in the world, this is significant. Not surprisingly, this area is also known as the "Soy Bowl" of India. Ruchi Soya Industries is a leader in the agribusiness sector, and has become the largest producer of edible oils, soy foods, and processed foods in the nation. The company has a large manufacturing capacity and several respected consumer brand names to its credit, including Nutrela and Ruchi Gold—both have captured leading spots in the soy foods and edible oils categories. The firm has also ventured into related businesses, including bakery specialties, vegetable fats, and soaps, which is now the number-one brand in the Indian market.

India's primary centers of commerce, transportation, and mining are to the west of Madhya Pradesh. Bordering southeastern Pakistan are the powerful western states that serve home to India's rapidly growing copper, zinc, and salt mines, and transportation, financial services, and entertainment industries. Rajasthan, India's largest state, is home to the nation's oldest archaeological ruins and the world's oldest mountain ranges, the Kalibanga and Aravallis ranges. The area looks a lot like the American West, and if it were not for the language, culture, and other traditions, you might think that you were in southern Utah or Arizona. Honda Motor Co., Japan's third-largest carmaker, is building its second Indian car factory in the western state of Rajasthan. Honda chose Rajasthan to supply its biggest market, the northern and eastern parts of the country.

Honda will spend an estimated US$ 450 million to set up this factory. The carmaker, which has a plant near New Delhi that assembles Accord and Civic sedans, will have an annual production capacity of 150,000 vehicles in India by 2010.

Endowed with the natural beauty of the Thar Desert as well as a venerable history, tourism is one of the pillars of Rajasthan's economy. The palaces in Jaipur, lakes of Udaipur, and forts at Jodhpur are preferred tourist sites. The Taj Hotels Resorts and Palaces have been recognized as one of the leading hospitality firms of the world, operating one of Asia's largest and finest groups of hotels, composed of 59 hotels in 40 locations across Asia. Although the company's hotels range from world-renowned landmarks to modernized business hotels, it is especially renowned for its authentic Rajput palaces, located in Jaipur, Jaisalmar, and Jodhpur. These accommodations, all formerly palaces of the most illustrious of India's kings and princes, have been transformed into luxurious destinations for travelers.

Gujarat, India's most industrialized state, produces 19.8 percent of the nation's total manufacturing output, an influence on a national economy similar to that of Detroit's contribution to the United States. Gujurat has established itself as a leader in textiles, transportation, and petrochemicals, and is home to Reliance Industries' Jamnagar oil facility. With a refining capacity of 661,000 barrels per day, Jamnagar is the world's largest greenfield refinery and the third largest globally. Gujarat is one of India's most progressive states when it comes to encouraging private sector investment, and that policy is clearly paying off. The state is also home to the world's largest shipyard (Bhavnagar). The state has also been aggressive in developing a dependable power grid, ranking first nationwide in gas-based thermal electricity generation, with a national market share of over 18 percent. It is home to scores of National Stock Exchange conglomerates, such as Adani Exports, Indian Petrochemicals Corporation, Vishal Exports Overseas, Nirma, Arvind Mills, and Cadila Healthcare.

To Gujarat's south lies Maharashtra, India's third-largest state in terms of size and second largest in terms of population. Favorable economic policies in the 1970s transformed Maharashtra into India's leading industrial and financial state, similar to New York City in its importance in the worlds of finance, entertainment, and culture (its urban population is 42 percent). Major industries include petrochemicals, agriculture (mangoes, grapes, and oranges), and electrical products. Fiat Auto and Tata Motors recently announced the formation of a joint venture to produce passenger cars and diesel engines at a new facility here for India's fast-growing auto market. This venture will create 3,000 to 4,000 jobs over the next 3 to 4 years. With the capacity to produce in excess of 100,000 cars and 200,000 engines and transmissions annually, the Ranjangaon plant will manufacture vehicles for both the Indian and overseas markets. Both Fiat and Tata vehicles will be manufactured at the same facility, and will be managed equally by the two shareholder partners.

Mumbai (formerly Bombay) is the financial capital of India, and is the home to many of India's major banks, insurance companies, and brokerage firms. It is also the site of Asia's oldest stock exchange—the National Stock Exchange—which is the third-largest exchange by volume in the world. There are over 6,000 companies listed on India's stock markets, compared to less than 1,700 in China, and another 150 companies expect to go public this year alone.

South India is a modern Tower of Babal, with a distinct language for each of the four states in the region. Composed of Andhra Pradesh, Karnataka, Kerala, and Tamil Nadu, this region is a real challenge for any marketing executive. It stretches south from the Narmada River and spreads from the west to the east coast. Over 48 percent of the population are involved in agriculture, cultivating crops such as paddy, sorghum, millet, sugarcane, and chili. Hill regions of the Western Ghats (mountain ranges) primarily produce coffee, tea, vanilla, rubber, and pepper. On the other hand, the area's major cities—Chennai, Bangalore, Hyderabad, and Trivanduram—are home to the manufacturing units of many information technology, automobile, and electronic manufacturers. Chennai is also home to Nokia, the Finnish mobile handset company. Nokia is leading the development of an electronics hardware zone—within 2 years, along with eight of its suppliers, it will invest over $200 million dollars and employ some 20,000 people. One of Nokia's suppliers is a Taiwanese company, Foxconn. When the company set up their operation in India, they soon learned that their Indian employees quickly adapted to the Taiwanese style of work—with uniformed employees performing both manual and highly skilled tasks well—once trained—and consistently maintaining international standards of quality. The automaker BMW has also recently built a plant here, to manufacture their series 3 and 5 models for the Indian market.

Bangalore, often referred to as the Silicon Valley of India, is located in this region. The city is India's IT and outsourcing center, accounting for approximately 38 percent of India's software exports. Many world-class companies have their roots in this city, Infosys being one of them. When you visit the corporate headquarters of Infosys you could easily believe that you had somehow stepped into the corporate campus of a U.S. technology company in Washington state. Employees ride bicycles to and from the various buildings that make up the campus, on pathways that are lined with all types of trees and plants. On campus is a fitness center that would give an L.A. Fitness a run for its money, and a lecture hall that is reminiscent of the Sydney opera hall. The Silicon Valley look doesn't end at the office park, as the company offers highly competitive compensation packages to their employees; with a healthy mix of stock options, many of Infosys' original employees are now millionaires. Infosys delivers information technology (IT)-enabled business solutions to more than 500 hundred global clients. The company provides end-to-end business solutions, including consulting, design, development, software re-engineering, maintenance, systems integration, package evaluation, and implementation and infrastructure management services.

Infosys also provides software products to the banking industry. The company first went public in India in 1993—in 1999 the company was listed on NASDAQ. With 2007 revenues in excess of US$3 billion dollars and a market capitalization of over US$26 billion, you could say the company is on a roll. It expects to add over 30,000 employees in 2007, giving Infosys an estimated headcount of over 100,000 employees by 2008 and a revenue target of over US$4 billion dollars the same year! And that is just one of the many international players located in Bangalore.

The state of Karnataka is India's largest producer of coffee, raw silk, and sandalwood. It accounts for 75 percent of India's floriculture and 59 percent of the country's coffee production. Over 90 percent of India's gold comes from the southern region of this state; that's important, since India has some of the world's top jewelry designers. Recently there has been increased activity in the extraction of manganese in these districts, a direct result of India's rapidly growing steel industry. Like Gujarat, Karnataka is one of India's most industrialized states.

Kerala, a landmass wedged between the Arabian Sea and the Western Ghats, is primarily made up of Malayali-Dravidian, Jewish, and Arab citizens. Since its inception, democratic socialist principles have guided Kerala's economy. The state is gradually liberalizing its economy and attracting more foreign investment. Kerala has India's highest literacy rate—its service sector forms the foundation of its economy, followed by agriculture (cereals and grains) and fishing. Also, Kerala plays a significant role in India's spice industry. India accounts for 45 percent of black pepper imports to the United States, almost all of which come from Kerala.

The southeastern tip of India is comprised of Andhra Pradesh and Tamil Nadu. Andhra Pradesh has long been recognized for its agriculture production, in particular rice, sugarcane, cotton, and tobacco. Recently, it has begun to invest heavily in its information technology and biotechnology industries; it hopes to increase its standing in the rankings of top IT-exporting states in India.

Andhra Pradesh, has entered into a formal agreement with Reliance Industries for planting jatropha for high-quality biodiesel fuel. Jatropha has been recognized as a critical component of India's desire to achieve energy independence by 2011. It is unique in its ability to be grown in wastelands, and once harvested it has a yield per hectare of more than four times that of soybeans and ten times that of corn. The government has identified 400,000 square km of land where jatropha can be grown, hoping it will replace 20 percent of India's diesel consumption by 2011. In September 2007, Hindustan Petroleum Corporation Limited joined with the Maharashtra State Farming Corporation for a jatropha seed-based biodiesel venture. The fuel is already being used on Indian Railways. In fact, more than 250 engineers from various R&D groups have come to India to work on the biodiesel program in the past year alone. Mahindra & Mahindra, India's largest tractor manufacturer, is aiming to produce the country's first biodiesel tractor as well as a passenger vehicle, to be launched under the Scorpio brand.

Tamil Nadu, India's southernmost state, has had continuous human habitation since prehistoric times. Its long history and cultural traditions are among the world's oldest, which has resulted in the oldest surviving literature in India. Currently, Tamil Nadu holds the position of having the highest level of urbanization in India (43.86%). Furthermore, it ranks as one of India's most industrialized states, with more than 110 industrial parks (and their supporting infrastructure). The state is a leading producer of agricultural products (corn, rye, and sugarcane) in India, second only to Punjab. It is also India's largest producer of turmeric, of which India is the largest producer, consumer, and exporter of in the world. It is the only state to have a formal biodiesel policy that stipulates the use of jatropha plant crops. Tamil Nadu distributes wasteland to poor farmers for planting. One would have to wonder why a country like India, with an economy one-fifth the size of the United States, would have a more progressive energy policy than the United States.

Eastern India consists of the states of West Bengal, Bihar, Jharkhand, and Orissa, where climates vary from tropical savannah in the southern portions bordering the Bay of Bengal to humid subtropical in the north. West Bengal is agrarian and is one of India's most populous states. It is unique for having been led by the Communist Party of India (CPI) Left Front for three decades, which makes it the world's longest-running democratically elected communist government. Rice and jute are the state's principal food crops. The service sector is the largest contributor to the gross domestic product of the state, contributing 51 percent of the state's GDP. State industries are localized in the Kolkata region and the mineral-rich western highlands. Numerous steel plants are located in the Durgapur region of the state. Mittal Steel, the company that recently acquired the European steel company Arcelor, is building a new plant here. The plant will be one of India's largest, built in two phases, with a capacity of 12 million tons per year.

West Bengal was also the scene of violent protests, which occurred when the government tried to seize land from local farmers under an eminent domain law. Local farmers weren't about to be bullied by politicians who were eager to hand over land to a multinational corporation. The resulting riots forced the courts to intervene, and the local government has now backed away from the deal. The lesson to take from this is to make sure that the local populace is aligned with government policy before you get into a major business deal!

Bihar is often recognized as being one of India's poorest and least-developed states. Its annual per capita income of US$94, compared with India's average of US$255, is a pretty good indicator of the wide variance between Indian states in terms of government policies, lack of direct foreign investment, and a lack of investment in agriculture, infrastructure, and educational facilities.

In 2000 Bihar was divided; the industrially advanced and mineral-rich southern half was carved out to form the separate state of Jharkhand, a new state that had previously produced 60 percent of

Bihar's material output. Jharkhand, known for its mineral wealth—iron ore, coal, copper ore, mica, bauxite, kainite, and forestry products—this small state, mostly covered by rivers and forests, has a concentration of some of the country's most highly industrialized cities.

Further south rests Orissa, a state with a long coastline and large resources of chrome, manganese, granite, and gemstone minerals. Because of this wealth, it frequently attracts foreign investment in steel, aluminum, power, refineries, and infrastructure. Furthermore, Orissa is emerging as a player in IT outsourcing and services. The current planned IT investment in the state is projected to be $90 billion. India's top IT firms—Satyam Computer Services, TCS, MindTree Consulting, IBM, Bosch, and Wipro—have set up development centers in Orissa. National Aluminum and Tata Sponge Iron have their corporate offices in the state. Recently the number of companies who have signed Memoranda of Understanding to set up steel plants has gone up to 50, including South Korea's Posco, which has agreed to construct a mammoth US$12 billion steel plant near the port of Paradip. Arcelor-Mittal has also announced plans to invest in another US$10 billion megasteel project. The state is also attracting an unprecedented amount of investment in aluminum, coal-based power plants, and petrochemicals. Vedanta Resources' 1.4 million-ton aluminum project in Kalahandi is the state's largest investment in aluminum.

The Seven Sister States comprise a region in northeastern India, consisting of the contiguous states of Arunachal Pradesh, Assam, Meghalaya, Manipur, Mizorum, Nagaland, and Tripura. The ethnic and religious diversity that characterize the seven states distinguish them from the rest of India. The *Seven Sisters* reference is symbolic of their relative isolation from mainstream Indian culture and consciousness. Originally, following India's winning independence in 1947, only three states covered the area. Four new states were carved out of the original territory, in line with the government's policy of reorganizing the states along ethnic and linguistic lines. Many industries in the region are tea-based, with others focused in crude oil and natural gas, silk, bamboo, and handicrafts. The Seven Sisters are heavily forested, with beautiful wildlife sanctuaries, tea estates, and rivers. However, for security reasons (intertribal tensions, widespread insurgencies, and disputed borders with neighboring China) there are restrictions on foreigners visiting, hampering the development of a potentially profitable tourism industry.

THE INDIA MARKET VERSUS THE CHINA MARKET

You now know that India is a worldwide leader in some key industries, and the country will soon become a global leader in a number of others, but why is it going to become the largest market the world has ever seen? Why not China, after all—that country has 1.3 billion people, compared to India's only 1.1 billion. China is clearly in the lead, as the world's manufacturing leader. China is a one-party state, and its government made a decision some years back to pursue economic development through exports, a lot of exports. Consumption was put on the backburner. In fact, two-thirds of China's GDP growth is driven by exports; less than a third is driven by consumption. The Chinese government also decided to pursue the "one child" policy, which has reduced population growth but has also created a graying population, with 265 million 65-year-olds by 2020. That number of retirees is going to put a significant strain on the economy—more importantly, retirees simply do not spend as much as younger workers. With fewer workers supporting larger numbers of retirees, the strain on the severely underfunded social pension system is expected to grow. The pension system currently only covers urban Chinese, not rural residents, who make up the majority of the population; even so, it has to be subsidized by other government revenues. Chinese already save prodigiously for retirement, and as their society ages, they are expected to consume less and save even more to fund their retirement.

The demographic challenge is bound to affect China's economic prospects. China is graying before it has fully developed. With more than 50 percent of its population living in poverty, it will have to grapple with the same age-related fiscal, social, and productivity challenges of countries like Japan and the European Community, with several times its per capita income.

The demographic picture for India is quite different—by 2005, India had nearly 500 million people less than 19 years of age; that's a lot of teenagers, which translates into a lot of iPods! And in another 40 to 50 years India is expected to have 220 million more workers than in China. But what does that mean in terms of consumption?

Everything hinges on education. Every year for the next 10 years an estimated 16 million Indians will be joining the workforce, and an additional 15 million Indians are expected to move from agrarian to nonagrarian livelihoods, meaning that over 30 million individuals per year will need some type of practical education. The problem is that the government does not have the resources required to meet this massive demand for education. Consider Infosys, one of India's premiere tech companies. They will spend more than US$150 million dollars on training and education for new employees this year alone. The reason is that India's universities are not providing graduates with the skills training that they require for the corporate world, so the private sector is being forced to fill the gap. The potential market for private education in India is expected to exceed US$25 billion per year, and some local players, like NIIT, the Indian equivalent of Devry, are already reaping the benefits of this vast market. The type of education that will be required will run the complete spectrum from electricians, welders, and plumbers to hotel managers, retail assistants, and bank associates.

But how will people pay for their education? After all, more than 60 percent of India's population are poor farmers, right? Not exactly. The fact is that almost 94 percent of rural households own land, including homestead land. There are more than 115.6 million farm holdings, with an average size of 3 acres. And that translates into capital—a lot of capital. Land is scarce in India, and property values are going to rise in a very big way. As the Indian market for mortgage-backed securities and asset-back securities is developed by global financial firms like Citigroup and ICICI Bank, liquidity will flow into the rural property market. Punjab National Bank, one of India's highest-ranked national banks, with a customer base of more than 36 million, grew from US$60 billion in assets in 2005 to more than US$80 billion in 2006. The portfolio varied from mortgage, lease rental, personal and education loans, to car and housing loans. The conservative estimate of this land value is US$3 trillion, and when that is freed up, capital will be available for education, starting a business, or buying an apartment. The process is already underway, with farmers selling their land to industrial groups, or in some cases taking part of the proceeds from the sale as equity in the new development.

EXPLOSIVE GROWTH IN INDIA'S MIDDLE CLASS

With education, assets, and millions of jobs being created in the fast-growing industrial base of the country, the Indian middle class is set to explode, from 60 million people today to more than 583 million people by 2025. In terms of consumption, India's consumer spending will exceed US$400 billion by 2010 and it will overtake Germany by 2020. By 2050—which is, of course, a long way off—consumer spending in India could surpass the United States. Today that consumption is concentrated in India's six major metropolitan cities: New Delhi (12,791,458), Mumbai (16,368,084), Chennai (6,424,624), Kolkata (13,216,546), Bangalore (5,686,844), and Hyderabad (5,533,640). These comprise the affluent, densely populated urban agglomerations endowed with high purchasing power. They are drivers of the economy, and while they represent only 6 percent of the total Indian population, they contribute 14 percent to India's GDP.

However, that is all set to change: As India's infrastructure is developed and large corporate parks are built in traditionally rural areas, consumption growth will increasingly be focused in the smaller cities. Today India's six major cities are home to just 6 percent of the total Indian population. The balance comprise the yet-to-be-tapped hinterland. Ahmedabad, Pune, Kanpur, Surat, Jaipur, Lucknow, and Nagpur are the major Tier II cities, and Patna, Indore, Bhopal, Vadodara, Ludhiana, Agra, and Nashik are some of the major Tier III cities. Consider the fact that in 2001 the number of Indian rural households that owned a TV was 26 million. By 2004 that number has jumped to more than 41 million households. And that is just one TV per household; as disposable incomes grow, the number of TVs per household will grow, and that will equate to a market opportunity in excess of US$30 billion over the next 5 years for TVs alone.

That type of growth in consumption has not escaped the attention of Wal-Mart, which entered into a joint venture with telecom tycoon Sunil Mittal for supply-chain and wholesale businesses with Sunil Mittal's retail stores across the nation. (Sunil Mittal is a master in running a consumer business; the New York-based buyout firm Warburg Pincus LLC took home US$1.6 billion on the US$290 million it invested in Mittal's mobile-phone network from 1999 to 2001.) Mittal will fully own the front end of Wal-Mart's retail business. Indian law still doesn't allow foreign investment in stores with a large range of brand-name consumer goods. The government's communist allies are opposed to its plan to open up the industry to overseas investors. The present policy restricts foreign direct investment in retail to single-brand ventures, with a foreign shareholding cap of 51 percent. However, 100 percent foreign ownership is permitted in wholesale cash and carry, where one can only sell to retailers and distributors, and not to consumers. Therefore, from a regulation point of view, Wal-Mart can hold a majority stake in the cash-and-carry venture. An equal joint venture between Mittal and Wal-Mart will run the supply chain and sell to wholesalers, something that German retailer

Metro AG is already doing successfully in India. It is still not clear whether the stores will carry the Wal-Mart brand.

Indian consumers expect value and are traditionally very conservative with spending, so expect consumers to initially focus on durable and semidurable goods like cars, TVs, and refrigerators. Only 1.6 million households, or slightly more than 1 percent of India's population, owned a car in 2006, and 160 in every thousand households owned a refrigerator. With more than 2 million new cars being sold a year, India is one of the fastest-growing auto markets in the world. And as more choices become available to consumers and competition drives down prices, consumption at all levels will accelerate. A case in point is the Indian automobile industry. Ten to twelve years ago a budget of US$ 5,500 could have bought an Indian customer a compact Suzuki 800CC car. Now, in 2007, within the same budget, the customer can choose from an array of financing options and can take home a Chevrolet 1600CC. And those with a US$ 1,000 budget 10 years ago, for a 2-wheeler? They have graduated to the Suzuki.

The Indian retail sector is changing rapidly; multiplexes with retail outlets have combined movie watching and shopping. PVR, a cinema chain spread across 10 cities in India, recently opened a multiplex with 11 screens in the IT city Bangalore. The public limited company recently entered the field of movie production, with Oscar-nominated Indian film star Aamir Khan; it also offers tickets on mobile phones. Multiplexes have grown to 150 in India as of 2006—with a seating capacity increasing to 160,000, 40 percent of the total revenue comes from multiplexes.

The number of retail malls in India is set to rise from 158 in 2005 to 600 by 2010.

Ahmedabad, a city known for low crime rates, has multiplexes like Fun Republic, Wide Angle, and the IMAX theatre, which is often touted as the biggest in India. E-Square multiplex, Adlabs, and Inox are among the popular multiplexes of Pune. Kanpur, India's supplier of flavored pan Masala, has few multiplexes and malls. Rave 3 is the most popular multiplex-cum-shopping mall. Surat, the land of diamonds and saris, is high on malls and multiplexes as well. FAME and Valentine multiplexes are the well-known ones. Entertainment Paradise and Inox are the popular multiplexes of Jaipur. Lucknow's multiplexes-cum-shopping malls include Fun Republic, Wave cinemas, and the Saharaganj mall. Inox is the most favorite multiplex in Nagpur.

Indian consumers have started favoring big retail stores more than the neighborhood grocery. They would like to visit a multiplex rather than a cinema hall. They would like to buy their daily vegetables from Reliance Fresh, retail chain division of Reliance Industries of India, rather than a roadside vendor.

What will the largest market the world has ever seen mean for you? Consider the following: Based on current GDP growth rates over the next 5 to 10 years, India will have 500 million mobile phone customers, 400 million new laptops, 50 million iPhones, 650 million new TV sets, 140 million new vehicles, 150 million new refrigerators, 95 million new dishwashers, 2.5 billion new tires, 5 billion light bulbs, 12 billion DVDs, 20 billion CDs, 40 billion bars of soap, 3 billion new shirts, 2.8 billion new jeans, 8 billion pairs of shoes, 24 billion tubes of toothpaste, 9 billion bottles of shampoo, 22 billion magazines, 200 billion newspapers, 9 billion books, 240 billion cans of beer—and that's just the beginning. India is going to need a lot of just about everything, and Indian consumers are quickly becoming savvy to international brands and trends. That level of consumer spending is going to create immediate opportunities for domestic and international manufacturers and retailers of just about every size and shape.

2

Bulls and Bears in Mumbai: India's Financial Markets

TV 18 CNN Newsroom

Going forward, you have a broad and beautiful street, full of rows of fine houses and streets of the sort I have described, and it is to be understood that the houses belong to men rich enough to afford such. In this street live many merchants and there you will find all sorts of rubies, and diamonds and emeralds, and pearls, and seed pearls, and cloths, and every sort of thing there is on earth and that you may wish to buy.

Domingos Paes (1520)

AN INDIAN ENTREPRENEUR'S STORY—TV18

Raghav Bahl, the founder of media company TV18, was huddled with Haresh Chawla, the group CEO, and his senior management team in their corporate offices on a hot, muggy Sunday night in New Delhi, reviewing the company's public offering document for what seemed like the millionth time. On Monday the company's second IPO would be officially listed on the National Stock Exchange, and public trading of the new issue would begin. The publicity surrounding the IPO, which was limited to Indian investors due to regulatory restraints, had been well received. Actually that's an understatement, as the IPO was sixty-five times oversubscribed. Still, the sense of anxiety and anticipation was apparent, as this was the culmination of a journey that had begun 15 years ago, when Raghav started a production company with the princely sum of thirteen hundred dollars (Figure 2.1).

Going public became a reality for Raghav thanks to a thriving financial market in India that's helping to underwrite the risks Indian entrepreneurs are taking. If you are a businessperson or an investor you may be interested to know that over one hundred and fifty companies plan to launch IPOs in India this year alone. If you are an online discount broker like Ameritrade or Scott Trade you might be

FIGURE 2.1 *The National Stock Exchange*

interested to know that last year over 12 percent of India's National Stock Exchange volume was from online trading. (The number of online trading accounts is expected to grow by 40 percent a year, and that is a conservative estimate.) If you are an asset manager or mutual fund company you should know that mutual fund coverage is extremely underrepresented in the Indian market, and that with high rates of savings (exceeding 28 percent) and homes with savings accounts set to double over the next 5 years, indirect investment by Indian investors is set to skyrocket.

How did Raghav build a public company from the ground up in 15 years? His story is exceptional but his entrepreneurial spirit is very typical. Years ago, working out of an air-conditioned hut in New Delhi with two tables and an assortment of plastic chairs, Raghav and seven other dedicated employees managed to produce two pilot programs they hoped to sell to the BBC, the India Show and India Business Report. At the time, producing a pilot program was no easy task. You needed a license for production equipment, and even if you were lucky enough to procure one, finding the necessary equipment was another matter all together. Raghav flew to London on the cheapest flight he could find to pitch the shows to the BBC. It was a gamble, and he knew it—after all, he didn't even have enough money left to get his shirts pressed. Staying with friends at their flat in central London, Raghav waited for what seemed like an eternity. On the third day, he received a call from a producer at the BBC. They wanted to buy not one, but both of his shows, and Raghav nearly passed out upon hearing the news. With a contract and sizeable advance in hand, he flew back to New Delhi and TV18 was on the map.

By 1999 the company had 80 employees and 19 shows in production. No longer operating out of a hut, TV18 had well-appointed offices and a state-of-the-art production facility. The money was good, and with a customer like the BBC you could count on a check arriving every Monday. Still, Raghav wanted something more—producing shows for the BBC and other networks was profitable but you were always at their mercy. Competition had increased and the constant dog-and-pony shows were getting old. Raghav is representative of many Indian entrepreneurs—never content with the status quo, he is constantly looking for new avenues of growth and is not afraid to take a chance.

In 1999 Raghav decided to take his second big gamble. TV18 would become a broadcaster. He made a pitch to MSNBC and they liked what they heard. There was one catch. MSNBC would agree to franchise the show to TV18 but TV18 would be responsible for all local content, marketing, and production costs. Raghav estimated the total investment at three million dollars—just about every dollar the company had managed to put away over the past 7 years. He decided to take the plunge and struck a deal with MSNBC. But not more than a year later Raghav received some bad news from the Indian broadcasting authorities. Indian media companies would be required to have majority ownership in any venture with a foreign company. Raghav tried to explain the new regulations to MSNBC as best he could. The producers at MSNBC were understanding, but this was still business and if they were going to be the minority partner then TV18 would need to carry the full weight of the deal. Raghav countered that if TV18 was going to take all of the risk, then he wanted to be in the driver's seat. The channel would be cobranded as MSNBC/TV18 and would be an Indian channel with 10 hours of local content and 2 hours of international content. MSNBC agreed and the deal was done.

(Investors in India should take note: There are still a lot of lawmakers in India with a protectionist bent, and that mentality becomes evident when you get into sectors that evoke nationalistic appeal. Retail may be the most talked about sector, with companies like Wal-Mart still being barred from direct entry into the Indian market. But there are many others, and you should do your homework before making any major foray into the market.)

Raghav had one small problem to deal with—the cost of creating an Indian channel with 10 hours of local content; also, the expense associated with getting the channel up and running would exceed 10 million dollars. Fortunately for Raghav and TV18, the timing could not have been better; in 2000 the Indian equity markets were on a roll, and with Internet and media convergence in the spotlight, new-economy companies like TV18 were hot. He decided to take the company public, and a few months later, TV18 was successfully listed on the National Stock Exchange. The IPO created a war chest of 15 million dollars in cash for TV18. Raghav was aware of his strengths and his weaknesses—he was a creator, and he had a vision, but he was not a professional manager. In 2001 he brought in Haresh Chawla, a seasoned professional, to run the company. Haresh quickly built a top-tier management team, and working closely with Raghav, he developed a long-term business strategy for the company.

Haresh and Raghav focused on building a world-class journalistic team. They invested heavily in analysts and journalists, increasing the company payroll to over 500 employees. Their strategy paid off: By 2003, TV18 was the leading English news channel in India, with over twenty million viewers. Seizing on their momentum, they decided to launch a Hindi language news channel, recognizing that there would be some degree of cannibalization but also aware that the move would capture additional viewers. By 2004 they had a combined audience of over 30 million viewers. Contrary to a lot of the propaganda you might hear, India is not the largest English-speaking country in the world. In fact, it is doubtful if more than 5 percent of the population is fluent in English. That is rapidly changing as more of the population gains access to education, but it is still an important point to keep in mind if you plan on doing business in India.

TV18 now focused on acquisitions to broaden their media base and to become an integrated media company. Unlike the United States, where traditional media portals like print media and radio are saturated and audiences are declining, India is at the other end of the spectrum, with low rates of penetration in print media and radio. Advertising expenditures are also quite low when compared to mature markets. The combination of these two factors is going to give media companies in India explosive growth potential. TV18 first targeted New Delhi Television Limited (NDTV), the top news channel in India for over 15 years. Not having the capital to acquire the station outright, they did what any other good capitalist would do—they acquired the management team. With the additional talent they inked a deal with CNN, winning the CNN franchise for India. Within 8 months CNN had gone from a market share of 1 percent to a market share of over 40 percent, with 25 million viewers in India. They decided to replicate their model, creating a CNN Hindi language channel, acquiring Channel 7 (IBN) as their platform.

With the traditional news channels in place, Haresh and Raghav began acquiring Internet portals, launching online news content and online shopping Web sites as well. They now plan to move into other key media outlets, and with a combined market capitalization in excess of 1.5 billion dollars and over 3,000 employees they are well positioned to do it. And what about employee loyalty? Well, consider the fact that the employees of TV18 hold 12 percent of the shares from the first offering and 5 percent from the second. And what about the seven original employees? They are all millionaires and the majority of them are still with TV18.

THE EMERGENCE OF INDIA'S FINANCIAL MARKETS

Raghav's success as an entrepreneur and TV18's success as a listed company can be traced back to a story that began over 170 years ago, when traders began buying and selling property rights under an old banyan tree in Bombay, ushering in what would become Asia's oldest stock exchange. Soon after the Bombay Stock Exchange was formed, and over time a number of other regional or city exchanges were created. While India may have been home to the oldest stock exchange in Asia it was hardly the most efficient exchange the world had ever seen.

At the time, all of the exchanges in India were mutual in nature and tightly held by a few brokers in each city. All of the trading was floor based and no one knew what the actual transaction costs really were. The brokers acted like a secret society, using an obscure local language to post notices and other financial information to the public, a practice that didn't change until the late 1980s. When transactions were finally settled, often a month or more after they were initiated, the buyer could be sure that he was paying the highest price for the security and sellers could be certain to receive the lowest price for the transaction. In the middle stood the brokers, reaping in fees that were far beyond any acceptable transaction fee.

The brokers were making a killing and they had plenty of friends in high places to make sure it stayed that way.

In 1992, as oil prices surged as a result of the Gulf War, India found itself in the middle of a foreign exchange meltdown. The government knew it had to act, and began looking to attract both foreign and domestic sources of capital into the market. The problem that the government faced was that the stock exchanges were tightly held, extremely opaque, and virtually devoid of modern technology. To make matters worse, the futures and derivatives markets that had been put in place years earlier had been dismantled by the socialist government after independence, and the stock exchanges themselves had been deemed to be charitable institutions exempt from income tax. Reforms had been tried in the past, but resistance was so great from the brokers that if regulators attempted to look at the books, the Bombay Stock Exchange would actually go on strike. You can imagine the lack of comfort that a foreign investor would have had in that type of environment—you would have felt more comfortable playing craps in Las Vegas.

Faced with limited choices, the government pushed forward with reforms, creating the Securities Exchange Board of India (SEBI) and creating a working group that included top financial experts in the country to make recommendations for radical reform. While there was certainly reason enough for reform of the financial markets, the real catalyst may have come in the form of the Hashad Mehta scam of 1992. That same year foreign capital had begun to find its way into the Indian market and the Indian economy was beginning to benefit from the economic reforms introduced by the government earlier that year. The Indian stock market began to take on the go-go feel of the U.S. stock market a decade earlier, when the phrase "Greed is good" was the mantra of the day.

Brokers and promoters knew a good thing when they saw one, and with foreign capital beginning to flood the market in search of a limited number of listed companies, the stage was set. The challenge was to inflate the value of the listed companies so that they would be ripe for the foreign investors to pick, and when that happened, fortunes could be made. The problem was money: You needed a lot of money—in fact, to make the scheme work, billions of dollars would be required. Enter one Hashad Mehta, a first-generation broker with a grand plan and plenty of friends working at India's public banks. At the time, there were no private banks in India, and as a result all of the personal savings in the country flowed into treasury accounts administered by the banks or into a mutual fund known as the Unit Trust of India, also administered by the government. In 1992, working at a public bank in India wasn't exactly the most exciting job in the world. Lacking the most basic technology, bank managers working in the treasury department would record daily interest rate changes in ledgers and the concurrent change in value of the billions of dollars of savings they were responsible for. Without competition, public banks in India performed as would be expected—badly! At the time, Indian bankers were notorious for the hours they kept, often beginning work at 10 A.M., taking a 2-hour lunch and then going home at 2 P.M.

Hashad Mehta, with the aid of several other brokers, convinced the State Bank of India—the largest bank at the time—that the money they were holding could be put to much better use in the stock market. There was just one small rub; banks were not allowed to invest in the stock market. Not a problem, considering the lack of technology—and with the use of ledgers, no one would ever know that any money was missing—and besides, they would be doing their customers and themselves a favor. The latter was especially true, with generous bribes being lavished on willing participants. Using a series of bank checks, billions of dollars were deposited in the brokers' accounts, with full discretionary responsibility. At first the scheme worked, with easy millions being made in foreign exchange arbitrage and stock market manipulation, but soon cracks began to appear. The State Bank of India launched an internal investigation, which soon caught the attention of Sucheta Dalal, a young investigative reporter working for the *Times of India*. Sucheta is an attractive woman with a natural grace and a disarming sense of humor. But beneath the soft exterior is a no-nonsense reporter that has an obsession for the truth. Sucheta soon learned that the scope of the scam was enormous, involving just about every major bank in India. The scope of the scheme was so great that in many cases brokers were actually running a bank's treasury department, using it as their own private credit line. The first bank to feel the heat of day was the National Housing Bank; soon, the daisy chain began to unravel. After Sucheta ran her story, the entire scheme imploded. Hashad Mehta, along with a number of other brokers, was arrested, and the Indian parliament launched a massive investigation.

The stock market tumbled, with the key index falling more than 40 percent—from 4,500 to 2,500—in a matter of hours, and with that, parliament moved quickly to enact the reforms to the capital markets that had been stalled just 6 months earlier. The Securities and Exchange Board of India was given full statutory authority and independence and they began enacting a full spectrum of regulatory reforms for India's capital markets. What ever happened to Hasha Mehta? He died in prison in 2002, awaiting trial on over 40 additional charges. Ironically, he had guessed it right, as foreign capital flooded the Indian market on the heels of the regulatory reforms, quickly erasing the correction that his scam had caused months earlier.

With regulatory reform underway and foreign capital entering the markets, Indian institutions and investors quickly grew tired of the opaque nature of the traditional Indian stock exchanges. With the support of government regulators and key institutions, the National Stock Exchange (NSE) was created (Figure 2.2). The NSE was the brain child of a working group headed by Ravi Narain that was formed in 1993. After assessing key markets around the world, his team developed five key principles that would form

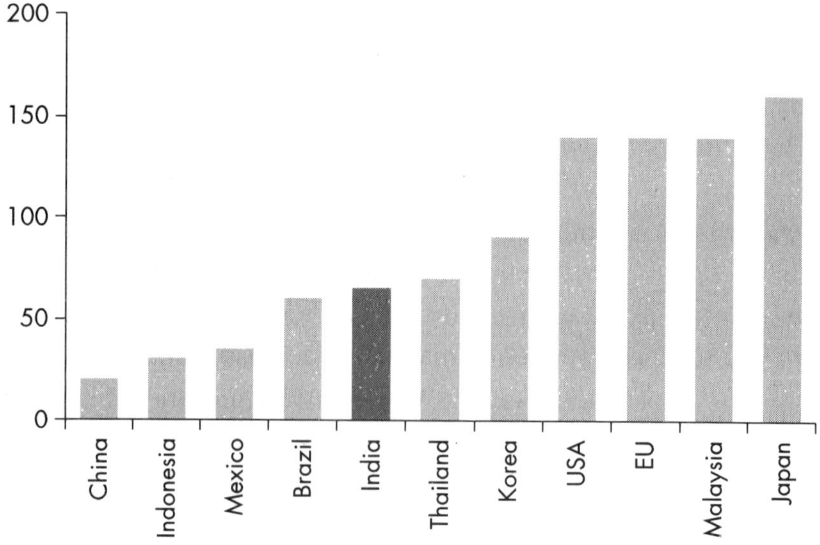

FIGURE 2.2 *India's Equity Market Comparable to Other Emerging Markets*

the bedrock of the NSE. The first principle was based on the belief that if brokers owned and managed the exchange there would be an inherent conflict of interest—similar to a baseball player acting as the umpire for his own game. Based on that premise, it was agreed that the exchange should be owned by large institutions, that it would be professionally managed as an ongoing profitable concern, and that all brokers would be required to pass a rigorous licensing exam. The second principle was based on the belief that the exchange should be a nationwide transparent electronic market with one national book of business. This posed a slight problem, as it would take over 3 months just to lay 4 miles of dedicated phone line in Bombay alone. At that rate it would take about 30 years to create the national exchange that they envisioned. The answer was technology. Using dedicated VSAT technology and state-of-the-art encryption codes, a nationwide exchange that operated in real time and was completely transparent was created. The third principle was that the exchange should be rule driven, with no exceptions. Stories of investors being bilked on other exchanges were commonplace and the NSE was determined that that would not happen on this exchange. All rules would be published for all investors to see. If a rule was open to question it would be reviewed, but the rule would stand until changes were deemed appropriate. The fourth principle recognized that high transaction volume would create volatility, and as such, the most advanced risk management tools would need to be put in place. The last key principle was to ensure that settlement terms would be strict, initially mandating a 5-day settlement term. When I met with Ravi Narain, now the chairman of the NSE, I got the sense that these principles were like a religion to him. He is adamant that the NSE be the most transparent and well-regulated exchange in the world, and he is determined to continuously look for ways to keep the exchange on the cutting edge of technology. By almost any standard he has already achieved those goals.

On November 4, 1994, the NSE commenced trading; with only marginal trading volume for the first 6 months of operations, it looked like the experiment might fail. But suddenly, as if the markets had all become simultaneously aware of the existence of the NSE, trading volumes shot up, and by November 5, 2005, almost one year to the day that trading had begun, the NSE had become the largest exchange in India. There were still a few people that wanted to spoil the party, which became evident during the end of one of the settlement days. At its inception the NSE was renting a floor in a commercial building. Young college graduates were intensely focused on the arduous task of physically counting shares for the day's trades when municipal authorities burst into the room, announcing that the office was illegal. They then proceeded to begin demolishing the room with hammers and pickaxes! The young employees of the NSE were stunned—cement, ceiling debris, and dust filled the office. They didn't panic, but instead pulled handkerchiefs from their pockets, moistened them with water, and the counting continued and settlement was made. The NSE's fifth principle had been kept, and with it the credibility of the institution. It also speaks volumes for the determination of the Indian people—something worth noting if you decide to invest in this market.

The brokers affiliated with the Bombay Stock Exchange (BSE), long resistant to change, finally recognized the changes taking place in the market and began to move aggressively to institute their own technological framework, and with it, heightened disclosure requirements and much greater market participation. The BSE is now one of the five largest stock exchanges in the Asia Pacific region, after Japan, Australia, Hong Kong, and Korea. The BSE's performance reflects that transformation, with the primary index of the BSE (Sensex) gaining 42 percent in 2005 and over 46 percent in 2006 (see Graph 2.1). Not exactly a mediocre return, and considering the fact that the Indian economy is at the beginning of a growth turnpike, you should expect more of the same.

In comparison, the Dow Jones Industrial Average and the NYSE Composite have moved by less than 15 percent over the last 3 years on an annualized basis. The Shanghai Stock Exchange's SSE

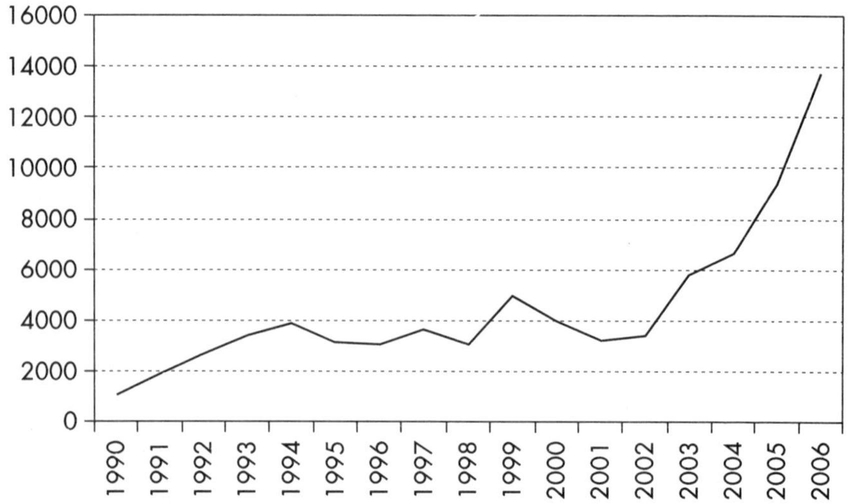

GRAPH 2.1 *India's Stock Markets: Scaling New Highs*

180 index has been on a roller coaster ride all this while. It fell by 16.5 percent in 2005 to 2,362.06 on December 31, 2004, falling further to 2,166.78 on December 30, 2005. It bounced back by 120.6 percent in 2006.

The differences between the Indian and Chinese capital markets are worth noting at several levels. Because China has manipulated its currency and restricted the number of companies listed on the exchanges, you have a lot of money chasing a relatively small number of companies. That excess liquidity is one of the reasons behind the overheating of China's capital market. This overheating started with the central bank of China's US$1 trillion reserves, bought from exporters. The trade surplus that emerged dramatically increased money in the market. The recent step, in April, 2007, to increase reserve ratios on bank deposits by a further 0.5 percent was the fourth time in the last 10 months when this was done. It was aimed at reducing the volume of money reaching the stock market, but the move had almost no impact on the market. By any metric, the Chinese stock market is at the peak of a classic asset bubble, and that bubble is going to burst sooner rather than later. Transparent markets, free from government interference and manipulation, will not eliminate asset bubbles, but it does tend to limit their extremes, a point that may seem prophetic by the time this book is published.

There are a number of other significant differences between the Indian and Chinese capital markets, and those differences are directly linked to their political systems. India is a democracy with an independent and credible judiciary that maintains strong intellectual property rights and patent protection and a vibrant entrepreneurial class that does not compete with the state for resources or customers. Add all of this up and you come up with some startling facts; of the approximately 6,000 companies that are listed in India, less than 1 percent are state-owned companies (see Table 2.1).

The remaining 99 percent are privately held mid-cap companies like TV18. Of the approximately 1,800 companies listed on

Table 2.1 Resource Mobilization from Public Issues

	2004–05		2005–06	
Issue	**Number**	**Amount**	**Number**	**Amount**
IPOs	23	123,820	79	109,360
Issues by Listed Companies	37	158,740	60	164,460
Public Issues	11	122,580	24	123,580
Right Issues	26	36,160	36	40,880
Total	**60**	**282,560**	**139**	**273,820**

Source: SEBI Annual Report 2005–2006.

the Chinese exchanges, more than 90 percent are state-owned companies, known for their sheer size, not their nimbleness. With that kind of composition, where do you think the next Microsoft will come from?

The NSE has an average trading volume of over seven billion dollars a day, making it one of the largest exchanges in Asia. If the exchange is measured by the number of daily transactions, it would be ranked the third-largest exchange in the world after the NASDAQ and the New York Stock Exchange. What makes the NSE somewhat unique is the composition of the trading volume that it handles. Retail is by far the largest component of trading volume: When you consider the fact that only 4 percent of Indian households currently participate directly or indirectly in the market, it gives you a sense of what is yet to come. Couple this point with the fact that less than 50 percent of Indian households even have bank accounts, and that Indians have the highest savings rates in the world, and you really begin to understand the scope of the opportunity (see Graph 2.2).

That opportunity is quickly being recognized by leading global financial institutions. On January 10, 2007, it was announced that the NYSE, Goldman Sachs, SoftBank, and the private equity firm

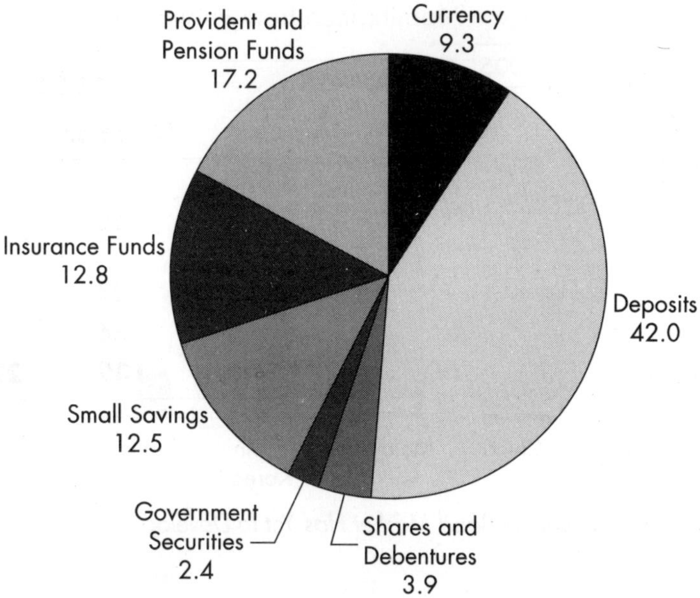

GRAPH 2.2 *Households are Ultraconservative in Their Investment Decisions*

General Atlantic had entered into an agreement to acquire a 5 percent stake each in the NSE. The deal gave the NSE a market valuation of US$2.3 billion, and by the end of 2008 that market capitalization is expected to exceed US$7 billion. The board of the NSE and the Securities and Exchange Board of India both recognize that additional reforms to the capital markets are needed. While the NSE has a regulatory framework that is equal to the New York Stock Exchange, the Indian corporate debt markets are extremely underdeveloped (see Graph 2.3).

This situation is not unique to India, with most corporate debt markets across Asia and Latin America sharing similar commonalities. Still, it is universally recognized by government officials and financial institutions alike that a mature corporate debt market is critical to the long-term financial success of the economy. That point is underscored by the massive investments India needs to attract in improving its infrastructure (see Graph 2.4).

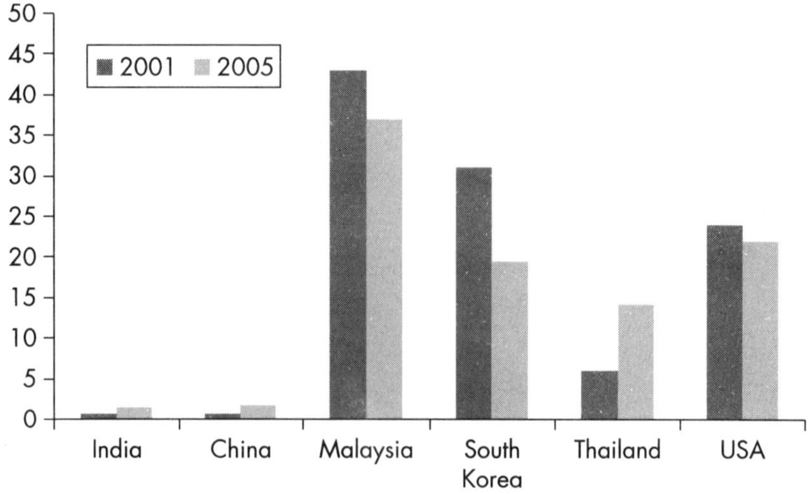

GRAPH 2.3 *Corporate Bond Market Has Yet to Develop*

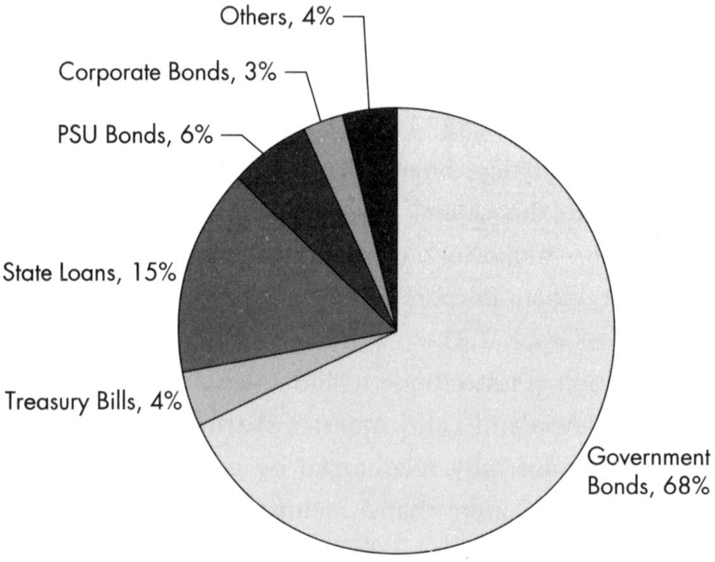

GRAPH 2.4 *Government Issuance Leads to the Local Bond Market*

The other two areas of India's capital markets that are still developing are the derivatives markets and mutual funds. The regulatory framework for derivatives was developed in 1996, based on a report by the Securities and Exchange Board of India. On June 12, 2000, the NSE began trading derivative instruments, and that market has grown substantially since, with total volume in 2004–2005 of US$6.5 billion, almost doubling to over US$12 billion in 2006 and averaging over US$7 billion per month in 2007. Mutual funds were originally a monopoly in India, created and managed by the government, known as the Unit Trust of India. Since 1998, open competition—and with it, a wider range of choices—have existed. Still, market participation is light, with 38 mutual funds registered with SEBI with a total market value of US$2.3 billion as of March 2006 (see Graph 2.5).

The transparency and regulatory nature of India's capital markets are important components of the overall investment environment, but India's overall credit rating is a critical factor as well. On January 22,

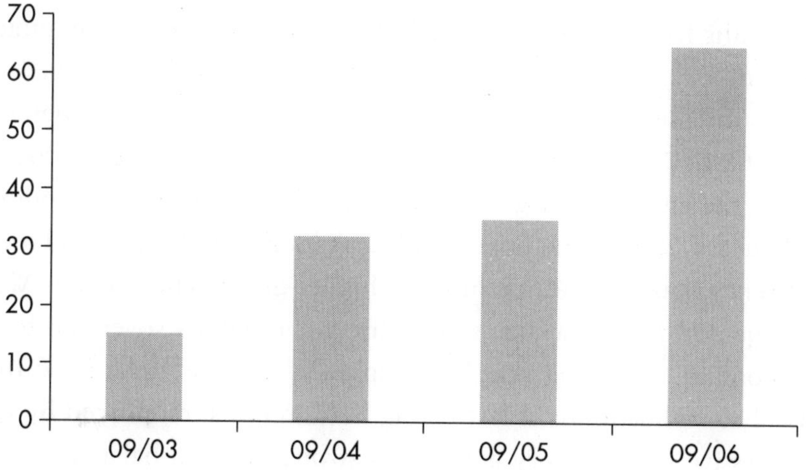

GRAPH 2.5 *Assets Under Management of Mutual Funds Have Soared*

2004, the credit rating agency Moody's upgraded India's foreign currency rating to "investment" grade. Moody's concedes that the ratings are a reflection of foreign currency transfer risk and systemic risk in a nation, and are considered an important factor in investment decision making. The steady performance of external payments and increase in foreign exchange reserves to US$100 billion were presumed to be the reasons behind the Indian promotion. Reflecting on the appraisal, the Indian finance minister had famously remarked "India was always investment grade." Later, the improving debt profile of the country resulted in Moody's upgrading India's domestic currency debt rating from "negative" to "stable."

In January 2007, Standard & Poor's ratings services raised India's sovereign credit rating to "investment" grade. The rating is understood by many as a reflection of the attractiveness of a nation as an investment destination. The rating agency, however, remarked that large government fiscal deficits serve as a deterrent, and the ratings can fall back. Reuters quotes S&P credit analyst Ping Chew as stating that "India's economic prospects remain strong and are rising gradually, with GDP trend growth likely to average more than 7.5 percent in the medium term." The news agency also reported that in the 6 months from April 2006, the Indian economy grew at an annual pace of 9.1 percent.

With the general government deficit declining to 7.5 percent in 2005 to 2006, from 10.1 percent of GDP in fiscal year 2001 to 2002, the Fitch agency gave another rating to boost India's standing. In January 2007, Fitch upgraded India's long-term foreign and local currency issuer default ratings to a higher grade. The agency's Web site quoted Paul Rawkins, senior director in Fitch's sovereign team in London, as stating that "This upgrade reflects Fitch's view that fiscal consolidation is at last taking hold in India, reinforced by the impressive growth story and India's strong external balance sheet." The drop in fiscal deficit levels to 4.1 percent of GDP last year and a consistent GDP growth have influenced India's ratings.

KEY INVESTMENT BANKS IN INDIA

India's robust economic performance has attracted numerous international brokerage and investment banking firms. Here is an overview of some of the leaders:

- Morgan Stanley first arrived in India in 1999, when it entered into two joint ventures (JVs) with JM Financial, the brokerage house JM Morgan Stanley Securities, and the investment banking arm JM Morgan Stanley. Those joint ventures ranked third in investment banking revenue in 2006. But early in 2007, Morgan Stanley decided to exit the relationship and pursue individual goals. It bought complete ownership of the brokerage and research business and sold the investment banking stake to JM. It was important for Morgan Stanley to partner with an Indian firm in 1999, when the market was still heavily regulated; but with the easing of rules and regulations, many feel it is the right time for Morgan Stanley to go solo. Vishal Kampani, JM Financial's director, told Forbes.com, "We would have preferred a joint venture but they wanted a divorce, so we accepted it." The U.S.-based investment services major is expected to kick start its investment banking, capital markets, fixed income, and private wealth management platforms soon in India. Together with JM Financial, Morgan Stanley executed several major offerings in the Indian capital market, which includes the US$620 million IPO of Reliance Petroleum Limited.
- The New York-based investment banking firm Goldman Sachs (GS) entered the Indian market in 1992 in a JV. In March, 2006, however, GS sold its stake in the relationship and decided to go it alone. Brooks Entwistle, chief executive of Goldman Sachs India, stated that "There is a compelling case for us to build an onshore presence." He did just that,

and the bank's Mumbai offices were opened last year in May 2006. Goldman Sachs India is wholly owned investment banking and securities firm of Goldman Sachs.

- DSP Merrill Lynch is a joint venture between India-based DSP Financial Consultants Limited (DSP) and Merrill Lynch and Co. The partnership was initiated in 1995 and is one of the few domestic-foreign relationships in the Indian capital market that have survived. The JV started as a 60–40 arrangement in favor of DSP. Merrill Lynch, however, has now gained a majority stake in the association. It bought a 50 percent stake in December 2005, for approximately $500 million, to gain control of 90 percent of the firm. Apart from mutual funds, the firm also manages IPOs and offers mergers and acquisitions (M&A) advisory.
- Deutsche Bank is one of the few investment banks that has entered the Indian market on a stand-alone basis. It established a presence in India in 1980 and is one of the top five foreign banks in the country. It has around 3,050 employees on its payroll. Apart from investment banking services, its products and service offerings also include fixed income sales and trading, OTC derivatives, equity broking, and M&A advisory. In March 2004, Deutsche Bank India lead managed the US$300 million Eurobond issuance of the Industrial Credit and Investment Corporation of India (ICICI) bank. It was the advisor on the largest FDI deal in India, involving Bharti Televentures and Singapore Telecom.

While there is a large and growing number of international investment banks in India, a number of large domestic firms also operate in the market:

- Kotak Mahindra Capital Company (KMCC) is the investment banking arm of the Kotak Mahindra Bank, a Mumbai-based commercial bank. The bank has 3,600 employees and was incorporated in 1985. KMCC is one of the leading investment banks in India and was earlier associated with Goldman Sachs. Kotak, however, bought back the 25 percent stake in their joint venture to gain complete control of KMCC. The Kotak-Goldman relationship started in 1992, forming an equity joint venture in 1996. It has managed IPOs in the Indian market to the tune of US$200 million and acts as a conduit for Indian corporations for global depository receipts (GDRs) and foreign currency convertible bonds (FCCBs) in international markets. It also managed the US$2,267 billion deal for Oil & Natural Gas Corporation of India (ONGC). It caters to firms ranging from banking and financial services, pharmaceutical and health care, energy and infrastructure, telecommunication, IT, retailing and media, and entertainment.

- JM Financial is a Mumbai-based firm. It started off as a business engaged in stockbroking and securities in 1986. Its partnership with Morgan Stanley in 1999 was among the first domestic-foreign JV in the Indian capital market. JM, however, bought back a 49 percent stake in their joint venture JM Morgan Stanley for US$20 million to gain solo control. The services of securities brokerage, investment banking, and trust and asset management are offered by 656 employees at JM Financial. The firm also has the corporate private equity (PE) fund, JM Financial India Fund, run in partnership with U.S.-based PE firm Old Lane Partners.
- The Industrial Finance Corporation of India Ltd. (IFCI) was established in 1948 by the government of India. The idea behind conceiving IFCI was to provide upcoming companies with financing options. It was the very first financial institution of post-independence India. Once it was decided that IFCI should access the markets directly for its fund requirements,

it was chartered as a company in 1993. Over the years, the breadth of services IFCI offers has grown, and now includes investment banking. Its economic contribution is exemplary, as it has contributed more than US$300 million to the government accounts over the years. It is a 487-member strong company, headquartered in New Delhi.

- Avendus Advisors is an investment bank based out of Mumbai. Founded in 1999 by three investment bankers, it offers M&A advisory and fixed income and strategic advisory services. It focuses on IT, Information Technology Enterprise Solutions (ITES), health care, and media firms. Avendus has facilitated the acquisition of New Jersey-based Power Software Services by India-based technology firm Wipro. It was also an advisor in Aditya Birla Group's Business Process Outsourcing (BPO) firm TransWorks' acquisition of Canada-based BPO Minacs. More recently, Avendus was on the advisory team of ChrysCapital, whose BPO firm Global Vantedge was taken over by Essar Global.

BLUE CHIP COMPANIES INVESTORS SHOULD LOOK AT

The companies selected for this section were done so on the basis of their growth, profitability, and leadership position in the market. These companies also occupy key vertical markets within the Indian economy, which include finance, infrastructure, pharmaceuticals, agribusiness, Telecom, IT, steel, real estate, and high-tech manufacturing. The majority of these companies are becoming global players through targeted acquisitions in key markets. Interested investors should note that many of these companies are now listed on the New York Stock Exchange through ADRs (American Depository Receipts). Investors should also look at India-focused or emerging market-focused mutual funds that hold these companies in their portfolios.

- Bharti Tele-Ventures, a part of Bharti Enterprises, works through three individual business units—mobile services, broadband, and telephone services (B&TS) and enterprise services. The company, established in 1995, is a public limited company and is headquartered in New Delhi. It was founded by Sunil Mittal (remember the Wal-Mart JV?). The mobile services business unit offers mobile services across India over 23 telecom circles. The B&TS business unit provides broadband and telephone services and the enterprise services business unit provides national and international long-distance services that includes integrated voice and data communications solutions to corporate customers and small and medium-size enterprises. As of March 31, 2006, the company had 20,925,948 million customers. For the 9 months ending December 31, 2006, Bharti Airtel Limited's revenues increased 59 percent to US$3.9 billion, and net income rose 84 percent to US$708 million. Headquartered in New Delhi, it has an employee base of 18, 213. Its market value as of March 2, 2007, was US$30.2 billion. From 2000 to 2005, Bharti Televentures has grown its revenues at a CAGR of 80 percent.
- Infosys Technologies Limited is a global technology services firm founded in 1981. It delivers IT-enabled business solutions to its clients. The Company provides end-to-end business solutions, including consulting, design, development, software reengineering, maintenance, systems integration, package evaluation, and implementation and infrastructure management services. Infosys also provides software products to the banking industry. Through its majority-owned subsidiary, Progeon Limited (Progeon), the company provides business process management services. Infosys' wholly owned subsidiaries are Infosys Technologies Pty. Limited (Australia), Infosys Technologies Co. Limited (Shanghai), and Infosys

Consulting Inc. For the 9 months ending December 31, 2006, Infosys Technologies Ltd.'s revenues rose 47 percent, to US$2.469 billion. Net income before extraordinary items rose 52 percent, to INR$660 million. Headquartered in Bangalore, it has an employee base of 69,432. Its market value as of March 2, 2007 was US$26,478 million and its net profit CAGR for the past 5 years is 36 percent.

- Hindalco Industries Ltd. is an Indian producer of aluminum and copper, founded in 1962. It was recently in the news for its US$6 billion purchase of Novelis Inc., the world's largest producer of aluminum rolled products. The company produces specialty alumina, primary aluminum, and downstream products. Hindalco's integrated complex at Renukoot houses an alumina refinery, an aluminum smelter, and facilities for the production of semifabricated products. Their captive bauxite mines are located in western and eastern India; their alumina refineries are located in Belgaum in southern India and Muri in eastern India. Hindalco's copper division is in Dahej, in the Bharuch district of Gujarat. For the fiscal year ended March 31, 2006, Hindalco Industries Ltd.'s revenues increased 19 percent to INR$3 billion. Net income increased 23 percent, to INR$385.3 million. Headquartered in Mumbai, it has an employee base of 19,593. Its market value as of March 2, 2007 was US$3,606.5 million. In July, 2005, Hindalco showed a 10 percent CAGR in annualized returns for the past 5 years.
- DLF Limited (DLF) is a real estate development company headquartered in Gurgaon. The company's primary business is the development of residential, commercial, and retail properties. Its operations span all aspects of real estate development, from the identification and acquisition of land, the planning, execution, and marketing of its

projects, through to the maintenance and management of its completed developments. In its residential business line, DLF builds and sells a range of properties, including houses, duplexes, and apartments of varying sizes. In its commercial business line, the company builds, sells, or leases commercial office space. DLF's retail business line develops, manages, and mainly leases shopping malls, which in many cases include multiplex cinemas. As of January 2, 2007, DLF had signed lease agreements or letters of intent for office space aggregating 10 million square feet. For the 8 months ended November 30, 2006, DLF Ltd.'s revenues totaled INR$810 million. Net income totaled US$446 million.

- Tata Steel Limited is an integrated steel company in India. The company's long products division produces billets, blooms, and slabs. The flat products division manufactures hot- and cold-rolled and galvanized coils and sheets. The tubes division provides standard pipes, precision tubes, and welded-line pipes. The rings division offers rings for bearings, gear blanks, and helical gears. The ferroalloys and minerals division produces ferroalloys, chrome ores, and manganese ore. The automation division specializes in implementing total automation solutions involving instrumentation, system integration, process modeling, communication, and software development. The Growth Shop manufactures heavy engineering equipment. The agricultural products division manufactures agricultural implements. The raw materials division operates coal mines, and produces coal, iron ore, and dolomite. For the 9 months ended December 31, 2006, Tata Steel Ltd.'s revenues increased 18 percent, to INR$4.3 billion. Net income increased 10 percent, to INR$783 million. Tata Steel was recently in the news for acquiring Europe's second largest steel maker, the Anglo-Dutch Corus Group.

Headquartered in Mumbai, Tata Steel has an employee base of 38,182 and had a market value of US$5.528 billion on March 2, 2007. For 2004 to 2005, net profit grew at a 3-year CAGR of 156.9 percent.

- Ruchi Soya is the flagship company of Ruchi Group, a pioneer soya processor group, which started operating back in 1972 to 1973. For the fiscal year ended March 31, 2006, Ruchi Soya Industries Ltd.'s revenues increased 63 percent, to US$1.879 billion. The company manufactures soya foods, edible oils, vanaspati, bakery fats, and soaps. The company is headquartered in Mumbai; its soya food brand Nutrela offers soya granules, chunks, and mini chunks, and is the most popular in India. It enjoys more than 50 percent of the market share. India is one of the top five producers of soybeans globally, and Ruchi Soya has taken it to the consumers. Ruchi Soya forayed into a new line of business last year with the introduction of Ruchi, the number-one soap in the Indian market.
- Adani Enterprises Ltd. (AEL), also known as Adani Exports Limited, is the flagship company of the Adani Group. It started off as a partnership firm in 1988 and went public in 1993. Adani Enterprises Ltd. is one of the largest trading houses in the country; its commodity portfolio includes yarn, fabrics, cereals, pulses, groundnuts, grains, dry fruits, sugar, oilseeds, marine products, chemicals, coal/coke, petrochemicals, petroleum products, metals, and fiber-reinforced metal (FRM). The group houses firms like Adani Petronet (Dahej), Port Pvt. Ltd. (APPPL), a joint venture between Petronet LNG Ltd. and Adani Enterprises Ltd., which wants to develop a multipurpose port to handle solid cargo at Dahej in the state of Gujarat. Gujarat Adani Port Ltd. is a preferred port on the western coast of India. Adani Willmar Limited

(AWL), a joint venture with Singapore's Willmar Trading, has set up India's largest integrated edible oil refinery at the Mundra port. Gujarat Adani Energy Ltd. (GAEL), Adani Retail Ltd., and iCall India Ltd. are the other firms that fall under the umbrella of the Adani group. Mundra Port and Special Economic Zone Ltd. has developed state-of-the-art, all-weather multipurpose port facilities at Mundra. For the fiscal year that ended March 31, 2006, Adani Enterprises' revenues were US$3.01 billion. The next expansion for this group will be its retail division. At present Adani Retail operates in nine cities across the state of Gujarat, with a chain of 47 stores that include neighborhood stores, supermarket stores, and hypermarket stores. Adani Retail plans to reach 19 cities with 60 stores in the state of Gujarat. It also plans to expand its operation in the states of Rajasthan, Madhya Pradesh, Maharashtra, and Chhattisgarh.

- Kotak Mahindra Capital Company (KMCC) is the investment banking arm of the Kotak Mahindra Bank, a Mumbai-based commercial bank. The bank has 3,600 employees and was incorporated in 1985. KMCC is one of the leading investment banks in India and was earlier associated with Goldman Sachs. Kotak, however, bought back the 25 percent stake in their joint venture to gain complete control of KMCC. The Kotak-Goldman relationship started in 1992, forming an equity joint venture in 1996. It has managed IPOs in the Indian market to the tune of US$195 million, and acts as a conduit for Indian corporations for GDRs and FCCBs in international markets. It also managed the US$2,267 million deal for Oil & Natural Gas Corporation of India (ONGC). It caters to firms covering banking and financial services, pharmaceutical and health care, energy and infrastructure, telecommunication, IT, retailing, media, and entertainment. For the 9 months ended December 31, 2006, Kotak Mahindra Bank Ltd.'s interest income rose 65 percent, to US$331 million.

- Moser Baer, a publicly held company, is principally engaged in the manufacture of storage media products. It was founded in New Delhi in 1983. It has a product range of floppy disks, compact discs (CDs), and digital versatile discs (DVDs). The firm's manufacturing facilities are spread across six different sites in the twin cities of Noida and Greater Noida, in the state of Uttar Pradesh. Their Greater Noida manufacturing facility is spread over a total land area of over 100 acres. This facility manufactures 150 million discs every month—that's 1.8 billion a year. The firm is one of India's largest manufacturers of optical storage devices. For the fiscal year ended March 31, 2006, Moser Baer India Ltd.'s revenues rose 28 percent, to US$390 million. The firm is truly an Indian multinational, with a presence in more than 82 countries. Earlier this year the firm announced that it will set up the world's largest thin film solar fabricator, in collaboration with U.S.-based Applied Materials, Inc., to achieve new cost benchmarks. The unit will make thin-film solar modules, which are ideal for energy farms and rural applications The company's subsidiaries include European Optic Media Technology, Moser Baer Photo Voltaic, and Moser Baer SEZ. During the fiscal year that ended March 31, 2006, the company entered into a new business, Solar Photo Voltaic, and also set up a subsidiary, Moser Baer Photovaltaic Ltd., for the photovoltaic cells and modules business. In 2007 the subsidiary received a US$22.5 million (INR1 billion) loan from International Finance Corp. (IFC), the private sector arm of the World Bank, to promote solar energy in India. The subsidiary is engaged in a US$92 million expansion project near New Delhi to produce electricity from sunlight.

- Biocon was founded in 1978. The firm produces a wide range of biopharmaceuticals, industrial enzymes, and food additives. The firm serves customers across 50 countries and is only the second Indian firm to achieve a market capitalization of US$1 billion on the first day of going public. The firm also provides custom research and clinical research services via its subsidiaries Syngene and Clinigene, respectively. The pharmaceuticals business manufactures and develops active pharmaceutical ingredients as well as bulk drugs. The majority of its products involve fermentation and synthetic conversion. The enzymes division includes single-component enzymes, formulations, and enzyme systems for the food and beverages, textiles, starch, brewing, and distilling industries. Molecular biology, synthetic chemistry, bioinformatics, and clinical research on patients suffering from chronic diseases such as diabetes, osteoporosis, and asthma are provided by its contract research arm. The firm is headquartered in Bangalore, one of the metropolitan cities of south India, and has representative offices in New Jersey, and other Indian metropolitan cities of New Delhi, Mumbai, and Kolkata. The firm is known for the host of "firsts" it has attained. It is the first biotech firm in India, the first Indian biotech firm to attain the ISO 9001 certification, India's first biotechnology company to export microbial enzymes to the United States and Europe, and its subsidiary, Syngene, is India's first biotech custom research company in drug discovery. For the fiscal year ended March 31, 2007, Biocon Ltd.'s revenues increased 25 percent, to US$220 million. The Planning Commission of India's "India Vision 2020" report says that investment in the biotechnology sector is expected to increase from US$2 billion to US$10 billion by the end of this decade. Biocon has already committed US$125 million of this by investing in a special economic zone in the city of Vishakhapatnam. The investment is a part of its growth plans. The firm has always been among the top performers in the Indian biotech industry turnover-wise, leading the market on most occasions. Total biotech exports from India were US$451 million in 2005, and Biocon accounted for more than one fifth of this with its total exports during the period coming close to US$100 million.

- The Industrial Credit and Investment Corporation of India (ICICI Bank) is India's largest private sector bank and the country's second-largest scheduled commercial bank in terms of balance sheet size. ICICI Bank is also ranked third among all the companies listed on the Indian stock exchanges in terms of free-float market capitalization. The ICICI was formed in 1955 as a joint initiative of the World Bank and the Indian government. Prior to the 1990s, ICICI operated primarily as a development financial institution, providing only project finance. It then remodeled its business to become a diversified financial services group delivering a wide portfolio of products and services, both directly and via a number of subsidiaries and affiliates such as ICICI Bank. ICICI has been listed on the New York Stock Exchange (NYSE) since 1999. It was the first Indian company and the first bank or financial institution from non-Japan Asia to do so. In 2001, the merger of ICICI and ICICI Bank was approved, keeping in mind the emerging competitive scenario in the Indian banking industry. Headquartered in Mumbai, ICICI Bank has a network of about 950 branches and 3,300 ATMs across India. It has a presence in 17 other countries. ICICI Bank has 16 subsidiaries operating in segments such as investment banking, general and life insurance, home finance, asset management, venture funds, and so forth. Its major subsidiaries include ICICI Prudential Life Insurance Company, ICICI Lombard General Insurance Company, Prudential ICICI Asset Management Company, ICICI Securities Limited and ICICI Venture Funds Management Company Limited. For the year that ended March 31, 2007, (FY07), ICICI Bank's operating profit increased 51 percent from last year to US$1.35 billion. Net interest income for FY07 increased 41 percent, to US$1,527 million. ICICI Bank's deposits reached US$53 billion March 31, 2007, from US$38 billion at March 31, 2006. In recent developments, ICICI Bank will raise its share sale to US$5 billion from US$4.3 billion, a record for an Indian company. The share sale by ICICI accounts for 50 percent of the US$10 billion that India's banks plan to raise in the year ending March 2008. The share sale was split equally between the Indian and overseas investors. While the Indian shares were sold at INR 940 each, it sold American depository shares at US$49.25 each. The company plans to meet the higher loan requirements of companies expanding overseas and also expects to substantially invest in India's rural economy. In June, 2007, ICICI Bank announced that it expects to add 60 million new rural customers. Through novel partnership with shopkeepers and nongovernment organizations, ICICI Bank aims to bring banking to rural areas.

- Videocon, an Indian multinational, was founded in 1979. Controlled by the Dhoot family, the group operates in four key sectors—Consumer Durables, Color Picture Tube (CPT), CRT Glass, and Oil and Gas. Headquartered in Aurangabad in Maharashtra, Videocon Industries Limited is a leading manufacturer of consumer products such as color televisions, washing machines, air conditioners, refrigerators, and microwave ovens. The company launched its range of color and black-and-white televisions as well as washing machines in 1987. It was during 1989 to 1990 that Videocon introduced the home entertainment system and air conditioners; refrigerators and coolers were launched later, in 1991. Videocon has technical and design collaborations with companies such as Samsung, Matsushita Electric, and Techneglas. The company possesses one of the most extensive sales and distribution networks in India. With the acquisition of Thomson in 2005, the company has emerged as a leading CRT manufacturer, with operations in Mexico, Italy, Poland, and China. Last but not least, the Ravva oil field is a crucial asset for the company. Having one of the lowest operating costs in the world, it produces 50,000 barrels of oil per day. The group plans for a global expansion in this sector. For the year ended September 30, 2006, Videocon reported consolidated revenue of US$2,819 million. The company, whose main export markets include Europe and the Middle East, plans to double its export turnover to US$187 million in 2007 to 2008. Recently, Videocon bought Normandie, a European brand of color TVs. Through this acquisition, Videocon hopes to penetrate the Italian, German, and French markets. The company plans to set up India's first thin-film transistor chip facility in Kolkata. In early 2007, Videocon reported plans to set up a manufacturing unit in Dubai as well as a greenfield liquid crystal display (LCD) panel manufacturing facility in Italy. The company's ambitious plans and strategies indicate that it's expanding abroad in order to stay competitive in the domestic front. It aims to become one of the top five consumer-electronics and home-appliance companies in the world by 2010. Faced with increasing pressure from foreign companies, Videocon has had to switch from primarily selling brand-name appliances to manufacturing components, to ensure its survival. Now the company is looking to acquire a global brand.

- Dabur India Limited (DIL), headquartered in New Delhi, is India's fourth-largest FMCG Company. The company's core operations cover three main segments—health care, personal care, and food products. It was established in 1884 by Dr. S. K. Burman for making health care products, and is one of India's oldest brands. The company's most reputed brands include Dabur Amla (hair oil), Dabur Chyawanprash (Ayurvedic health tonic), Vatika (personal care), Hajmola (digestive tablet), and Real (fruit juices). Dabur products are available in the markets of the Middle East, Southeast Asia, Africa, the European Union, and the United States. Recent reports suggest that Dabur is in negotiations with Actis and Standard Chartered Private Equity for buying out their 60 percent (30 percent each) stake in Unza Holdings, a leading Southeast Asian manufacturer of personal care products. The deal is expected to cost Dabur between US$100 to 150 million. Dabur Pharma also plans to acquire an international distribution and marketing company, most likely in China. In other recent developments, Dabur plans to enter the retail health and beauty business in India through its wholly owned subsidiary, H&B Stores Ltd. (HBSL). The HBSL outlets will sell pharmaceutical products, health foods, confectionery, personal and baby care products, and general merchandise. New strategies include adding more products in its soaps portfolio and increasing its market share in India's processed foods sector. Dabur's cancer diagnostics arm, OncQuest, can be expected to enter the clinical trials domain soon. Further, Dabur India is working on an aggressive marketing strategy to capture a larger market share in south India. Overall, Dabur is focusing on strengthening its distribution network to increase sales and is raising its advertising outlay by 20 perent in 2007 to popularize its brands. For the year ended March 31, 2007, Dabur India's consolidated net profit increased 32.2 percent to US$65.15 million; revenues recorded a 17.6 percent growth to US$514.2 million. The company also reported significant gains from overseas markets.

3

Why India Will Outperform China

The Future Look of India's Airports

India conquered and dominated China culturally for 20 centuries without ever having to send a single soldier across her border!
Hu Shih (former Chinese ambassador to the United States)

Recently I (William) attended a dinner party with a guest list that included several venture capitalists and a number of executives from large multinationals, all of whom had made large bets on China. The dinner conversation quickly moved to the China-versus-India topic, at which point I voiced my opinion that India would ultimately outperform China. "That's ridiculous," one of the guests blurted out. "India doesn't have the infrastructure that China has, and furthermore, the Chinese government is much more organized than India's." "You mean it's a dictatorship that doesn't have to deal with political dissent or debate, correct?" I replied. "No," another guest retorted, "it's just that the Chinese don't consider democracy to be that important . . . it's an Asian model." "Okay. Before we get into the values-and-principles side of the argument, let me try to articulate in quantifiable terms why I believe that India will ultimately outperform China. India has the three Ds in its favor." "What are the three Ds?" my fellow guests asked. I replied (with a smile), "The three Ds are *democracy, demographics,* and *determination!*" My guests were intrigued but not even close to being convinced.

So I proceeded to explain my position, starting with the first D, *democracy,* which surprisingly has been conveniently absent from most strategic business planning discussions that focus on China. Democracy is an entrenched institution in India with participation rates that are higher than the United States. In fact, simply witnessing a general election in India is an experience not soon forgotten. Think about this: In a general election, the 600 million-strong electorate elects about 500 representatives to the national parliament. A national election requires 900,000 polling stations, scattered from Cape Cormorin at the southern tip of India to the Himalayas in the north. The electoral process requires 4.5 million persons to administer; some of these individuals use elephants as transport to reach remote villages and polling stations in an effort to ensure that every eligible voter has a chance to vote.

I am not going to tell you that democracy on its own will ensure economic prosperity and social justice for the Indian populace. In fact, India has been a glaring example of government incompetence and corruption that helped keep more than two thirds of the population in abject poverty. Its government failed to provide the most basic social services, like clean drinking water and good health care. But India is a young democracy—in fact, the first elections didn't even occur until 1952—and the legacy of British colonialism didn't help matters much. And what would be the alternative—scrap their system and opt for some type of dictatorship, or reform the democracy they already have? I personally would choose the latter, and as India emerges as an economic power so I believe will its democratic institutions.

There is a new breed of politicians taking the stage in India. Many of them are successful entrepreneurs, tired of the old politics and determined to make a change. One such is Suresh Prabhu, a chartered accountant by training. Now a member of India's parliament, he got into politics in 1996, and after his term is completed he plans to go back to the private sector. He will be the first to tell you that corruption is still rampant and that the system can be incredibly frustrating. In the past, many Indian politicians were beholden to the party bosses and not to the electorate. Such a model created a sense of favoritism, so you ended up with individuals appointed to positions based on loyalty, not ability. To make matters worse, key ministerial positions often changed hands like a game of musical chairs, based on shifting parliamentary relationships. That doesn't tend to create steady, long-term policies. But Suresh will also tell you that things are changing: One example is the fact that more than one third of the members of Congress are women, and they are taking their work seriously. Indian politicians are also beginning to see the benefits that free markets and open competition bring, and as a result, even the most ardent communists are now buying into the new India. Another example of evident change is that elections are happening at the grassroots level, with unusual coalitions of voters.

The most recent example of the new India occurred during the 2007 elections in the state of Uttar Pradesh (UP). With more than 170 million people, UP is one of the most crowded regions on earth and is India's most populous state. Like all other elections in India, just having a fair and open election was a challenge in itself. With 6,070 candidates, 450,000 election personnel, 350,000 security personnel, and 120,000 electronic voting machines, the election was unprecedented. More than 50 million people voted, representing 44 percent of UP's 114 million registered voters, and by almost any account the election met the toughest international standards of fairness. But what made the election truly unique was that the winning party had put together a coalition consisting of India's poorest citizens—once referred to as "untouchables"—and the Brahmins, the traditional elite of Hindu society. The election represents a historic departure from the divisive, caste-based politics of the past. Old India is now being replaced by much broader coalitions of voters who have common economic and social interests. This is important; it is not an anomaly, but rather is a fundamental change in the way the Indian people are voting.

The Bahujan Samaj Party (BSP) is a relatively obscure regional party led by Miss Mayawati, a member of India's oppressed *dalit* caste (untouchables). Constituting about 22 percent of India's 1.1 billion people, *dalits* are often politically sidelined by most mainstream parties. Poor and discriminated against as well as disadvantaged in social and educational terms, *dalits* have historically been pushed to the fringe in India. Mayawati, born in the slums of New Delhi to a low-level government employee and his illiterate wife, has spent her life fighting the marginalization of her caste. A single woman who struggled to obtain an education, she is the new chief minister (CM) of UP.

As you can see, the Indian people take their voting seriously—and they expect their votes to count. The entire election process in India is overseen by the Election Commission (EC), a constitutional body. The EC consists of a Chief Election Commissioner and "such number of other Election Commissioners, if any, as the President may from time to time fix. . . . When any other Election Commissioner is appointed the Chief Election Commissioner shall act as the Chairman of the Election Commission." The commission's independence is assured by the Constitution, which provides that "the Chief Election Commissioner shall not be removed from his office except in like manner and on like grounds as a Judge of the Supreme Court," that is, by each house of parliament, by a special majority, and on the grounds of proved misbehavior or incapacity. Other election commissioners may not be removed by the president except on the recommendation of the Chief Election Commissioner.

China, on the other hand, has an authoritarian political system controlled by the Communist Party, which allows little recourse or voice by the Chinese people. The party committees formulate all major state policies before the government implements them. And by the way, there are no women holding senior leadership positions within the Chinese Communist Party. The party dominates Chinese legislative bodies such as the National People's Congress (NPC) and fills all important government positions in executive and judicial institutions by an internal selection process, more like a private club or fraternity. The State Council's White Paper on "Building Political

Democracy in China," issued in October, 2005, states that: "Party committees serve as the leadership core over all [government and mass] organizations at the same level . . . and through Party committees and cadres in these organizations, ensure that the Party's policies are carried out. . . . Through legal procedures and democratic discussion, Party committees ensure that Party proposals become the will of the state and that candidates recommended by Party organizations become leaders in the institutions of state power." Does that sound like a democracy to you?

Party control extends throughout institutions of local government. Party institutions control the selection of judges, and local party committees influence which judges are posted to their localities. Many local party secretaries serve concurrently as head of their Local People's Congress (LPC). County and township party secretaries also control LPC and village elections through the election leadership groups, which they often head.

Under the Chinese system there is a complete lack of popular and/or legal constraints to check the behavior of party officials, which, as you might have guessed, has led to widespread corruption. Although party policy documents assert that one-party control is necessary for social stability, senior Chinese officials have acknowledged that the inability of local party cadres to respond to citizen grievances is contributing to rising social unrest. That means riots—when power is concentrated in the hands of the party secretary and standing committee, corruption and other abuses of power are likely to occur: After all, once you have your hand in the cookie jar it's difficult to take it out! This type of corruption is widespread, with thousands of local Chinese officials using their positions to acquire financial interests in local mines, hampering efforts to improve their safety. How often do you read about a Chinese mine disaster? In some localities, police collude with criminal forces. In June 2005 local officials hired armed thugs to break up a protest by farmers in Shengyou village, Hebei province, killing six villagers and wounding more than one hundred. Villagers had opposed local government efforts to seize their land, and claimed that local officials had embezzled money that should have gone to them. Ministry of Public Security statistics show that incidents of "mass gatherings to disturb social order" rose by 13 percent from 2004 to 2005. Weak protection of labor rights and worker discontent over unpaid wages and benefits resulted in an increase in mass labor disputes, from 1,482 in 1994 to 11,000 in 2003. Both collective and individual citizen petitions seeking official redress have increased steadily from 1993 to 2004.

Party secretaries can block access to local information sources that might challenge their control, which stifles the role of the media as a check on the abuse of government power. In November, 2005, Jilin provincial officials prevented the news media from reporting on an industrial accident and massive benzene leak on the Songhua River for more than a week. The delayed local government response impeded central government efforts to manage the crisis, caused panic among the citizens of Harbin, and created a diplomatic incident with Russia. In June, 2005, Hong Kong news media reported that party propaganda officials issued a directive limiting publication of critical investigative reports by local news media through a requirement that state-run news media first clear the articles with the local party committee. If you are planning to invest in the Chinese capital markets, this should be of special concern. Do you really believe that the Chinese government would allow the dissemination of news that was adverse to their own financial interests?

Chinese authorities have ruled out building representative democratic institutions to address citizen complaints of corruption and abuse of power, and are recentralizing government posts into the hands of individual Party secretaries. Officials are also relying on top-down personnel controls to address local governance problems, but these measures have increased incentives for some local party secretaries to conceal problems from their superiors, and thus risk compounding the issue. Consider the fact that a recent survey by the Chinese Academy of Social Sciences found that of the 20,000 richest men in China, more than 90 percent were directly related to Communist Party officials!

In 2005, Communist Party officials called for strengthened controls over society to address mounting social problems and suppress dissent. In January, 2005, party leaders launched an "advanced education" campaign to strengthen party organizations and to conduct political education for Party cadres. In October, 2005, the Party Central Committee and State Council issued an opinion calling for strengthened controls over society, and the accompanying press statement set a 2006 goal to reduce the number of "mass incidents" that disturb public order, including strikes, marches, demonstrations, and collective petitions to government authorities. In November of that year, officials expanded the campaign to rural areas. Party officials assert that this propaganda campaign will help reduce social unrest. A December, 2005, Party and State Council joint opinion called for strengthening village autonomous institutions (such as elected village committees), but "under village Party leadership." Government officials tightened controls over the press and imposed new restrictions on the Internet. Authorities issued warnings about the activities of civil society organizations, and are preparing new measures to monitor and control them. The problem with an authoritarian system is that it creates distortions in society, and in due course those distortions have a way of blowing up.

The Chinese government has made it clear that it will definitely not imitate Western political models—they are strengthening Communist consultative institutions instead of creating representative political bodies. At the March, 2005, meeting of the Chinese People's Political Consultative Conference (CPPCC), Central Party School Vice President Li Junru contrasted the Chinese system of "elections plus consultation" with "discredited" Western liberal democratic models. The CPPCC is a party-led organization that includes party members, representatives of party mass organizations, and non-party members who closely align themselves with party goals, including members of the eight minor "democratic" parties permitted under Chinese law. Li said, "In order to address foreign and domestic challenges regarding the issue of democracy, particularly the challenge of the 'color revolutions,' the advantages of the CPPCC need to be brought into play more effectively." That's Orwellian-speak for toe the party line or face the consequences—not exactly a recipe for innovation.

Okay, so India is a democracy and China is a dictatorship, but anyone that has ever been to Shanghai and witnessed firsthand the world-class airport, high-speed trains, and gleaming skyscrapers might be tempted to wonder if a good authoritarian system might not be better than a bad democracy? If the measurement is economic growth, then India is clearly a democracy that is getting better—after all, India will most likely surpass China in GDP sometime in 2008. So if India's democratic institutions are becoming more responsive to the will of the people, then what will that mean for the country economically and socially and why will it give India an advantage over China?

First, it is important to define what the key elements of democracy are and how exactly that will translate into a competitive advantage for India. Let's take a look at property rights—a fundamental aspect of most modern democracies. While far from perfect, India has property rights that extend to 65 percent of the population that lives in rural areas. These property rights were originally codified in the British Land Act of 1896, which defined land as agriculture, non-agricultural, or forest. Certain additional restrictions were placed on the sale of land between various castes so that a nonfarming caste could not acquire land from a farming caste. Certain hereditary rights were also given to sharecroppers, who worked the land but had no direct ownership, ensuring that they would receive some compensation when the landowner sold the property. While that may sound like a lot of dry legalese, it is important for you to remember.

Land is in short supply in India and farmers and other landowners understand that their land has value. A number of large multinationals and a few Indian companies have found their expansion plans stymied by irate farmers who have refused to sell their land at less-than-fair market value.

As India becomes urbanized many families will choose to sell or borrow against their land so they can start businesses, buy apartments, or provide educational opportunities for their children. Currently, close to 65 percent of the Indian population lives in small villages, with over 100 million Indians directly involved in farming while another 500 million are indirectly linked to the agricultural sector. India is at the beginning of a gradual migration, driven by the development of high-end manufacturing and other startup industries that will require a vast pool of semiskilled and skilled labor.

This migration will create an increasingly urban India that is expected to attract over 200 million rural inhabitants to urban centers by 2025, primarily in class B & C cities. This transition will involve the sale of landholdings by an estimated 30 million farmers and 170 million other individuals who are indirectly tied to the agricultural sector. While the transition will not be uniform—driven in part by politics and the policies of the different states—it will nevertheless occur. Some states, like Punjab—which has progressive property sale regulations that require buyers to negotiate directly with sellers without interference from the state, thus ensuring that the seller receives fair market value—will transition quickly. States like West Bengal, however, which attempted to use a corrupt government policy of eminent domain to take land from farmers at unfair values, will transition at a much slower pace. It should be noted that the latter state's policy resulted in violent riots that ultimately forced the government to abandon the policy.

The sales of these landholdings, catalyzed by rural-urban migration, is expected to generate over US$3 trillion in capital by 2025. This capital will, in turn, have a multiplier affect on the Indian economy that could exceed US$6 trillion. Now let's take a look at China. China has no rural property rights, and China's 750 million rural residents who lease land are at the mercy of their local and regional government as to what compensation they will receive, if any, when they are forced from the land as a result of development, infrastructure growth, and so on. Additionally, the Chinese rural population have no right to borrow against their lease, and as a result they have few assets. In fact, the Chinese government's official figures state that over 500,000 acres of rural land are taken from rural residents every year, with little or no compensation. The result is not unexpected: over 87,000 mass incidents (riots) were reported in 2005, a 50 percent increase over 2003. Many provincial governments in China have begun to use plainclothes policemen to beat, intimidate, or otherwise subdue any peasant who dares to oppose these land grabs. And as might be expected, the beneficiaries from these policies are developers and corrupt government officials. The Chinese government did enact a property rights law in March, 2007, but it's practically worthless—and after all, who controls the courts in China?

The second, equally important element is the presence (or lack) of the rule of law: The rule of law is a fundamental cornerstone of any modern society. India inherited a legal system from Britain that has been in place for well over 100 years. This legal system is internationally respected and includes laws that protect intellectual property as well as physical property. The rule of law creates predictability and stability, which allow entrepreneurial behavior to flourish. This is clearly evident in India, with more then 6,000 companies listed on the stock exchanges, compared to approximately 1,700 in China. More telling is the fact that of the 6,000 listed companies in India, only approximately 60 are state owned. This stands in stark contrast to China, where more than 1,500 of the 1,700 companies listed on the exchanges are state owned. The reality is that in China entrepreneurs compete with the state for resources and capital. And if you are a successful entrepreneur in China, do you really believe that you are not going to be beholden to the communist government?

On the other hand, more than one 100 Indian companies that completed IPOs as mid-cap companies now have a market capitalization of over a billion dollars. These include: Jet Airways, Bharti Tele-Ventures, Infosys Technologies Limited, Reliance Infocomm, Tata Motors, Wipro Technologies, and Hindalco Industries Limited. Companies such as these are becoming multinational competitors with globally recognized brands. China also has numerous companies that have a market capitalization of over a billion dollars, but the majority of these are state-owned behemoths recognized by their sheer size, not their competitive nimbleness. China uses its capital markets to shore up lumbering, state-owned companies, not as a tool of entrepreneurial expression. China also manipulates its currency: By most estimates, the Chinese currency is at least 40 percent undervalued. The Chinese government has used an undervalued currency to create an unfair trade advantage, and the countries that suffer most are other large emerging markets like India and Brazil, which allow their currencies to freely appreciate, even when this has a negative impact on exports.

When the rule of law is recognized by investors and foreign companies alike as something that is beyond question, it serves to facilitate additional investments in research and development. This is evident in the form of R&D of the Fortune 500 companies, 150 of which now have R&D bases in India. Additionally, the U. S. Food and Drug Administration has certified more companies in India than in any other country outside the United States—a testament to the innovation fostered by the combination of free markets and the rule of law.

The case for a democratic India receives further endorsement in the *World Competitiveness Report,* 2006–2007, published by the World Economic Forum (WEF), based in Switzerland. Property rights, judicial independence, and freedom of the press are three important facets of a democracy. The report ranks India far above China on all three parameters and gives it a rank of 43, compared to China's 54. In fact, India ranks higher than Russia and Brazil as well who come in at 62 and 66, respectively. The report says that China's most worrisome development is a marked drop in the quality of its institutional environment, as witnessed by the steep fall in rankings from 60 to 80 in 2006, with poor results across all 15 institutional indicators, spanning both public and private institutions. Factors that influence the institutional environment ranking are property rights and quality of the judicial system, among others. Comparatively, India attains a rank of 34 in institutional environment, close to the United States' 27 (see Graph 3.1).

A third important pillar of democracy is a free and dynamic press—after all, in a free society the press often exposes corruption and other issues of public importance. Remember Sucheta Dalal, the reporter from *The Times of India* who broke the Hashad Mehta scam in 1992? China, which is not a free society, not surprisingly is among the worst offenders of free press in the world. According to the Committee to Protect Journalists (CPJ), China has the highest number of imprisoned journalists (as of December 1, 2006)—31. Not exactly something that would inspire investigative reporting. At the peak of the student-led prodemocracy movement in Tiananmen Square in 1989, journalists chanted "Don't force us to lie!" The press was reduced to being the Communist Party's mouthpiece. The *People's Daily*, the official party organ, tried desperately

Graph 3.1 Comparison of India and China by the *World Competitiveness Report, 2006–2007*

Country	Property Rights	Judicial Independence	Freedom of Press
India	43	25	26
China	64	62	99

to get permission for the press to publish reports on crimes and malfeasance committed by public officials. One article, titled "What If the Media Is Absent?" thanked the journalists who uncovered the true reasons behind the death of some 80 people in a tin mine in Guangxi province in July 2001. Journalists defied local officials and, at great personal risk, revealed the truth. When the story came out, the government, which had earlier proclaimed that there were no casualties, fell flat on its face. When you have a corrupt government those in power never permit a free press to enjoy the light of day.

It should be made clear that the *People's Daily* was not calling for a free press. It can never do that, knowing that it serves as the party's principal mouthpiece. It suggested, however, that if its reporters are given more independence it will be a more effective mouthpiece and will serve the party's interests better. But high-placed officials could not offer even that much. The *People's Daily* article said that "some people" have different perspectives on the advantages and disadvantages of media exposés; "some say" exposing the details of accidents, or investigative journalism in general, can lead to instability and hurt the reputation of the party and the government.

In June 2001 the Chinese authorities imposed one of its biggest media crackdowns. This was after concerns were raised about the media's reporting the rising unemployment, stagnant wages, and growing corruption in China before the party's 80th anniversary on July 1, 2001. Do you really believe that the upcoming Olympics will be any different? An internal document that somehow found its way into journalists' hands said that newspapers and magazines reporting independently on corruption scandals, crime, disasters, and speculation over leadership changes were to be immediately shut down. Journalists who report controversial news (known as "*ca bian qiu*," shots that kiss the edge of the ping-pong table) will be arrested. A yellow card (warning) and red card (dismissal) system was also in place earlier and only reports by the state-run Xinhua news agency on controversial issues could be printed. The ruling party launched a campaign to promote a "Marxist outlook on journalism," and an internal party memo is reported to have said that the movement is aimed at "maintaining the correct opinion orientation and preventing the corrosive influence of a Western outlook on journalism." The memo said that the campaign is to prevent "press liberalization" and "valuing professionalism and circulation more than politics and guidance."

Failure to follow party dictates meant newspapers in Guangxi and Sichuan provinces were shut down. In March 2001, *Guangxi Business* Daily was merged with the party's *Guangxi Daily* under coercion from Guangxi party officials. In June, the paper's staff clashed with party officials after refusing to obey their orders. A problem in China is that a business can only operate at the pleasure of the authorities, and exposés of official misdeeds only tend to anger corrupt officials. Editor Ma Yunlong of *Dahe News*, a private paper in Henan province, was sacked. Ma had approved an article that uncovered health insurance officials' misbehavior when they accepted female escorts sent by drug and medical companies at an industry conference. He also did not stop articles on complaints by foreign investors about corruption, chaotic management, and obstruction by local bureaucrats. In early 2007, contaminated pet food that had been exported from China to the United States resulted in the deaths of thousands of pets. In May the head of the Chinese FDA was sentenced to death for corruption. *Southern Metropolitan News* and its sister publication, *Southern Weekend*, were banned for reporting corruption. The crackdown was in relation to the government's efforts to establish a more firm control over the media market. State-run broadcasters were merged into powerful conglomerates and cable TV firms came under the control of provincial or municipal TV networks.

In December 2004, China shut down several newspapers and detained a number of dissident academics. *The New Weekly*, which had been in circulation for fewer than 2 months, was run by former members of another popular paper, *Southern Weekend*, which had earlier seen many of its editors ousted by the government. Another paper, the *China Youth Daily,* lost its top editor about the same time. The state-run daily had reported that a Shenzhen party official made public-school students watch a movie made by his daughter. "This administration is no different from the past in the sense that all people in power do not want to rock the boat. Their challenge is to not encourage dissenting views on either side of the political spectrum," *The Seattle Times* (December 18, 2004) quoted Linda Chelan Li, a political scientist at the City University of Hong Kong. The article also said that clampdowns can be seasonal and unpredictable. Enforcement will keep investigative journalists at bay, fearful of breaking the rules, and as a result reporters would censor themselves. The threat of a trip to the Public Security Bureau is a strong motivator to keep independent journalistic tendencies in check.

Around mid-2006, the World Association of Newspapers (WAN) called for the release of all journalists jailed in China. "More than 30 journalists remain behind bars in China. The vast majority of them have faced long periods of detention before even being charged. Most trials result in lengthy prison sentences, often under extremely harsh conditions," the association said. "Two of the world's longest-held journalists are imprisoned in China. Chen Renji and Lin Youping were arrested in 1983 for distributing pamphlets on democracy. More than 23 years later both remain incarcerated. They are both serving life sentences; in the case of Lin Youbing, this came after a reprieve from a death sentence. A third colleague, Chen Biling, who was arrested along with the journalists, was sentenced to death and executed," noted the WAN board in a resolution.

In 2006, Beijing decided to restrict domestic news circulation by foreign media. According to new rules set by China's Xinhua News Agency, any foreign news agencies should obtain approval from Xinhua before bringing news to the public eye in China. They would be represented by agents allotted by Xinhua and cannot independently develop Chinese subscribers. Foreign news agencies, which include agencies from Taiwan, Hong Kong, and Macau, will now need to get their articles approved by Xinhua before circulation. China has not only imposed censorship on news but has also blocked online news sites operated by Taiwan's media, including the *China Times, United Daily News, Liberty Times, Apply Daily,* and *Ettoday*.

China has also imposed controls over online search engines and restricted the release of books and magazines in the country. Where does the Chinese government get the technology required to censor news content? The unfortunate irony is that they purchase the technology from companies like Google, Yahoo, Microsoft, and Cisco Systems.

The continued control over the Chinese press led German Chancellor Angela Merkel to press Chinese Premier Wen Jiabao on the issues of human rights during a meeting in Berlin last year. During the meeting Merkel stressed a need for a free press, which would be crucial for the 2008 Summer Olympics in Beijing. In the run-up to next year's Olympics, the Communist Party has relaxed the rules a bit for foreign journalists. The new set of rules declares that foreign journalists will "travel freely and interview anyone with the interviewee's consent, dropping cumbersome official approvals which were often denied anyway by security-conscious authorities," the *Taipei Times* reports. But is it genuine, and will it continue after the Olympics? Agence France Presse doubts that "foreign journalists in China began a new year of supposedly more open reporting; there is lingering skepticism over how faithfully local-level officials will implement relaxed media rules."

On the other hand, a free and vibrant press is a cornerstone of India's democracy and an entrenched part of its social fabric. A free press helps to ensure transparency and an equitable social response by the government and markets. Remember Channel TV18? They now have a show similar to "Sixty Minutes," which uses hard-hitting investigative journalism techniques (like hidden cameras) to expose all types of corruption. There are more than 5,000 newspapers in

India and countless magazines and journals, all of which have complete journalistic freedom. In fact, the Press Council of India is a statutory body in India that governs the conduct of the print and broadcast media. It is one of the most important bodies that sustain democracy, as it has supreme power in regard to the media, ensuring that freedom of speech is maintained. It is also empowered to hold hearings on receipt of legitimate complaints against the press for libel and to take suitable action where appropriate. It may either warn or censure the errant journalists on finding them guilty. The Press Council of India is protected by the Constitution and its actions may not be questioned unless it is proven to be in violation of the Constitution, which makes it an exceedingly powerful body. The Indian press has been instumental in exposing numerous government and corporate corruprion scandals, resulting in the arrest and imprisonment of numerous government and corporate officials. Notable examples include the Bofors case, the Fodder scam, the Jain dairies case, and the petrol pumps' largesse scandal.

According to the World Economic Forum, India ranks 26 on the freedom of press ranking, compared to China, which is ranked at 99. The Indian Supreme Court has laid great emphasis on the value of the freedom of press in India. There are also exclusive press laws, like Working Journalists and Other Newspaper Employees Act, Press Council Act, and the Press and Registration of Books Act. The Press Council of India deals with complaints against newspapers and was created by the Press Council Act. The Working Journalist Act is a newspaper employees' measure that regulates the working conditions and working hours and wages. The Indian Parliament recently enacted a law named "Right to Information Act," for the benefit of its citizens.

One of the most important aspects of a democracy may in fact be a credible and independent judiciary—after all, if you have a business dispute and you are forced to file a lawsuit you expect the case to be handled fairly, don't you? Unfortunately the Chinese judiciary is not a fully coequal branch of government, even on paper. At the national level, the Supreme People's Court (SPC) is subordinate to the National People's Congress (the Chinese legislature) and on the same level as the Supreme People's Procuratorate (the organ responsible for prosecuting cases on behalf of the Chinese government). And party interests continue to influence judicial reforms in China. The party's "harmonious society" campaign aimed at reducing social unrest and the Chinese Ministry of Justice's efforts to strengthen the role of local judicial bureaus in resolving local disputes are correlated. Social unrest in China is growing. Even according to official Chinese statistics, the number of public protests in China increased every year between 1993 and 2004. In 2003, public security authorities reported 58,000 public protests involving more than 3 million people. In 2004, public security authorities reported 74,000 public protests involving more than 3.5 million people, and a seven-fold rise from the 10,000 protests recorded in 1994. In October 2004 alone, more than 2 million farmers reportedly took part in more than 700 protests. Not exactly the economic miracle you often read about, is it?

In 2004, news surfaced about judicial reform proposals that had been prepared by two well-known legal scholars at the Supreme People's Court's request. The proposals were expansive; they included a proposal for guaranteeing independence to Chinese judges in deciding cases and forbidding court officials and adjudication committees to interfere in trial judge deliberations. The SPC, which had commissioned the proposals, publicly distanced itself from the authors and criticized them. In April 2004, the *People's Daily* reported that the "Supreme People's Court has ruled out the scenario of radical judicial reform in the short term." It is obvious that Chinese authorities are cautious of creating an impression that they want to Westernize China.

Chinese judges are often rendered powerless due to external interference. Local governments protect personal interests, and through their control over judicial funding and appointments, they influence courts. Party authorities often intervene in politically sensitive cases. Since the early 1990s, local people's congresses have exercised increasing influence over court decisions. "Case closure ratios," or the ratio of closed to filed cases is an important criteria used by Chinese courts for evaluating judicial efficiency. This ratio is used during appraisals and for assigning bonuses. Courts in China pressure parties to agree to mediate outcomes or refuse to accept cases filed late in the year in order to manipulate this ratio. Judicial responsibility systems discipline judges for a range of errors, including appellate reversals for legal error. According to this system, judges may rely on internal advisory requests (*qingshi*) for guidance from higher court authorities as to how to decide cases in order to avoid punishment. Chinese scholars and officials have both criticized this system. These internal administrative practices, commonly used in Chinese courts, reduce judicial effectiveness and independence. What do you think will happen when the Chinese economy suffers a real downturn and state-owned companies look for protection from multinational competitors? You may want to dust off those contingency plans.

India has a credible and clearly independent judiciary, where the Supreme Court has insulated lower courts from any interference in their judicial work by high court judges, saying their independence is as important as that of the superior courts. Under the Indian Constitution, the high courts monitor the district and subordinate courts in each state, ensuring that they function within the limits of authority. The power of judicial review is a basic feature of India's Constitution. The legality of all legislative and executive acts can be examined in India. This is pragmatic, as the Indian Constitution prescribes restrictive orders and laws to be "reasonable." Other Articles in the Constitution also allow the courts to examine the propriety of legislative Acts. It is recognized that when a judge announces his or her ruling, it can affect the entire community. A basic principle of majoritarian democracy says that public policymakers are accountable to the public. Judges are trained to ignore vested interests and political interference in resolving cases. Judges also must be isolated from the political pressures and prejudices of society in order to protect individuals and minorities from the potential tyranny of the majority. India realizes that a substantial degree of judicial independence is necessary for any credible legal system.

India's judicial system, although relatively young, often renders progressive settlements in favor of environmental and historical preservation, a trait possessed by less than a handful of emerging-market economies. Supreme and appellate court activity on behalf of environmental and other public issues has been as striking as judicial activity on behalf of victims of state lawlessness. Actions to save the Taj Mahal from the effects of pollutants have attracted extensive media coverage. By 1992, the Supreme Court had ordered the closure of 212 industries near the Taj Mahal that were in chronic violation of environmental regulations. It took similar action with respect to 190 polluters on the banks of the Ganges River. In 1996 and 1997, it extended its enforcement rulings to industrial violators in the heavily polluted Delhi area. Even more than its public interest litigation (PIL) decisions, its environmental enforcement efforts generated resistance from powerful interests and languished due to civic inertia. In 1999, the Delhi government was requesting 2 years' grace for noncompliant polluters. In February 2000, however, the Supreme Court ordered the closure of outlets emitting pollutants into the Yamuna River and threatened to jail for contempt state government officials who obeyed Delhi Environment Minister A. K. Walia's and Industry Minister Dr. Narendra Nath's orders to keep them open.

The second D in my argument is, of course, *demographics.* To put it in simple terms, China is aging as India is getting younger. That is a demographic challenge that is bound to affect China's economic prospects. In 1994, the British Broadcasting Company reported that China's over-65 population was the fastest-growing in the world.

It said at that time that it will take only 21 years for the over-65 population to increase from 10 to 20 percent, whereas the same development took Sweden 85 years, the Netherlands and Germany 50 years, and Japan 32 years. The BBC noted that the aging of China's population is outstripping its economic development, whereas the population in the developed world is aging at the same rate as its economic growth. This article, published more than a decade ago, said that statistics indicated that worldwide, all of the 57 countries with a predominantly older (+65) population have a per capita gross national product (GNP) above US$1,000 per year, and 21 of them enjoy a per capita GNP over US$10,000, but China's average GNP will not reach US$800 to US$1,000 until the end of this century.

In 1994, China had more people over 65 than any other country in the world. It is estimated that by the year 2025 there will be 250 million people over the age of 65 in China, representing about 24 percent of the aged population around the globe. Moreover, China's pension deficit, which reached US$40 billion as of the end of 2005, is not a good sign. State-owned enterprises once provided pension and health care benefits, while Confucian traditions compelled children to support their parents and grandparents. But the shift to a market economy has sent half the Chinese workforce into the private sector, where pensions are rare. Last year China had 46 million retirees, who took a total pension exceeding 500 billion yuan (US$64.1 billion). Estimates for how big China's pension shortfall will be by 2035 vary, with the World Bank estimating it at 9 trillion yuan (US$1.2 trillion) and one Chinese government department estimating it at 2 trillion yuan. In simple terms, that's a pension time bomb.

China's aging population is the by-product of the one-child policy introduced in China in 1979. The number of children who have received certificates showing their status as an only child has dramatically increased, from 6.1 million in 1979 to 35.467 million in 1990, a 580 percent increase in just 12 years. According to data collected in 1990 by the Fourth National Population Census, the percentage of one-child families in the Beijing and Shanghai urban districts was 49.9 percent and 50.3 percent, respectively, and 87 percent of children born in that year were the first children born into families, the great majority of whom were to become part of the cohort of only children. This shows that the ratio of one-child families is steadily increasing in cities. The "young elderly" (people between the ages of 60 to 70) accounted for 60 to 70 percent of urban elderly in the 1980s. Most of them enjoy state pensions, reducing their reliance on their children. Another problem is that a great proportion of the population receives no education after graduating from primary school. Only one in fifty of those 25 years old and over had a college education. In developed countries that proportion is one in four.

China's population is becoming old before it has attained significant economic development. With more than 50 percent of its population living in poverty and a per capita income not even 10 percent of that of Japan, China's age structure is rapidly approaching that of Japan. A greater proportion of China's population will mature in the next generation than that of Europe over the past century. It will have to grapple with the same age-related fiscal, social, and productivity challenges of countries with several times its per capita income. Just think of how Japan's economy has stagnated over the last 15 years because of its aging population. China will face a similar problem in less than 20 years while still having hundreds of millions of its population struggling to rise out of poverty.

The impact of these problems is only beginning to be understood, but many agree that China's aging population will lop multiple percentage points off its economic growth rate, beginning in the middle of the next decade. Tinkering with nature always creates unintended consequences. The Chinese already save prodigiously for retirement, and as their society ages, they will probably consume less and save even more to fund their retirement. Such a cycle contributed to Japan's recent economic malaise, and it similarly could starve the Chinese economy of investment and consumption spending. That spells bad news for the Wal-Marts of the world—and any other retailer hoping for long-term gains in China. And if you are a manufacturer in China leveraging labor arbitrage (cheap labor), then consider the fact that an aging population could lead to labor shortages, which will drive up wage rates.

Today India has the largest population in the world of people 25 or younger, and by 2015 there will be 550 million teenagers in India. That's known as a *demographic dividend,* and with the majority of Indian households owning property the potential economic benefits could be enormous. The Indian middle-class, currently defined as those earning between $4,400 and $22,000 annually, exceeds 60 million people, or approximately 5 percent of the population. By 2025 that number is expected to grow more than tenfold to over 583 million people, or 41 percent of the population.

One thing that the Chinese government has failed to understand is that as people achieve economic prosperity they tend to have less, not more, children, and that when a society moves from an agrarian to a nonagrarian lifestyle that effect is reinforced. In India, consequently, if educational opportunities can be provided to this incredibly large youthful population—and all indications are that they will be—then India stands to gain a significant advantage over China in terms of both its labor pool and the proportion of the population that will require retirement benefits. India's estimated elderly population in 2050, based on historic trends, which are coupled with economic prosperity, will be at 220 million. India's total population is projected to stand at 1.1 billion in 2010, which means the share of elderly in its total population will be close to the world average of 21 percent. That's good news if you are a manufacturer, retailer, or service provider.

The third D in my argument is *determination,* and before I proceed I want to be clear that I believe that the Chinese are very determined, industrious people. In fact, I believe that determination is part of human nature. When I had the privilege to serve as a member of the Army Special Forces I was able to witness countless examples of human determination—individuals in the most extreme and often desperate situations would prevail against seemingly impossible physical odds, rising above any challenge set before them. I saw the same type of determination again when I participated in climbing expeditions in North and South America with individuals who were physically exhausted but who continued to push themselves, using sheer mental willpower.

Human beings are capable of truly amazing things but they cannot really flourish economically and socially if they are oppressed or inhibited by their own government. China has many successful entrepreneurs; however, they succeed in spite of the state, and more often than not they compete with the state for resources. The overwhelming majority of large companies in China are state owned, and until that country adapts democratic institutions the totality of China's entrepreneurial spirit and its economic capabilities will never be realized.

India is a country of entrepreneurs: It is often called the land of a million shopkeepers. for many years the true entrepreneurial capabilities of the Indian people were shackled by misguided government economic policies. But that was the old India: Today, the Indian people are beginning to realize the true extent of their capabilities. That fact is self-evident in the thousands of Indian companies that have successfully gone public, such as TV18, Infosys, Mphasis, and the GMR Group. All of these companies were started by determined entrepreneurs who often had little more than a vision and a few dollars in their pockets.

Infosys, like so many other companies in India, was founded by a determined individual, N. R. Narayana Murthy, who graduated in engineering from the University of Mysore and then completed his MS in technology from the Indian Institute of Technology, Kanpur. Murthy started Infosys, which is often touted as the largest publicly traded software services exporter in India, with US$250 in 1981. Murthy borrowed his initial capital from his wife. Murthy brought together a group of likeminded individuals in the venture, among them Nandan Nilekani, who is currently the CEO and Managing Director of Infosys. Murthy focused on a most challenging market, since there was no market for software in India at the time. Infosys opened its first international office in California in 1987 and became a public limited company in India in 1992. The revenues grew and surpassed the US$100 million mark in 1999. The same year, Infosys was listed on NASDAQ and ventured into consulting services. Within a year its annual revenue doubled, to surpass the US$200 million mark. Last year the 50,000 strong company celebrated its 25th year of existence and revenues passed US$2 billion. Murthy's "out-of-the-box" attitude is apparent in a statement quoted by Rediff Money; he states that "We were the first company in the software industry that adopted the campus approach. In 1992 to 93 we took a decision to build a campus for $4.75 million, when our revenues were $3 million." From the beginning, a key marketing strategy for Infosys has been to always believe in doing unusual stuff, and thereby be in a position to secure its future and growth. It is ironic that Murthy was interviewed and rejected by Azim Premji, the founder of Wipro, a firm that is Infosys' closest Indian competitor. Murthy is considered to be a favored candidate as the next president of India, an example of the new breed of politician that is taking India forward.

Determination also manifests itself in a desire to help others. Mr. Anil Agarwal, chairman of Vedanta Resources, a U.K.-based mining group, recently made an endowment of US$1 billion to create Vedanta University, which would make his contribution the largest donation ever made to a single Indian higher education institution. Vedanta University will be a research-oriented educational hub spread across 8,000 acres on the Puri-Konark marine drive in Orissa. The university will receive additional financial support through investments of more than US$3.6 billion. The university will begin enrolling students in 2008. It promises to be home to more than 100,000 students from around the world. Vedanta University plans to hire more than 10,000 full-time faculty members, and a proportionate number of support staff for the effective running of the institution.

What does this mean for you? If you are the CEO of a company and long-term economic growth and political stability are important factors in your investment decisions, then India will be an important market for you. If you are a businessman or investor and you are looking for a market that has the same entrepreneurial spirit as Silicon Valley, then India will be important for you. And if you believe in democracy, and believe that democratically led countries make better trading partners, then India will be important for you. Consider the currency manipulation issue: How long do you think it will be before the United States Congress takes punitive action against China for unfair trade practices? The problem for China is that Chinese manufacturers are already operating on razor-thin margins—15 percent or less, in some cases. If the Chinese government is forced to allow its currency to appreciate, or if the United States and other countries place an equivalent tariff on Chinese goods, you will see a large number of Chinese manufacturers go out of business overnight.

4

The Road Less Traveled: The Gold That Lies under India's Crumbling Infrastructure

Narmatha Bridge—One of the Countless Infrastructure Projects Under Development in India.

> *I believe that the civilization India has evolved is not to be beaten in the world. Nothing can equal the seeds sown by our ancestry. Rome went; Greece shared the same fate; the might of the Pharaohs was broken; Japan has become westernized; of China nothing can be said; but India is still, somehow or other, sound at the foundation.*
>
> Gandhi

Kumar has been sitting in his truck for over 4 hours waiting for his paperwork to be processed at a border checkpoint. The temperature outside is over a 100 degrees Fahrenheit, and the temperature inside his cab is about 10 degrees higher, owing to the fact that he does not have air conditioning (or even a heater, for that matter!) He travels at night, since trucks are not permitted on India's overcrowded roads during the day. With minimal training and even less education, driving a truck is hardly a lucrative profession. Kumar earns the equivalent of $250 per month, barely enough to support his family, who he sees all too seldom. Many of his fellow truck drivers have turned to less-than-honest ways to make ends meet. They often wear lead belts around their waist, sometimes weighing more than 120 pounds, so that when the truck is weighed the excess weight will also be included. If the driver was transporting lubricants he could discard the belt and siphon off the equivalent weight in product, selling it in the open market.

However, Kumar's lot in life, like that of many of India's other truck drivers, is going to improve—slowly at first, but the change will be significant. Kumar is what is known as an owner/operator, which accounts for over 70 percent of India's truck drivers. He, however, is under contract with Delhi Assam Roadway Corporation, the largest road transport company in the country. Delhi Assam was founded in 1962 by Shri Tekchand Agarwal and his brothers, with just two trucks. Today, Delhi Assam Roadways manages over 1,000 trucks and directly owns a fleet of 150 vehicles. I had the opportunity to meet Krishan Agarwal and his family at their modest office, located on the outskirts of New Delhi. Mr. Agarwal is a humble individual and one who is eager to share and debate his vision openly with family, friends, colleagues, and even an inquisitive writer. This spirit of debate and willingness to share opinions is a hallmark of Indian business practice, which serves to hone the strategic planning process through a type of trial by fire.

Our discussion quickly delves into the challenges and opportunities that India's infrastructure presents. Currently, trucks in India travel an average of less than 200 miles a day, compared to an average of approximately 1,000 miles a day in the United States. The reasons for this disparity are many, but the important ones include poor roads, a lack of automation and computerization at checkposts, and old-fashioned bribery. Additionally, only between 1 and 2 percent of domestic cargo is containerized (cargo bound for export fares somewhat better, at about 65 percent). But while the current transport situation seemingly looks bleak, one only needs to look a little further to understand the dramatic transformation that has now begun in earnest.

It is common knowledge that India's infrastructure is in bad shape. In the past, government regulations had deterred private sector participation in infrastructure projects. One glaring example of this restrictive government policy is the fact that until recently the government did not permit private sector investment in power distribution and transmission as well as in airports. Areas such as power generation, which were open for private sector investment, did not hold much interest because of the poor financial state of the state electricity boards and the uncertainty of local politics. Simply put, half-baked regulations and a lack of a comprehensive approach to reforms discouraged badly needed private sector investments in infrastructure. In certain parts of India the infrastructure is in such bad shape that you would be tempted to think that the country has fallen into some type of time warp.

The Indian government finally got its act together. Even the most ardent socialists within the government know that without dramatic improvements to the country's roads, ports, railways, power grid, irrigation channels, and airports, it will not be possible to sustain the current rate of economic growth. Last year India embarked on an ambitious infrastructure modernization program that has not been seen in a free market economy since the United States developed the interstate highway system and regional airport network in the 1950s. At its peak, that investment will reach 8 percent of India's GDP per year. The program, called the Public-Private Partnership for Infrastructure Investment and Development, has already produced tangible results. More than 60 percent of that investment will go to roads and power, and for the transportation sector the impact is already quite visible.

At the national highway level India has developed a new six-lane highway system, called the Golden Quadrangle, that connects the four corners of the country. This highway is 92 percent complete and will be finished by early 2008. The Indian highway authority also plans to build an additional 10,000 miles of secondary highways and improve and widen 25,000 miles of existing roads within the next 5 years. This would be equivalent to the United States' building a new six-lane superhighway that connected Chicago with Orlando and Pittsburgh with Dallas, building additional highways that would span the country, and improving the combined road system of the midwest—all within 5 years.

Some of the more important projects include the National Highway Development Program (NHDP), which involves improving 16,000 miles of single/intermediate-lane national highways to two lanes, at an estimated cost of about US$5.7 billion. It also includes widening of about 4,500 miles of national highways to six lanes on a built-operate-transfer (BOT) model basis with an estimated cost of US$3.9 billion. Development of 900 miles of expressways, with an estimated cost of US$3.4 billion, and construction of ring roads, bypasses, and overpasses in several important cities, with an estimated cost of US$3.4 billion have also been mapped out on a BOT model. Under the BOT model, the private sector finances, builds, and operates the project according to performance standards set by the government, and is allowed to run the establishment long enough to pay off the construction costs and realize a profit, after which the government takes ownership. India is only about one third the size of the continental United States in terms of land mass, so building that many highways will have a major impact on the economy, creating major opportunities for the distribution and logistics sector. The first BOT deals that the Indian government negotiated placed almost all of the risk and most of the potential profit on the back of the company that won the bid. But after seeing the success of various toll roads and other BOT projects, the government quickly changed the composition of the contracts, with the government taking on more risk—and, of course, keeping more profit—capitalism at its best!

While the development of a national highway system will create immediate returns for the Indian economy, it is only part of India's transportation equation. India also relies on railroads—it has the second-largest sytem in the world, with 1.6 million employees. India's rail system transports over 15 million people every day, which is equal to the combined population of New Zealand, Hong Kong, and Singapore. The India Railroad Authority is an agency that was almost bankrupt 10 years ago but is now generating over $5 billion in free cash every year and has begun a massive modernization program of its own. Recognizing the fact that within 5 years freight movement will increase by more than

50 percent—to 1,100 million tons per year—and that passenger traffic will increase by more than 31 percent, to over 8.4 billion passengers per year, the railroad authority has shifted into high gear.

The Indian Railroad Authority plans to invest over $56 billion over the next 5 years for the development of new tracks, new passenger cars, station modernization, and the development of high-capacity containerized freight cars. The railroad authority plans to finance this investment with the surplus cash that the company is generating every year, supplemented with traditional bank financing. Within 2 years, two dedicated freight rail lines will be completed, running from Mumbai to Delhi and from Ludhiana to Kolkata. These will be supplemented with 14 privately contracted freight rail corridors. With an eye on the future, the railroad authority has begun talks with a Japanese high-speed rail manufacturer to develop a 2,500 mile high-speed rail system that would utilize the new fastest "bullet" train, which has top speeds in excess of 320 miles per hour. With India's large population, mass transit systems will continue to be a critical component of the country's transportation infrastructure and longer-term energy self-sufficiency objectives of the government. If you ever get the chance, you should travel by train in India in a first class cabin. It's a bit like stepping back in time to the British Victorian age, with white-glove service, bar cars, and fantastic cuisine, while an incredible landscape passes by.

With so much passenger traffic, the railway authority recognized the need to create world-class stations. Nineteen stations have been identified by the railway board for conversion to this standard. The new stations will have state-of-the-art buildings, complete with all modern passenger amenities such as food plazas, currency exchange, hotels, retail outlets, ATMs, and more. That is a big difference from what Indian train stations look like today and a big opportunity for the Starbucks of the world.

Investments will also be made to develop heavy-haul trains, which can carry more while using 25 percent less fuel, and to develop the freight cars they will pull. It is not possible to load freight cars beyond 64 tons, except with certain heavy commodities. Research Design and Standards Organization (RDSO), an Indian ministry of railways undertaking, is designing new high-capacity freight cars. Commodities such as coal can be loaded up to 70 tons in these new cars. Prototypes of these cars will be developed in the coming year, and trials will soon be completed. Regular production of the new cars, with a payload-to-tare weight ratio of even better than 3:1, will start from 2007 to 2008. Efforts will also be made to start manufacturing aluminum and stainless steel cars in 2006 to 2007 to improve the payload-to-tare weight ratio. In the future, India will need to manufacture 25-ton axle load cars that can carry loads up to 80 tons and whose payload-to-tare weight ratio is around 4:1. The new freight cars will increase Indian railways' share in the transportation of commodities such as motor vehicles, petrochemicals, and so on, and concurrently drive down transportation costs. That's important, since lower transportation costs will make Indian exports more competitive and create additional opportunities for national and multinational corporations.

There has been a remarkable improvement in the operating efficiency of freight transportation with the help of Freight Operating Information System. In the first phase of this project, Rake Management System has been implemented at a few locations. In the second phase, Terminal Management System will also be implemented at all major locations. Work has commenced on control charting, crew management, and Coaching Operations Information System. Next year, Control Charting System will be implemented on all the divisions. The complete computerization of Control Office, Coaching Operations Information System, and the interfacing of both these systems with National Train Enquiry System will directly benefit passengers and other rail users. Railways run more than 2,500 ordinary passenger trains every day, and the new system will enhance the line capacity of various rail sections and also reduce travel time.

What may in fact be the most ambitious aspect of India's transportation plan are the modernization and greenfield development of 12 airports. In India, the number of people traveling by air is expected to grow by more than 25 percent per year, but like so much of India's infrastructure, Indian airports are considered by global standards to be some of the least efficient. Indian airports lack terminal capacity, parking, modern ground-handling facilities, night landing systems, and cargo-handling facilities. To put this in perspective, imagine the United States embarking on a 5-year project, with a completion date of 2012, to build two new airports the size of Chicago O'Hare with an annual capacity of 85 million passengers each, 10 others the size of Dallas-Ft. Worth with a capacity of 45 million passengers. Now realize that 30 percent of these projects have been completed—and that is just the first 5-year plan! Indian airline companies are also adding capacity and routes. Kingfisher has ordered the new super jumbo A380 Airbus airliner and is expanding its international routes. Paramount Airways is planning to acquire 40 Embraer jets for US$2 billion. Air India has placed a US$9 billion order for 68 new aircraft, of which 50 are meant for Air India and the rest for its budget subsidiary, Air India Express. The company also plans to add four new destinations to the United States by the end of 2008.

Ports are also an essential component of India's transportation infrastructure and a critical aspect of the country's growing trade flows. Currently India's ports can handle a combined capacity of 660 million tons; this capacity will be doubled to roughly 1,300 million tons by 2012. As part of this modernization program, the government is developing interconnectivity for all of the 12 major ports in the country through a Port Community System (PCS). The system will link the various stakeholders, such as shipping agents, exporters, importers, banks, and terminal operators, through the centralized web-enabled PCS to facilitate paperless transactions through e-filing of all applications or electronic data interchange. Right now it takes 2 days to unload a container ship at an Indian port, compared to 10 hours at a port in Singapore. Closing that gap will translate into big savings for just about everyone involved in the process.

What does this mean for Delhi Assam Roadways and Kumar, the truck driver? Delhi Assam is focused on becoming a leading multimodal transportation company with an emphasis on developing containerized trucks, computerized tracking and transaction systems, connectivity with the freight rail corridors, and the creation of port staging facilities. The ramifications of these investments play out in a dizzying array of projections. The percentage of domestic cargo that is containerized is expected to increase from 2 percent today to 75 percent within 5 years. The amount of distance a truck travels, on average, is also expected to jump from 200 miles a day today to 800 miles a day within 3 years. For Delhi Assam, which had revenues of approximately $200 million in 2006 and a CAGR of 35 percent, the future looks quite bright indeed. In February 2007, a private equity fund acquired a minority stake in the company—and for good reason. By 2012 the company expects to have over 10,000 trucks under management and to have gross revenues approaching $1 billion dollars. Not surprisingly, the company is planning an IPO within the near future.

But what about Kumar—where does he stand in this story? There is already a shortage of drivers in India, and the reasons for this are well known. Right now, driving a truck is not a preferred profession, but with a rapidly developing infrastructure the need for well-trained professional drivers will grow dramatically. Those drivers will need a combination of good driving skills and basic computer skills, so that they can interact with information-driven multimodel transport system. All of these requirements, coupled with a rapidly growing economy, will require additional vocational training—which, in turn, will lead to a commensurate increase in compensation. So as the infrastructure story unfolds, Kumar's job will change from one of bare survival to one that provides a comfortable living for both him and his family.

If Delhi Assam Roadways Corporation and Kumar are intermediaries in India's infrastructure boom, then who is implementing it? The government calls this ambitious plan the public-private partnership (PPT). Recognizing the fact that the public sector does not have the capital required to meet the mammoth sum of $60 billion a year in investments that will be required—a sum equivalent to $180 billion a year, when purchasing power parity is applied—the government has turned, not surprisingly, toward the private sector for support.

Founded by G. M. Rao, the GMR Group might be considered to be one of the armored divisions spearheading higher command's strategic directive. The company, with a market capitalization of $4 billion, has successfully won the bids to develop the Hyderabad and New Delhi airports. However, Mr. Rao was not always a titan of infrastructure, and he certainly was not born with a silver spoon in his mouth. G. M. Rao's road to success began in the 1970s when his father split up the family estate between the four brothers. The family fortune amounted to approximately $6,700, along with a truck for each brother. Recognizing that their capital was limited, they pooled their assets and started a business trading jute. In the 1970s the license Raj was king, but Rao and his brothers managed to transfer the license of an existing jute mill in Tamil Nadu and build a mill in their native village in Andhra Pradesh. The mill did well and the Rao brothers began acquiring whatever licenses they could get, ending up with licenses for a brewery and a ferrous alloys business.

Rao's big break came in 1985, when he acquired a stake in Vysya Bank and was invited to join the board. Vysya is a community bank that has launched an IPO to improve its capital base. The issue was not fully subscribed, and Rao, sensing a target of opportunity, made his move. Rao liquidated any personal asset he could find; jewelry, land, and his car, using the proceeds to pick up the unsubscribed portion of the offering and a subsequent rights issue, so that he became a major shareholder in Vysya Bank.

In 1991, he left his village and moved to Bangalore so that he could focus on the bank's activities. Recognizing the need to instill best practices and technology in the bank, he enticed Bank Brussels Lambert of Belgium to take an initial 5 percent stake in the bank, which BBL later increased to 10 percent. With the help of BBL, the bank's balance sheet was cleaned up, technology was brought online, and more focus was brought on core banking. Soon after, Vysya Bank acquired a local life insurance license with ING, and in 1998 ING acquired BBL. In 2002, ING approached Rao and offered to buy him out at a rate far in excess of what he paid for his majority stake only 10 years earlier. Flush with his winnings from the Vysya deal, Rao turned to infrastructure—although he readily admits that he had no vision and no goal, just a gut instinct.

The first project was a power plant in Tamil Nadu, the first of its kind in that region. He then set up two others in Karnataka and Andhra Pradesh. In 2003, Rao identified another target of opportunity, partnering with Phaneesh Murthy to setup a business process outsourcing unit, with plans to focus on banking, insurance, card services, and investment banking. Within 6 months Rao cashed out of that venture, sold the brewery that he had started with his brothers some years back, and prepared to go for the brass ring! His first coup was winning the bid to build the new airport in Hyderabad, an airport that will ultimately have three times the passenger capacity of Dallas-Ft. Worth and is slated for completion in 2008. Rao hit paydirt in January, 2006, when a consortium led by his group, which included Fraport AG, IDFC Private Equity, and Malaysia Airports Holding Berhard, won the contract for the modernization and expansion of the New Delhi airport. When the refit is completed in 2012, the airport will have four runways and a total passenger capacity of 100 million per year, besting both O'Hare and Heathrow airports by a significant margin.

Rao is not your typical billionaire, but he is representative of the unassuming nature that you can find in most successful Indian entrepreneurs (he drives a Honda). As I sat with him and his team in their offices in Bangalore I could not help but think that I was with a group of old fraternity brothers. The conversation came easy, and it was impossible for the GMR team to mask the sense of pride and passion that they had for India's development as an emerging giant. As Rao explained it, infrastructure development is just the beginning. Try to think of an airport as an oasis with water and shade in the middle of the desert. What happens at an oasis—people congregate so that they can enjoy a respite from the heat and sun. That is what will happen with India's new airports, and Rao is ready for the opportunity. His group is now moving into the real estate sector, sensing that airports will require hotels, offices, restaurants, and all the other trappings of a modern city. Will there be delays as a result of politics? "Of course, that is the price we pay for democracy and we wouldn't have it any other way," Rao explains with a smile.

But where will all the capital that is required for this massive infrastructure buildout come from? The government calls it a public-private partnership—a diplomatic way of saying that they don't have all of the money that this giant endeavor will take, so private sector involvement is going to critical if this bold vision is to succeed. The answer to that question might be found in the persona of Luis Miranda, the founder of the IDFC Private Equity or (IDFCPE). Founded by Miranda in 2002 as a subsidiary of the Infrastructure Development Finance Company Limited, his private equity fund has raised over $630 million and invested in more than 20 infrastructure projects over the past 5 years, including three airports, 31 highways, four power plants, hospitals, and a private university.

Sitting with Luis Miranda in his well-appointed office in Mumbai, you get the sense that you are attending a briefing by General George Patton as he briefs the high command on his plans for the invasion of Sicily. A large map of India dominates the room, with numerous colored pins stuck in various strategic places around the country. The map looks like a running tally of bombing runs, with a corresponding damage assessment report next to each one. But these are infrastructure projects, and the reports objectively assess the progress of each one and the return on investment to date. The list is impressive—GMR Group, Manipal Health Systems, Delhi Assam Roadways, Gujarat Pipavav Port, Ashoka Buildcon, and Quipo Infrastructure Equipment, just to name a few.

Miranda motions to the map. "You see those projects; they are just a drop in the ocean. We have forty more projects currently being analyzed, and those are worth over $1 billion." "But what about german artillery? I mean, government bureaucracy," I ask. "Bureaucracy exists in all countries and India is no exception, but even the old-school politicians understand the benefits of infrastructure. India needs modern infrastructure, but power is the key to it all," elaborates Miranda. "Without sufficient supplies of power India's economy will grind to a halt."

And he is absolutely right: India has desperate energy needs, with large parts of the country suffering from daily brownouts, and in the case of the countryside, no electricity at all. Progress on this front has been mixed at best. In the last 5-year plan, the government targeted 41,000 megawatts of additional power, but only about half of that capacity is expected to be added by the end of the plan. Power distribution is also a mess, with more than a third of all power generated failing to reach consumers.

The current 5-year plan (2007 to 2012) is even more ambitious than the previous one, with a targeted power capacity addition of 76,000 megawatts. The majority of that capacity will come from thermal power plants, with hydroelectric and nuclear power plants accounting for the remaining capacity. There are also plans to create a national power grid with a transmission capacity of 37,000 megawatts by 2012. As Miranda pointed out, this is one area of the infrastructure that simply cannot be permitted to fail; however, in a free market system, investments have to show a profit—is there any money to be made by investing in India's infrastructure?

The short answer is yes, there is a lot of money to be made! A political consensus among the various parties on the need for infrastructure improvement and acceptance of user charges by the general public have kick-started private investments in this area. Until recently, the concept of a toll road or other types of user fees was a foreign concept in India. That has rapidly changed, as consumers quickly bought into the benefits that a modern infrastructure creates. The Indian government has also developed an improved regulatory framework by setting up independent regulatory authorities to ensure fair competition, dispute resolution, and competitive tariffs across various segments, thereby ensuring stable returns. Remember the GMR Group? They have invested US$660 million into power, roads, and airports, which have netted a current equity valuation of US$2.4 billion and an IRR of 67 percent with a holding period of 7 years. In short, infrastructure investments in India are creating cash cows with long-term returns on capital. And that is why so much capital is now flowing into the market, with groups like TransAsia Infrastructure Holding creating a US$1 billion India-specific urban infrastructure fund and Eden Reality Ventures creating a US$500 million fund.

India's infrastructure boom has extended to other areas as well. For years, the urban areas of India had fallen into various states of disrepair, with inadequate or nonexistent water supplies, poor sewage systems, and a lack of mass transit. This situation is now changing, with the creation of the Jawaharlal National Urban Renewal Mission (JNURM) a program aimed at accelerating the development and expansion of physical infrastructure in 63 cities. Under the JNURM program a $12.5 billion dollar assistance fund has been created, to be paid out as grants of up to 35 to 90 percent of the project cost. Is it working? Well, consider the Delhi Metro part of the Mass Rapid Transit System (MRTS).

New Delhi was long overdue for a mass transportation system. The number of vehicles in the city was more than the combined number of vehicles in India's three other major cities and that number was growing fast! In 1980, Delhi had 521,000 motor vehicles. By 1995 that number had grown to 2,700,000; and by 1998 that number had expanded to 3,167,000. Adding to the mess, the city relied entirely on buses for its mass transit needs, which created traffic bottlenecks on the city's bad roads. Autos and taxis were not affordable alternatives for the average individual. Adding insult to injury, the number of road accidents involving motorcycle/bus collisions was growing dramatically, and pollution levels within the city were becoming intolerable.

Enter one Mr. Tiwari, Joint General Manager, Delhi Metro Rail Corporation (DMRC). What is his take on the inspiration and ultimate success of the project? "Initially, a system like the local trains of Mumbai was thought to be the ideal solution. But later on our consultants suggested it would need manually monitored barricades and also eat up a lot of road space, so we had to dump that idea." Studies to find a solution were commissioned as early as 1965. The metro trains were always identified to be a viable solution but India's earlier experience with the Kolkata metro train was not very fruitful, and it deterred other cities. There were many obstacles for New Delhi. Obtaining land, resettlement of jhuggies (hutments), permission for cutting trees, clearances from various city agencies for carrying out constructions, all had to be done professionally and quickly, since the day-to-day life of the citizens of New Delhi could not have remained affected for long.

Fortunately the chief minister of Delhi, M. L. Khurana, was very supportive of the project, and in 1995 the plan took a decisive turn. The Delhi Metro Rail Corporation, founded in 1995, was entrusted with the responsibility of connecting Delhi through metro trains and establishing a mass rapid transit system. It was to be a 50/50 joint venture between the government of India and the government of Delhi. Road-safety measures that matched international standards were adopted to avoid accidents during construction. Trained personnel were deployed to manage traffic at metro-construction junctions and major construction took place at night. DMRC promised to replace every tree that it cut down. The corporation prepared to plant over 30,000 saplings; remember that Delhi has one of the largest tree canopies of any major city in the world. It ensured that noise pollution is kept under check by layering train tracks with rubber. It ensured that rain-harvesting processes are implemented. Some stations have already started harvesting rainwater. Elevated tracks will mean that rail traffic remains unperturbed by what is happening on the ground level and also give a scenic view of the city to commuters. Construction was carried out at a rate that ensured that deadlines would never be a concern, and daily commutation is not affected over a long period.

For a city that had only buses as a mode of public transport, metro trains came as a welcome addition. The idea of linking the city with metro trains was to be executed in four phases. Officials from DMRC visited major international cities where metro trains were present to get a first-hand feel of things. Major support came from unexpected channels, with the Japanese government supplying the project with a loan covering about 60 percent of the total project cost. In fact, to a large extent the project typified globalization—Pacific Consultants International, Japan, were advisors on engineering, the initial shipment of coaches came from Korea's Rotem and Japan's Mitsubishi, and designing the automatic train control system was led by France's Alstom. This should reinforce the fact that India is a large and open market for foreign products and services.

As of now, around half a million commuters use the network on a daily basis. There is an automatic fare collection system to control ticketing and passengers—a first in the country, and the corporation has done well to connect its stations with feeder buses to increase ridership. "The Delhi Metro is a stunning example of how a government project can be done properly," Delhi Metro Rail Corporation managing director Elattuvalapil Sreedharan has stated. The transport system is gaining more popularity among commuters. Compared to peers like Singapore, whose metro trains carry close to 1.34 million people a day, or Hong Kong, where close to 2.4 million commuters use metro trains, Delhi has some catching up to do. But with a population of 13 million that is always growing, and tracks that are spreading their web like a jungle fire, the figure is bound to head north.

When Delhi commuters got their first look at the new metro, in 2005, they were visibly impressed. Equipped with jointless tracks, safety standards matching NFPA-130, an emergency evacuation system that could empty an entire station in 30 minutes, air conditioned lightweight coaches, an on-board communication facility and an automatic train supervision system (ATS), Delhi metro could easy rival the San Francisco system. Built at a cost of approximately US$2.5 billion, Phase I of the mega project, covering 55 miles, was completed in December, 2005, after 7 years and 3 months of construction. What is very impressive is the fact that the Delhi Metro Rail Corporation beat deadlines and finished a project that was earlier supposed to finish in 10 years and cover a distance of 40 miles. It also finished the construction well within the planned budget, with a US$220 million cushion. Delhi's metro resounding success prompted Prime Minister Dr. Manmohan Singh to declare, "It has become the symbol of a really 'New' Delhi." And the Delhi Metro Rail Corporation intends to be relentless.

The second phase, spanning 110 miles, will be available for athletes visiting Delhi during the 2010 Commonwealth Games. Mr. Ved Mani Tiwari, Joint General Manager, DMRC remarked that if DMRC succeeds in completing this phase in the stipulated time, it will set a world record of sorts. The previous construction record had been set by the Madrid metro and all expectations are that Delhi will beat that. Here are some numbers that might be worth noting: The trains run for more than 20,000 kilometers every day, they operate from 6:00 A.M. in the morning to 10:00 P.M. in the evening, and the doors of the trains open and close half a million times every day. "Our metro can handle 65,000 passengers in PHPDT which means 'peak hour peak direction traffic.' This is amongst the highest in the world," Mr. Tiwari said.

Delhi is very different from its global peers in that a significant number of people in Delhi travel to satellite towns like Gurgaon and Noida for work, and not the other way round, wherein people live in the suburbs and travel to cities for work. Keeping that thought in mind, the Delhi Metro Rail Corporation has started work to link these towns with the city as well. Falling under Phase III of the mega project, this stage intends to connect the GE offices in Gurgaon with the India Gate. The corporation is also developing properties around the metro stations that will give the terminals a totally new look. The information technology park located near an east Delhi metro station is an example. It is the first IT park in the city and is spread across 15 acres. It is developing residential property in North Delhi and is developing commercial property in Central Delhi.

The project has inspired other cities as well, and Bangalore, Hyderabad, Ahmedabad, Mumbai, Kochi, and Chennai are soon going to have their own metro trains. Managing director Sreedharan has said, "We have to support the urbanization of India by bringing in mass rapid transport systems in a big way in all our cities." DMRC is on the consulting team for the Mumbai metro train project. Mr. Tiwari said that the corporation is a prime consultant for the Jakarta metro project and it is also on the consulting consortium for Colombo's metro train dreams. Recently, when Mr. Sreedharan visited Karachi, Pakistan, he was confronted with questions on the high costs the metro project in that city is incurring. The man whose corporation is fast approaching a world record, in a short debrief to officials there, brought the project costs down by as much as 50 percent! Experience, as they say, is worth its weight in gold.

Metro trains have changed the way people travel within the city. Mobility has increased and business options have opened up. Visiting friends and families on weekends is now a pleasure, not an ordeal. Doing business in the remote but fledgling areas of the city is now a viable option. It has reduced the time Delhi's citizens used to spend on the road, stuck in traffic.

India's infrastructure boom is reaching every possible corner of the economy. Pipelines, the most cost-effective means for the transportation of oil and gas, are not surprisingly below global standards, with penetration rates of less than 25 percent compared to the global average of 75 percent. Recent discoveries of large natural gas deposits on India's coast, which include the discovery by Reliance Industries in the Krishna Godavari Basin, combined with a hot economy will drive the build-out of more than 12,000 miles of new domestic oil and gas pipelines over the next 5 years. That build-out, like every other aspect of infrastructure growth, will require large pools of skilled and semiskilled labor and significant quantities of equipment and technology.

What might be the most underrepresented area of investment and modernization in India's infrastructure is irrigation. India has some of the least irrigated farmlands in the world, and when more than 60 percent of your population is involved in agriculture, that's a big deal. Agricultural productivity has been the "crazy aunt" that no one wants to talk about—with a mediocre annual rate of growth of less than 3 percent it is not exactly a success story. Much of that lack of growth can be attributed to a poor supply chain and lack of mechanizing of farms, but another major factor is poor irrigation, which makes it very difficult to maximize crop yields.

As in so many other aspects of the economy, the government has finally woken up and has now created the Bharat Nirman program, which, if fully implemented, will bring an additional 25 million acres of farmland under irrigation by 2012. Initiatives are being undertaken at the state level as well, with the state of Andhra Pradesh developing the area around the Godavari River to benefit parched farmlands in Telangana. The total expected investment in the various irrigation projects over the next 5 years is estimated at $19 billion.

What does all of this mean for you? From a macroeconomic perspective, consider the fact that India didn't make any major infrastructure improvements for over 50 years. Over half of the villages that Gandhi loved so much do not have basic electricity and most do not even have paved roads. Investing the equivalent of one trillion U.S. dollars over a 5-year period is like introducing a feudal village to the Jetsons—the possibilities are endless. Most economists agree that a modern infrastructure will reduce inflation by reducing many of the inputs that drive it—reduced transport costs, lower power costs, greater efficiencies, and so on. However, very few analysts have taken a hard look at what a modern infrastructure will do for the outputs of the economy.

Agriculture accounts for roughly one fifth of India's GDP today, yet with average growth rates in the single digits it is also one of the feeblest sectors of the economy. Much of the sector's lackluster performance can be directly related to supply-chain issues, with over 30 percent of all produce that is harvested failing to make it to market. Of the remaining produce that does make it to market less than 5 percent is processed or semiprocessed—that means eat it today or throw it away! In the United States, less than 2 percent of all produce is lost in the supply chain and over 8 percent of all produce is processed or semiprocessed. Now imagine—what will happen when a modern transport network is developed in India with rural access? But that creates other opportunities—for the development of refrigerated warehouses, refrigerated trucks, processing plants, distribution facilities, and so on! But what about the actual infrastructure projects? Indian companies do not have the resources to complete these massive projects on their own—they will need partners. Take GMR Group—they have partnered with the German company that built and manages the Frankfurt International Airport and they are using the American consulting firm that developed Dallas-Ft. Worth Airport to help design and build the airports in Delhi and Hyderabad. The opportunities for engineering firms, consulting firms, interior design firms, and architectural firms are enormous. Just consider the fact that Larson & Toubro is planning to erect a mega shipbuilding facility in Gujarat, and the Shipping Corporation of India plans to spend US$4 billion to acquire 72 vessels—and that is just a small sampling of the opportunity that India's infrastructure build-out is creating.

Of course, you need equipment and materials to build infrastructure—a lot of equipment and materials. India's infrastructure investment is driving the demand for everything from cement trucks and heavy cranes to drills and saws. A number of international firms have already entered the market so that they can leverage this historic opportunity. An efficient transportation system is a prerequisite for any economy to prosper. It plays a vital role in connecting people and places. Road transportation contributes the maximum part of India's transportation network and facilitates 80 percent of passenger movement and 60 percent of freight in India. Commercial vehicles are closely linked with the movement of freight and in turn affect the economic activity and movement of goods in the country.

Tata Motors has been a leader in manufacturing commercial vehicles and has a product portfolio ranging from light, medium to heavy-duty trucks, buses, and tractor trailers. Seven out of ten trucks on Indian roads bear the Tata brand.

The company has been actively involved in the advancement of the commercial vehicle industry by continuous product innovation and focus on R&D programs. In 1992, Tata Motors formed a 50/50 joint venture with Cummins Engine Company USA, called Tata Cummins Limited (TCL), to bring diesel technology solutions to India. The US$75 million project started with a share capital of approximately US$62 million and was set up in Jamshedpur for manufacturing diesel engines to power Tata Motors' commercial vehicles.

The plant was inaugurated in 1995 and has since been manufacturing engines for medium and heavy commercial use, which vary in range of 80 to 235 horsepower and conform to Euro I, Euro II, and Euro III emission standards. Tata Cummins has received ISO-9002 certification, QS-9000 certification, and ISO 14001(EMS) Certification, TS 16949 certification, and also won several awards such as the Rajiv Gandhi Quality Award for 1999 to 2000 and TPM Excellence Award—First category—2005 for the high quality of its products.

In 2000, the company started production of eco-friendly, Euro-II compliant diesel engines for commercial vehicles. In 2001, the joint venture increased the scope of the alliance and decided to use engines for other applications. These were exported to new markets such as China, the United Kingdom, and Europe. In addition, Cummins decided to use Tata engines for genset and industrial applications across Indian and overseas markets.

The growth in auto sector and infrastructure has fueled the demand for B-series diesel engines, which are used in 25 different vehicles in the 12 to 40 tons gross vehicle weight segments, ranging from cars, carries, trucks, buses, and so on. In November 2006, Tata Cummins invested between US$60 million and US$70 million to increase the annual capacity of B-series engine to 120,000 in the next 2 years, from the current capacity of 69,000 engines. Though the majority of the engines are consumed by the Tata Group, some of them are also used for other applications, such as gensets, construction machinery, and marine applications.

Both Tata and Cummins have played a vital role in the Indian infrastructure development by contributing hugely to the country's transportation sector. Tata was the first company to launch low-floor, semilow-floor, and disabled-friendly buses in 2005. The success of these buses helped Tata secure the offer of supplying 500 low-floor CNG buses for Delhi Transport Corporation (DTC). The buses will have B Gas International (BGI) engines and will run on compressed natural gas. These engines will be manufactured by Cummins India. The new buses are expected to contribute to transforming the city's traffic system.

The deal benefits the DTC, as each bus costs DTC approximately US$100,000, which is approximately US$17,000 lower than the next lowest bid of US$120,000. The tender also includes maintenance of the bus till 750,000 kilometers.

Besides transportation, Cummins India also helps the power sector by manufacturing diesel gensets in the rage of 20 to 62.5 Kva, which cater to medium-sized organizations in various sectors such as IT and telecommunications. Hotel and residential complexes are an important product line when you consider the still delicate and evolving state of India's power sector. The Indian market still has a modest vertical penetration rate by foreign companies operating directly or indirectly in the infrastructure. That will change rapidly as the Indian economy continues to grow and the government accelerates various economic and social reforms.

5

The Next Wave: What Will Drive India's Growth After Information Technology and Outsourcing

GMR Ethanol Renewable Energy—A Key Component of India's Next Wave

I am convinced that everything has come down to us from the banks of the Ganges, astronomy, astrology, metempsychosis. It is very important to note that some 2,500 years ago at the least Pythagoras went from Samos to the Ganges to learn geometry. But he would certainly not have undertaken such a strange journey had the reputation of the Brahmins' science not been long established in Europe.

Voltaire (French writer/philosopher)

Let there be no misunderstanding—information technology (IT) and business process outsourcing (BPO) will continue to be key drivers of India's economic growth. Many of the companies in these sectors have become or are quickly becoming world-class companies, led by industry leaders such as Infosys, Mphasis, Wilpro, and others. These sectors will continue to see sustained growth for years to come, with an ever-increasing number of innovations. But India's entire economy is growing, and many of the obstacles that have hampered industrial development in the past have been removed. While many industry segments will benefit from this growth, there are a number that will drive it—and in the process, create additional competitive differentiation for India. When we began assessing the next-wave sectors that would drive India's growth, we first looked at the country's inherent strengths—a vibrant entrepreneurial culture, a large and growing pool of engineers, PhDs, and other professionals, a proven track record of innovation, a large agricultural sector, and so on. We then synthesized this information with external forces and trends, that is, massive investments in infrastructure, a growing middle class, increasing levels of direct foreign investment, rapidly growing exports, and increased levels of domestic consumption.

We then used the synthesized data to compile a list of next-wave sectors. In the majority of these sectors, foreign participation is still quite low and therefore opportunities are still quite large. From an evolutionary point of view, and based on our experience in these markets and others, we expect that initial forays by foreign corporations into these sectors will take the form of joint ventures and/or minority ownership positions in the host company in question. Longer term we would expect a significant amount of mergers and acquisitions, as these companies gain size and scalability, which has already happened in the IT and BPO sectors.

HIGH-TECH MANUFACTURING

A lot has been said about China's manufacturing capability, and it certainly is formidable. However, while China has touted labor arbitrage as a competitive advantage, with an export-driven economic strategy, India may have what could be deemed to be an *innovation* arbitrage advantage. This advantage, when combined with low wage rates and a large domestic market, will equate to a significant opportunity for international companies. To find a proven example of India's prowess in this field one need not look any further than to Moser Baer, founded in 1983 by Ratul Puri, an engineering graduate who had studied at the London Business School. The company began as a joint venture with a Swiss company to produce sophisticated timing devices for mechanical networks. If, for instance, you had 20 drawbridges that had to open and close at a predetermined time, these timing devices would perform the task. The problem for this initial venture was that there really was not much of a market. Undeterred, Puri looked for another opportunity. India's prime minister recognized at the time that Indian industry needed to computerize, and knowing a good opportunity when he saw one, Puri decided to ride the coming wave. He raised some money from local banks and began investing in floppy disc technology, acquiring software and hardware from Zydex. This was the period of the "license Raj," and Puri secured a license that allowed him to manufacture 100,000 floppy discs per month. In the government's infinite wisdom, it had granted licenses to 16 local manufacturers, believing that this would provide an adequate supply of floppy discs to meet Indian demand. The problem, of course, was that in order to be competitive on an international basis Puri needed to sell ten million discs per month. That type of market logic seemed to have escaped the socialist government of that time.

By the early 1990s the license Raj had been eliminated and Puri was able to begin scaling up production, and by 1995 Moser Baer was one of the top 10 disc manufacturers in the world. Puri was not content with the floppy disc sector, knowing that the entire high-tech industry was quickly evolving. He had been carefully watching the progress of Kodak and its research in the area of blank optical conversion. Kodak had probably made the most investments in this area of any company, and when its CEO announced that it was physically impossible to produce a recordable CD for less than five dollars Puri took notice.

In 1999, Puri decided to make a big bet on blank optical technology. With revenues of US$20 milion, his company could hardly afford the US$100 million investment required to build a plant with a capacity of 60 million units per year, especially since the total global demand for the previous year was only 40 million units! The big question was how to get the necessary financing. Puri decided to go to local banks for the capital; however, his challenge was that the banks did not understand the technology or the model. They were comfortable financing cement plants or steel mills, but blank optical disc technology—no way! Consequently, Puri pitched his plan to the International Finance Corporation (IFC) and a few strategic venture capital (VC) firms. The IFC and the VCs agreed to invest, and with that in place the banks had found their comfort level and the rest of the financing fell into line. Within 6 months of the time work began, a state-of-the-art disc plant had been built and was operational. There was one small but quite problematic issue—the local power grid was completely unreliable and could not handle the massive amounts of energy required to run a manufacturing facility of this type. No problem: Puri built a 50 megawatt gas generation facility on site. This facility generated enough power to run a small city and it was cost effective. Global demand for discs exploded, increasing by six-fold in 2001 and four-fold in 2002, and Puri kept investing in capacity to meet demand. By 2005 Moser Baer had become the third-largest disc manufacturer in the world, with 5,000 employees and an annual production of 3.5 billion discs per year.

By that time India's domestic market had exploded as well, and demand for CDs and DVDs was growing at a phenomenal rate. Entertainment technology and other advances in manufacturing processes had driven down the cost of prerecorded discs. With that Puri saw another opportunity, and he moved quickly to acquire local entertainment content. With over 7,000 movie titles and 40 percent of all local content, Moser Baer was now also in the entertainment business. The current market for CDs and DVDs in India is approximately 1.5 billion units per year, and that market is expected to grow to 4.5 billion units per year by 2010. But like the rest of the retail sector in India, distribution channels are fragmented and informal. Puri recognized that counterfeiters had the best distribution channels in India. You could find them everywhere—on street corners, walking paths, and even at subway stations. The question, of course, was how to make them part of the solution, not the problem. India has tough intellectual property rights (IPR) and patent protection laws, and pirates were already feeling the heat. So Puri turned to the counterfeiters and transformed them into sales representatives, showing them that they could buy legal CDs and DVDs from current content from his company and they could sell them at a higher markup than they had been receiving in the past, with no legal issues!

What's next for Moser Baer? What do you do when you have mastered the art of thin film technology and you have economies of scale? Well, consider a world that is facing the very real threat of global warming as a result of increased greenhouse gases, increasingly costly fossil fuels, declining fuel reserves, and an immense country that is drenched in sunlight? You guessed right—solar panels and solar cell technology. Moser Baer has made its next big investment, building the largest solar panel and solar cell manufacturing facility in the world. They have also brought together a leading team of scientists and engineers, many of whom had worked at Indian energy labs or in Silicon Valley. The potential is staggering when you consider that India has plentiful amounts of sunlight, a power distribution system not fully developed, wide geographical space—and no cheap energy alternatives.

Solar energy will not be the complete solution to India's energy needs but it will definitely play a major role in improving the situation. India is going to require 600 gigawatts of new energy generation over the next 10 years if its GDP growth rate is to be maintained. And unlike the United States, which consumes a continuous amount of energy through waste (e.g., leaving the lights on) 30 percent of India's current and future requirements will be based on peak demand. Solar energy is expected to account for 20 gigawatts of total supply, accounting for a sizeable percentage of current and future peak demand.

What does all of this mean from a business perspective? If you include lower installation costs, combined with an abundance of sunlight, the total cost of solar power generation in India is 50 percent less than in Germany! Moser Baer has not even considered government subsidies, tax credits, or a growing demand from the United States in their financial projections. But I am willing to bet that demand from the United States may be bigger than from India, and that government subsidies and tax credits will soon become a reality; that is, think California. Expect Moser Baer to achieve revenues in excess of $4 billion by 2102—unless, of course, someone decides to become a leading manufacturer of optical disk and solar technology before then. Indian companies have mastered the processes required for high-tech manufacturing and have now begun innovating. That spells opportunity for companies looking for a low-cost manufacturing platform, which could lead to the development of innovative products as well. That should be good news for companies like Kodak, Canon, 3M, Hewlett Packard, and many others.

DISTRIBUTION AND LOGISTICS

India is investing the local equivalent of US$1 trillion over the next 5 years to improve and modernize its infrastructure. That is going to create a tremendous opportunity for logistics service providers (LSPs) and third-party logistics providers (3PLs), which are still in their infancy in India. With massive investments in infrastructure and double-digit growth in the manufacturing sector, the Indian distribution and logistics market will exceed US$125 billion by 2010. Remember Delhi Assam Roadways, with their fleet of contracted trucks, containerized shipping, and computerized routing programs? They are the exception to the rule in India, where transporters with fleets smaller than five trucks account for over 65 percent of the total trucks owned and operated and more than 80 percent of revenues. Of the remaining transporters, only 17 percent have more than 20 trucks. In fact, there are only approximately 14 national players currently operating in the Indian logistics market with organized trucking accounting.

The majority of 3PL revenues come from inventory handling, transportation, warehousing, and IT services, but in India most warehouses are ill-equipped, often with no refrigeration or cold storage, and the shippers typically offer very few value-added services. Currently only 10 percent of Indian produce is handled through cold-storage facilities, with a grand total of only 3,500 cold-storage facilities in existence in India today. The result of these inefficiencies is that more than 30 percent of all produce, seafood, and meats are lost in the supply chain. Also, freight costs typically average 11 percent, compared to the global average of 6 percent and thus drive up costs and erode margins even further. The lack of a well-established LSP and 3PL network is further evidenced by the fact that the standard transit time between the factory shop floor in India and the shop shelves in the United States is 6 to 12 weeks compared to just 2 to 3 weeks for Chinese goods to make the same journey. India spends approximately 13 percent of its GDP on logistics, compared to 11 percent in the United States. If India can reduce its logistics costs by just 1 percent of GDP it would equate to more than US$7.5 billion per year in savings.

Logistics service providers in India have yet to develop state-of-the-art warehouses with high-security features. The warehouses are not integrated with each other and therefore do not support a shared inventory stock management program among the regional distribution centers (RDCs), local distribution centers (LDCs), and global distribution centers (GDCc). Warehouses are not TAPA-certified. They do not provide features such as CCTV, alarms, pre-theft and post-theft security measures, e-seals, and/or mechanical seals, all of which are prerequisites for multinational corporations.

Outsourcing among Indian shippers is more task based than for the entire manufacturing process, which largely limits the role of an LSP. Key performance indicators (KPIs) are not adequately measured to reflect the direct value in the business of the shipper, mainly in terms of cash cycle, delivery lead time, time to market, and time to cash. Indian logistics players do not invest sufficiently on research for newer markets and the requirements of shippers that are entering India now. Employees are not sufficiently trained, including drivers (remember Kumar?) to keep the systems and procedures intact. There is not enough cooperation between shippers and LSPs, limiting the end-use objectives of logistics service providers. There is a considerable lack of trust in LSPs to provide them better access to information and process know-how. Third-party vehicle providers do not often have any regard for the systems and procedures put in place by the 3PL or shipper. Currently only approximately 6 percent of the Indian logistics market is outsourced to 3PL providers, with more than 83 percent still perfromed in house.

With a rapidly growing middle class in India, consumer markets are extending beyond the five metros of Mumbai, Delhi, Bangalore, Chennai, and Hyderabad. Slowly, consumer markets are reaching the Tier-2 cities in the more rural areas of the country. This trend, combined with growing exports, will force firms to focus on product distribution and cost reduction, which will further drive the growth of logistics outsourcing in India. A reduction in government red tape will also foster growth and profitability in this sector, as the government moves to replace a myriad of state and central government taxes with a value added tax (VAT). The implementation of the VAT will lower transit times and reduce associated paperwork. All of this is going to create significant opportunities for domestic players like Delhi Assam and foreign 3PL providers like BAX Global, BNSF Logistics, Pacer Logistics, the Hub Group, and many more.

PHARMACEUTICAL AND MEDICAL DEVICES

With the most FDA-approved companies outside of the United States, India's pharmaceutical and medical device industry is poised to become a major component of India's next wave. From a turnover of US$2.2 billion in 1990 to a turnover of over US$10 billion during 2004 to 2005, the Indian pharmaceutical and medical device sector is still at the beginning of its growth trajectory. India has developed thorough clinical trial protocols and processes for Phase I, II, and III clinical trials, with substantially lower costs. Product design capabilities are also being generated, with a large pool of engineering talent that has significant experience at leading medical device companies like Boston Scientific. With these attributes India could capture more than 20 percent of the US$30 billion global contract research and manufacturing services (CRAMS) market in the near future.

Numerous Indian pharmaceutical companies have now become industry leaders. One company that has played a strong role in achieving this success is Ranbaxy. Founded in 1961, Ranbaxy is currently one of India's largest pharmaceutical firms. Ranbaxy went public in 1973. That same year it established a multipurpose plant in Mohali, Punjab, to manufacture active pharmaceutical ingredients (APIs), followed quickly by the establishment of numerous joint ventures, the first of which was in Nigeria.

By the mid-1980s Ranbaxy had developed a state-of-the-art research facility and a modern dosage forms facility, supported by a second pharmaceutical marketing division called Stancare. It soon became the largest producer of antibiotics in India, and the API plant received U.S. FDA approval. Two of its drugs, Cephalosporins and Doxycyline, received U.S. patents in 1991. Ranbaxy's joint venture with Eli Lilly & Co. in 1992 was its first clear show of intent to increase market share in the Indian market. The next year it established another JV with Guangzhou, China, to enter the Chinese pharmaceutical market.

Getting access to foreign capital and finding alternative financing resources in the Indian market were believed to be the key drivers behind the listing of Ranbaxy's Global Depository Receipts (GDRs) on the Luxembourg Stock Exchange in 1994. In its endeavor to become a research-based pharmaceutical firm, Ranbaxy developed a research center at Gurgaon that became fully operational in 1994. It then started acquiring firms at an accelerated rate and entered emerging markets like Brazil and Vietnam as well as the more developed markets of the United States, France, Italy, Spain, and Canada.

The company had sales in excess of US$1 billion by 2004, and the research facilities in Gurgaon had expanded to three state-of-the-art facilities. Among Indian pharmaceutical firms, Ranbaxy has the largest research and development budget, with more than 1,100 scientists engaged in R&D. In 2005, Ranbaxy spent approximately US$100 million on R&D activities, which represented 10 percent of its gross revenues. Not surprisingly, Ranbaxy has some of the largest numbers of pending approvals from the U.S. FDA for abbreviated new drug applications (ANDAs). The 88 pending ANDAs could represent a US$56 billion market opportunity for Ranbaxy.

Exports have always been a focus of Indian pharmaceutical firms, which produced more than 20 percent of the world's generics in 2005, making the country one of the largest global manufacturers of generic drugs. In 2003 India exported 30 percent of its pharmaceuticals, worth US$2.15 billion. Recognizing the potential market for exports, the Indian government established the Pharmaceutical Research and Development Support Fund (PRDSF) and Drug Development Promotion Board (DDPB) in 2004 with an initial investment of US$34 million. It intended to utilize the accrued interest on the investment to support R&D projects jointly proposed by industry and academic institutions/ laboratories and to extend soft loans for R&D. Soon after, Ranbaxy won U.S. FDA approval for an antiretroviral (ARV) drug under the U.S. emergency plan for AIDS relief in 2005—a first for India. Close to 10 drugs went off-patent in 2006 and became generic. The market for these drugs is estimated to be worth US$13.5 billion, which could create significant additional opportunities for Ranbaxy.

Ranbaxy was astute enough very early on to understand that its real opportunities lay in the international market, and its constant foreign marketing and analysis (M&A) activities are a good indicator of this fact. Ranbaxy's recent global M&A activity includes Terapia's purchase for US$324 million in 2006 and acquiring RPG Aventis (US$84 million) and Brand-Veratide from P&G-Germany

(US$5 million). About 75 percent of Ranbaxy's sales originate from these international markets. Currently, Ranbaxy has a presence in 46 countries, and in about 16 of them it has either formed a JV or has its own subsidiary. Ranbaxy has an aggressive strategic plan in place; it aims to grow, and expects to achieve sales worth US$2 billion by 2007, targeting US$5 billion sales by 2012, which would make Ranbaxy one of the top five generic drug manufacturers. The acquisition of Terapia, which was the largest independent generic company in Romania, fits well with this plan. The company also acquired Ethimed NV of Belgium in 2006, adding additional countries to its portfolio. Ethimed is a generic pharmaceutical distributor in a country that is the seventh largest pharmaceutical market in Europe. Around the same time Ranbaxy purchased the generic business arm of Allen S.p.A, a division of GlaxoSmithKline (GSK) in Italy. The purchases in Germany, Romania, Belgium, Italy, and France will serve to enhance Ranbaxy's focus on the European generics market.

Ranbaxy's involvement in the European market is fascinating. But equally aggressive are its activities in the U.S. market. In 2007 Ranbaxy acquired its first major brand in the United States by obtaining the right to manufacture and market 13 dermatology brands in the United States. The contract from Bristol-Myers Squibb (BMS) is believed to be worth US$25 million. The market size for these 13 brands is estimated to be a whopping US$4.5 billion. The company also launched 10 new products in the market in 2006 and grossed US$114 million from its U.S. operations the same year. Ranbaxy continues to expand its presence in the contract research and manufacturing services sector, having recently entered into a partnership with Merck for clinical trials.

The growth in the Indian medical devices and equipment sector is a natural progression of the growth in high-tech manufacturing, pharmaceuticals, and private health care. The Indian private health care sector is now experiencing a high growth rate, which is further driving the growth of the medical device sector. Revenues for the private health care sector are estimated at US$2.31 billion, and the industry is growing at 15 percent annually. The private health care industry is expected to reach US$5.20 billion in revenues by 2012, with the demand for medical equipment rising annually at an impressive rate of 13 to 16 percent.

The cost advantages India offers are significant. Indian companies can produce cardiac medical sutures for US$10 in comparison to the US$200 in the United States. However, India imports more than half of its medical devices—mostly from the United States, Japan, and Germany. With the expansion of the health care infrastructure in the private sector, increasing medical tourism, and the increase in government spending for health care, however, local manufacturing will take off. Multinationals such as GE Medical Systems and Siemens already have a presence in the country. While GE Medical manufactures in India in partnership with Wipro, Siemens has an X-ray manufacturing facility in Goa, where it will begin making ultrasound equipment. Cancer diagnostic, medical imaging, ultrasonic scanning, and plastic surgery equipment are some of the products that are in high demand.

Lack of progress in this sector has been mainly due to government apathy toward the industry. Now, the government has undertaken specific steps that are expected to drive the growth of the sector in terms of both volume and value. In early 2007, the Indian national government approved the creation of an autonomous unit, the Central Drugs Authority (CDA), to regulate the import, licensing, quality, and safety of pharmaceutical and medical device products.

The agency's structure is modeled on the U.S. FDA and it operates as a part of the Ministry of Health and Family Welfare. The CDA comprises distinct divisions for drugs, vaccines, medical devices, cosmetics, clinical trials, quality control, and other regulatory oversight activities. The agency is funded through regulatory fees. Presently, companies have to deal with a plethora of state regulatory requirements that tend to delay the introduction of new drugs and devices and lead to problems such as misbranding. The centralized authority is expected to facilitate these regulatory procedures. Transition from the present system to the centralized licensing system will be phased in over 5 years. Currently, the unorganized market impedes efficient production; however, the recently created Indian Medical Devices Regulatory Authority will rapidly get the industry organized.

Growth in the telemedicine services segment is driving the demand for diagnostic medical equipment such as X-ray machines, CT scanners, and Dopplers. Most of the high-value equipment is marketed by leading international companies who have local support. These companies have set up manufacturing facilities in India to assemble equipment units to cater to the domestic market as well as for export.

Relisys Medical Devices Limited is a leading Indian medical device manufacturer engaged in the local development of medical devices such as coronary stents, catheters, and critical care products. The focal products of the company include drug-eluting stents, angiographic/angioplasty catheters, occlusive devices, cardiac surgery disposables, and critical care products. Relisys is, in fact, the sole domestic manufacturer of coronary stents. The company is emerging as a high-potential player in the international medical devices market. With a stent manufacturing facility and technology alliances, the company is well positioned to making low-cost, high-quality stents and catheters.

Global alliances are helping Relisys reach the U.S. and EU markets with cost-effective products. In its alliance with German technology company Cinvention, Relisys designs and makes stents and Cinvention provides the carbon composite coating and a super structure that facilitates proactive healing. Last year, Relisys formed an alliance with a German material-and-surface-engineering company, Blue Membranes, to get access to the highly competitive carbon-based drug-delivery platform. The firm recently brought Dr. William A. Haseltine, an internationally acclaimed scientist-entrepreneur, on its board.

In July 2006, the Association of Medical Devices and Diagnostics Suppliers of India (AMDDSI) appealed to the Indian government to sanction Special Economic Zones (SEZs) covering 200 acres of land so as to set up 20 companies that will manufacture medical and diagnostic equipment. The growing interest of domestic and international players in Indian medical device manufacturing is obvious. Philips Medical Systems has signed a partnership with Artemis Health Sciences, a corporate hospital promoted by the Apollo group. The partnership will conduct joint research in new medical technologies. Senior director and business head of India's Philips Medical Systems, Anjan Bose, has stated that "With the health care delivery boom, the medical equipment industry, including small devices, will grow between 15 percent and 20 percent in 1 to 2 years time, from the current 10 percent." 3M Health Care, a U.S.-based medical supplies major, is another party deeply interested in India.

China's Neusoft group, a US$700 million medical technology solutions company, is planning a foray into the Indian market via a joint venture with the Chennai-based Trivitron group. The intent is on setting up a medical equipment manufacturing unit in Bangalore to make linear accelerators, laser imagers, and bioanalyzers. Neusoft already has a direct service base in Bangalore, in collaboration with Trivitron, for its CT and MRI systems. "After the software, retail, and finance boom in India, it is our firm belief that the next big growth area for India is going to be in indigenous medical technology," observed G. S. K. Velu, managing director of the Trivitron group. The slashed import duties on medical equipment, announced in early 2007, is bound to increase foreign interest.

Another interesting facet is the impact that super-specialization in Indian corporate hospitals has had on medical device and equipment manufacturing. Wockhardt Hospitals' Dr. Vishal Bali states that

"The entire industry is focusing on super specialty and it has become imperative to increase investment in equipment to get the best technology. Indian hospitals today have state-of-the-art technology, and about 30 to 35 percent of the investment in a new hospital goes in procuring equipment." Industrial development body FICCI has created the Medical Technology Forum. Texas Instruments, GE, Philips, and TCS are some of the members of the forum, which intends to work with the Indian Ministry of Science and Technology to promote the domestic manufacture of medical equipment.

Proven manufacturing processes, a solid relationship with the U.S. FDA, low-cost clinical trials, and innovative engineering and scientific talent will certainly benefit companies like Eli Lilly and Boston Scientific, but these same attributes may prove even more valuable to newer players in the pharmaceutical, medical device, and biotechnology field. These capabilities will give new companies in these sectors the opportunity to get their products to market at a far lower cost. That's good news if your company happens to have a high burn rate and is still in the product development phase.

FINANCIAL SERVICES

The Indian financial services sector could prove to be significantly larger than that of China, as more than 70 percent of India's population owns private property and more than 50 percent of Indian households already own bank accounts. These facts, coupled with a rapidly growing middle class and dramatically increased consumption patterns, will drive profitability and growth in all segments of the financial services sector. Indian banks like ICICI, India's most valuable financial services company, and HDFC Bank, India's third-largest bank by value, are benefiting from the dramatic growth in consumer and commercial loans, which grew by more than 35 percent per year over the past 2 years. And with an estimated US$500 billion of investment required for infrastructure and manufacturing projects over the next 3 years, demand for loans is expected to increase dramatically. Mortgage-backed securities and asset-backed securities are still in the early stages of development, but with an estimated US$2 trillion in property loans or sales expected over the next 5 years, these markets will increase at a dramatic rate.

With a middle-class population that is expected to grow to 91 million households by 2012, the Indian debit and credit card markets are set to explode. India has now become the third-largest card market for Visa International in Asia Pacific, after Japan and Korea. Visa is the market leader in both credit and debit cards in India. As of March 31, 2006, Visa saw a 36 percent annual growth rate in the number of cards issued. The current number of debit and credit cards stands at 27 million and 12 million, respectively. The total number of debit and credit cards issued in India as of 2007 is estimated to be at around 47 million and 18 million, respectively. More debit cards are being issued as public-sector banks develop core banking solutions. Banks have started issuing credit cards in Tier II cities, and markets like airline ticketing are opening up. With 40 million Internet users—a number that is expected to grow to 200 million in the short term—the use of online shopping networks and other portals will also drive the use of debit and credit cards in India.

Traditional retail sales volumes (RSVs), which include customer spending at point-of-sales (POS) terminals, are also growing. Visa clocked a 61 percent growth in RSV, to US$5.37 billion, as of March 31, 2006, with annual consumer spending on credit cards increasing to US$380 from US$335 the previous year. As India's retail sector continues to modernize and expand, led by companies like Reliance and Wal-Mart, POS sales will also increase at double digit rates. The number of POS terminals in India has seen a significant growth, up from 40,000 terminals in 2002 to 306,000 in 2006. Visa card sales volume, which includes RSVs and ATM transactions, have seen a 47 percent rise, to $432 billion, as of March 31, 2006. An important point to remember is that Indian culture traditionally did not promote credit; it has only been in the past few years that the Indian consumer has begun to embrace the concept. With the growth of the middle class and a growing acceptability of credit, the Indian consumer will soon demand premium benefits, which will include gold card programs, special airport lounges and train station lounges, and easy access to ATM machines.

Of the total number of Indian households with significant financial assets, only 4 percent are currently investing in stock markets—yet 12 percent of the NSE's trading volume is due to online trading by retail investors. The level of investing by Indian households is also set to grow dramatically over the next 5 years, fueled by historically high rates of saving and a rapidly growing economy. The rapid growth of India's financial services market is going to create significant opportunities for a wide range of financial services companies such as Fiserv, Fidelity, Metavante, and TSYS. This growth also means opportunities for commercial banks and brokerage houses like Wachovia, Morgan Stanley, Prudential, and others. India's insurance sector is also expected to open up in the near future, creating vast opportunities for companies such as AIG and MetLife.

EDUCATION

With more than 30 million individuals leaving the agriculture sector or joining the workforce for the first time, India is facing an education shortfall. That shortfall is already being seen in the IT sector, with companies like Infosys and Tata Consulting spending millions of dollars on training just to get college graduates up to speed. In the construction sector there is an estimated 30 percent gap in skilled and semiskilled labor. Less than half of Indian students matriculate to college, and with almost two-thirds of India's universities and about 90 percent of its colleges rated below average in quality, the market need is big. The overall size of the education market is estimated to exceed US$35 billion per year. However, there is a common misconception that commercial education companies cannot succeed in India as the government is resistant to the concept. To the contrary, numerous Indian commercial education providers have been created and have prospered in the Indian market.

NIIT, a technology training and curricula development corporation based in India, was founded in 1981. The company claims that one out of every three software professionals in India is an alumnus, with an annual graduation rate of 500,000. Oriented toward IT aspirants, the flagship GNIIT program, with its focus on software engineering, systems engineering and networking, information systems management, and business process outsourcing management opens up many career paths and also offers placement partnerships with leading IT companies by customizing portions of the curriculum to match precise industry trends and emerging technology platforms. GNIIT provides generic and company-specific skills that create professionals who are industry-ready and able to contribute immediately. That's important, considering the fact that India's knowledge-worker population grew to 650,000 software and services professionals in 2003 to 2004, up from 6,800 in 1986. India's IT workforce could grow to 2 million in 10 years.

India's booming education sector is not limited to information technology. Manipal Education Systems, a provider of traditional degree programs was founded in 1953. With 100,000 students and 30 campuses, the company is the largest private sector player in the traditional Indian degree sector, and was the first private university to be accredited by the government, in 1993. Manipal Systems offers a full range of programs, including management, health care, and professional skills development for banking, retail, and hospitality sectors.

The university also provides an e-learning program, based on a hub-and-spoke model, that is used in conjunction with 450 education centers. There are 72,000 students currently enrolled in distance learning, which is an important aspect of any successful educational program in India, as the majority of the population still lives in rural areas. Manipal Systems recently entered into the vocational education arena, with Phase 1 of its program covering service sectors, including banking and insurance, retail, infrastructure services, telecom, IT and BPO, and digital media. They expect this initiative to involve over 25,000 students in 2007 alone. The university also offers online testing and assessment services for academic entry and academic and corporate assessment (including prerecruitment assessment) through 19 centers across India.

Manipal also operates twinning programs in medicine and engineering, as well as research programs (with a specific focus on biotechnology, medicine, and engineering). Many of their research programs are undertaken in conjunction with global leaders such as Philips and GE. Some of their other education services include a global nursing program that focuses on specialized nursing training and placement, e-content publishing and related services, and other related transaction support services. Manipal Systems also plans to implement several other strategic initiatives, which will include setting up a chain of "CityCampuses," which are university branch operations covering a spectrum of offerings, including corporate education and training, formal education, distance education learning center services, and professional education. In September 2006 the company received funding from one of the leading private equity (PE) funds in India, with over $650 million under management. That's not surprising, considering the fact that Manipal Systems has a CAGR of 35 percent per year and earnings before interest, tax depreciation, and amortization (EBITDA) margins that would rival any equivalent U.S. institution. The United States is a leader in commercial education services, and companies such as The Apollo Group, Career Education Services, and DeVry are well positioned to capture significant market share and profits in the Indian education sector.

RENEWABLE ENERGY

Renewable energy is in vogue these days—for most countries, it makes sound environmental sense for it to be a serious focus of energy policy. But for India, which was crippled by the oil shock of 1992 but has now rebounded as one of the fastest-growing economies in the world, renewable energy is critically important. Companies like Moser Baer will give India a global leadership position in the field of solar energy, and companies like the GMR Group are rapidly expanding the country's ethanol production, which will soon surpass that of Brazil. But that is only part of India's renewable energy equation, as the country rapidly develops global expertise in the area of biodiesel. A processed fuel developed from plant-based sources such as vegetable oils and soybeans, biodiesel is equivalent to oil-based diesel, and more importantly, it reduces toxic emissions from cars by as much as 50 percent. That is important in a country that has one of the fastest-growing automotive markets in the world.

Environmental degradation and foreign exchange outflow caused by an increasing consumption of petroleum products is a major concern for India. Ethanol and biodiesel have been identified as equally effective and less damaging options than conventional fossil fuels. To tackle this challenge, the Indian government created the Committee on Development of Bio-fuel to conduct a study on the feasibility and means of procurement of biodiesel. The committee identified two species of trees, namely *Jatropha curcas* and *Pongamia pinnata*, which should be used for biodiesel production, and identified areas where dedicated plantings of these species can be done. Close to one million acres of land across India have been identified as plantation areas for these trees.

The government has organized lectures, conferences, and special sessions for farmers across India to educate them on the utility of biodiesel. During one of these conferences, a farmer, Shravan Tripathi, got so infatuated by the idea that he bought a hundred saplings right away. He has been cultivating Jatropha trees for 3 years. "After having grown Jatropha trees for three years now, the best part is that from plantation to primary processing and from seed collection to oil extraction—I own every task. I produce for myself and am not affected by external factors," he told us. The first time he sowed the Jatropha seeds, almost the entire village watched him, he says. Shravan hopes that the government will take up the planting program on a large scale. He wants to organize road shows and mass awareness programs, with significant government support.

The committee also suggested measures to achieve a 5 percent replacement of petrodiesel by biodiesel by 2006–2007. To achieve this target a National Mission on Bio-Diesel has been created to bring all the interested parties together. The first phase of the mission, the demonstration project, with an investment of approximately US$370 million, will be implemented by the year 2007, and subsequent expansion of this project, in Phase II, is expected to result in the production of the required amount of biodiesel by 2012. The fact that extracting oil from the seeds is not a very complicated process helps—it is a simple process, very similar to extracting mustard oil, something that has been done for hundreds of years.

By the year 2007 the demonstration project alone will necessitate a total employment of 127.6 million days in planting and 36.8 million days in seed collection. Dr. R. Mandal, advisor, (Ministry of Environment and Forest) has stated that "The use of biodiesel blends will result in a savings of $5 billion annually on imports of crude oil. We are planning to produce 13 million tons of alternate fuel every year. However, this will require 11 million hectares of land and create 11 million jobs." What's more, the new fuel will be available at almost half the price of petrol. Shravan, the Jatropha enthusiast, insists that the government should speed up the program and take initiatives to make Jatropha cultivation more popular. He has suggested that steps be taken to allot government-owned lands to farmers for Jatropha cultivation. The government should also ensure that only Jatropha is grown in these areas.

Buoyed by the initiatives undertaken by the Indian government, the state of Haryana has deployed biodiesel-fueled buses on the streets of Gurgaon. The Indian Railway was next to buy the idea, and trains running on biodiesel have been put on trial runs. But the biggest deployment has come from India's auto sector, which will most probably be the largest consumer of the new fuel. Daimler AG is on the verge of completing a feasibility study on biodiesel derived from Jatropha. Two C-class Mercedes Benz have already been tested, and the results have been positive. In Pune, more than 40 buses are running on biodiesel. These mass-transportation vehicles are manufactured by the automobile division of the giant Indian corporation, Tata Industries, and are compatible with biodiesel.

But it is the largest manufacturer of agricultural vehicles in India, Mahindra & Mahindra, that has made the biggest splash. In 2007 the company introduced versions of its two most successful SUVs, Scorpio and Bolero, that will run on biodiesel. Scorpio is the first Asian vehicle in its class running on 100 percent biodiesel. In a move that will surely bring a smile to the faces of Indian farmers, Mahindra & Mahindra also unveiled a biodiesel tractor for the first time in India. The company set up its own biodiesel plant in 2001. It carried out extensive studies and worked in conjunction with IIT Kanpur, a leading Indian technology institute, and the R&D center of Indian Oil Corporation, the highest-ranked Indian company in the Fortune Global 500 listing. Mahindra & Mahindra is also working on the fuel adaptability for their other vehicles. It plans to be fully prepared for the time when the market matures and the infrastructure required for utilizing alternative and better sources of fuel is present across India. Renewable energy will provide investors and joint venture partners with significant returns over the coming years. And with opportunities in solar, wind, ethanol, and biodiesel, numerous global synergies exist between homebuilders, power companies, and automotive firms.

AGRIBUSINESS

By now you probably know that India is the largest producer of fruits in the world, the largest producer of milk, the second largest producer of sugarcane, the third largest producer of cotton, and the list goes on. You are also likely aware of the fact that India has a completely undeveloped supply chain, and as a result, the amount of agricultural product that is lost through waste and spoilage is mind-boggling. It is no secret that India's growing middle class is gradually altering its consumer patterns. Consequently, the growing presence of supermarkets and other large chain stores comes as no surprise. It is a sign that shoppers are ready to move past the small, open-air traditional shops.

The organized formation of retailing in India has never found a foothold. This was in large part due to poor economic policies. The retail sector, which was the second-largest employer in India after Indian Railways, could not emerge from its unorganized shadows. The retail industry is massive: It contributes close to 10 percent of India's gross domestic product. With that kind of an impact, it was mandatory for the government to change the sector from an unorganized, inefficient arrangement to a platform where everything could be accounted for and its potential could be realized, including its fiscal revenues.

The total annual retail trade in India is estimated at US$200 billion, with the organized retail sector constituting 3 percent of the total market, or US$6.4 billion. The unorganized segment, accounting for the bulk of India's retail trade, consists of the traditional formats of low-cost retailing. Known as "mom and pop" shops, these include the neighborhood shops, owner-run general stores, convenience stores, handcarts and sidewalk vendors, and so on. Some important aspects of unorganized retailing include the fact that more than 99 percent operate in less than 500 square feet of area and that a limited number of goods are stored, mainly consisting of low-priced brands. Unorganized retail caters primarily to lower-income sections, and their localized target audience is small. Unorganized retailers also practice differential pricing, and no separate accounts are maintained for trading and in-house consumption.

While these shortcomings are clearly being addressed by the organized segment of retailing, Indian retailers still face certain key issues. First, the high cost of real estate presents a major challenge, making it more difficult for the retailer to break even. Second, huge inefficiencies exist in the supply chain, since the retail sector is highly fragmented. The supply chain for food products in India, for instance, is characterized by heavy wastage as well as poor handling. This is attributed to the existence of multiple points of manual handling, poor packaging, and the lack of availability of temperature-controlled vans and warehouses. A study by the Federation of Indian Chambers of Commerce and Industry (FICCI) showed that almost 40 to 45 percent of fresh food is wasted due to inadequate handling and lack of adequate storage infrastructure. Lack of distribution networks connecting Tier II towns with regional logistics hubs is another concern. In this case, the services of regional transport companies as well as third-party logistics players can be leveraged to ameliorate the situation. A third major challenge is posed by the shortfall of trained manpower and professionals to manage stores.

The situation is rapidly changing, as India's infrastructure is rapidly expanded and modernized and the distribution and logistics sector develops. This, coupled with growing income levels, higher international exposure, and a stronger purchasing power, translates into a higher consumption rate, which bodes well for the agribusiness sector. As of now, the retail industry is witnessing a metamorphosis, with existing as well as new players experimenting with new retail formats that include malls, department stores, supermarkets, and convenience stores.

The Indian government announced in January 2006 that foreign single retail brands can open their own stores and own up to 51 percent of local joint ventures. This is expected to further encourage new players to enter the Indian market. However, India has yet to completely open up its retail sector.

With the enormous opportunities offered by India's flourishing agribusiness and retail sector, international players such as Wal-Mart and Tesco as well as domestic corporate giants like Reliance, the Aditya Birla Group, and the Bharti Group are eyeing to capture a share of India's agribusiness and retail market. The Aditya Birla Group is planning to invest US$2.5 billion over the next 3 years to develop 1,000 hypermarkets and supermarkets of approximately 10,000 square feet each.

Mukesh Ambani—the chairman of Reliance Industries, India's biggest company by market capitalization—announced in 2006 that the company will invest over US$6.2 billion in its latest retail venture. The undertaking includes the creation of supermarkets such as Reliance Fresh, investments in consumer electronics, footwear, apparel outlets and the construction of hypermarket stores. Aiming to become India's largest retailer by 2010, Reliance Retail plans to launch more than 1,000 multiformat outlets across the country.

Operated by Reliance Retail, the Reliance Fresh stores sell fruits and vegetables, groceries, and dairy products under its own brand, Reliance Select. Though Reliance Fresh had started off as a pure fruit and vegetable store in October 2006, it has decided to sell other groceries as well. This first mid-course correction was announced in May 2007.

Reliance Retail has embarked on a massive retail venture and has ambitious plans for its Reliance Fresh retail outlets. The first

Reliance Fresh retail store was launched in the city of Hyderabad in the South Indian state of Andhra Pradesh in October 2006. As reported in June 2007, there are about 169 Reliance Fresh stores in almost every part of India. In its latest development project, Reliance Retail plans to open 11 stores in the city of Nashik, in the state of Maharashtra (Central India). By July of 2007, the company aims to launch five stores there. Ranging from 280 to 550 square meters in size, the outlets will sell fresh groceries and dairy products. By the end of 2007, Reliance plans to open 150 new stores throughout the state of Maharashtra.

In March 2007, Reliance Fresh forayed into Eastern India by launching a store in the Jharkhand capital city of Ranchi. It is one of four planned for Ranchi. It revealed plans in April 2007 to launch over 180 Reliance Fresh stores in 16 cities and towns in the Western state of Gujarat over the next 6 months. In May 2007, Reliance Retail reported plans to set up 23 stores in Indore and another 20 in Bhopal, located in the central state of Madhya Pradesh.

One hundred Reliance Fresh outlets are proposed to open in the state of Punjab (Northern India) by the end of 2007. As of May 2007, it had already opened five stores in the city of Jalandhar. Earlier this year, it launched 27 stores in the city of Hyderabad in the South Indian state of Andhra Pradesh. Reliance Retail also secured the European Retail Parties Good Agricultural Practices (EurepGAP) certification in March 2007 for some of its fresh produce sourced from farmers in India.

Reliance is also considering the acquisition of a large Western retailer; a stake in the French retailer Carrefour is being touted as possible. With the objective of expanding its retail segment, Reliance Retail is creating a huge supply chain to support its "farm-to-fork" initiative. This includes vast contract farms for produce and an extensive refrigerated infrastructure, as well as its own fleet of planes to transport goods.

Reliance Fresh, with its fresh supplies, competitive prices, air-conditioned aisles, shopping carts, and automatic doors is pulling customers away from the small traditional neighborhood shops and local vegetable vendors. Earlier, Indian shoppers had little choice when it came to buying fruits and vegetables. One had to necessarily go to the vegetable market to buy fresh items and bargain with vendors. With the advent of retail outlets such as Reliance Fresh, shopping for fresh fruits and vegetables in a clean, air-conditioned ambience at prices lower than the local market comes as a blessing for most consumers. Besides buying fruits and vegetables, customers can shop for other provisions under the same roof. This eliminates the need to hop from shop to shop. Moreover, people working late into the night need not rush to the wholesale market at dawn every day. As the new outlets are open from early morning till late in the night, customers can shop at their own convenience. The advantages that Reliance Fresh offers over its local counterparts are numerous, including the fact that the company buys in bulk directly from farmers; Reliance Fresh enjoys economies of scale. The benefit is passed on to the customers in the form of lower prices. Historically a large portion of the country's fruit and vegetables rot before they reach the shelves or market stalls. Reliance Fresh, with its cold storage and refrigerated transport, is well-equipped to address this concern, thereby offering better quality. The stores also offer a barter-free shopping experience, which is welcomed by consumers, and of course there is better quality and hygiene compared to the local vendor.

Reliance has mastered effective supply-chain management with strong backward integration. It is setting up collection centers across the country for various commodities with the objective of procuring the produce directly from the farmers. It will also educate farmers on best farming practices. For instance, Reliance Retail has obtained a license to procure onions for its Reliance Fresh stores across India from the Lasalgaon Agriculture Produce Market Committee (APMC) in Nashik district.

Further, the company possesses cargo carriers to facilitate the movement of produce directly from the farms to the food processing plants or retail outlets. Heavy investments have been made to monitor the movement of goods and plan inventories. Also, small shopkeepers would be able to buy from Reliance on a wholesale basis, and thus benefit from its supply chain. The set up seems a win-win situation for all parties involved. With the intention of catering to Tier II cities, Reliance has ventured into cities like Ranchi, Jalandhar, and Indore.

Reliance has also mastered the art of manpower training and is setting up learning centers across the country to train people in modern retailing. This is keeping in line with the growing demand for trained manpower in the retail industry. In terms of skill as well as personality, Reliance Retail is recruiting people from diverse industries. That's going to be important, as Reliance Retail plans to open 100 million square feet of retail space by 2010 to 2011. The company has leased retail space at various prime locations across India.

With the view of entering into retail in a big way, Reliance has also taken over local cooperative stores. Besides having several branches in prime neighborhoods, these stores are cheaper in terms of land rentals and they already have a dedicated clientele. For instance, Reliance Retail has already taken over Sahakar Bhandar in Mumbai. Reliance retail claims that the new shops will create half a million new jobs within 3 years.

The mammoth company's venture in retail is not restricted to Reliance Fresh. Reliancedigital, Reliance Retail's pilot standalone consumer electronics store, was launched in the capital city of New Delhi in March 2007. It plans to open a second such store in Bangalore later, in August. Further, Reliance Retail is to roll out a chain of home stores in India during 2007.

By July 2007, Reliance Retail is expected to commission the first of its chain of Reliance Mart hypermarkets. The first one will be built in the South Indian city of Bangalore; the first hypermarket will cover 0.18 million square feet. It will offer a wide range of digital, lifestyle, and food products. The second hypermarket is planned for Gujarat. The size of each hypermarket will vary from about 40,000 to 0.2 million sq ft.

Reliance and the rest of India's rapidly developing retail sector is only part of the opportunity that agribusiness will present in the coming years. Consider mangoes, which made their reentry in the United States in June 2007 after having been banned from the U.S. market for nearly two decades. India is the world's largest producer of mangoes—it produces approximately 14 million tons annually—but it only exports 60,000 tons, less than 1 percent of total production. The opening of the U.S. market to Indian produce is a good indicator of the global opportunity that exists for India's agribusiness sector—in fact, the Japanese government followed suit and opened their market to Indian produce a week later.

As the global export market for India's agricultural products expands it will compel farmers to adopt more commercial aspects of agribusiness. One example is that farmers are now learning about techniques like high-density planting—this move will not just help mangoes, but other tropical produce as well. The benefits of the commercialization of India's agribusiness sector will extend far beyond farmers and processors. Companies involved in the irradiation business will benefit, as will cargo flight operators, wholesalers, and distributors.

FASHION APPAREL

India is the third-largest producer of cotton in the world, and the Indian textile industry has been completely reengineered using the latest technology and processes. These facts, combined with the increasing purchasing power of hundreds of millions of Indian consumers, will drive major growth in per capita consumption in textile and clothing. By the end of 2009 the Indian apparel market will exceed US$120 billion dollars; at that size India will be in the top 15 markets in the world, even considering the substantially lower retail price in that market. What makes the Indian market even more appealing is the large volume of apparel exports which exceeded US$35 billion dollars to the U.S. market alone in 2006.

An abundance of raw material availability, low-cost skilled labor, presence across the value chain and a growing domestic market are all driving the growth of India's fashion apparel market. Multinationals like Wal-Mart, Levis, Gap, JC Penney, Marks & Spencer, and other foreign labels are coming to India to buy garments and fabrics. Wal-Mart intends to increase its purchases to US$3 billion by 2009 and GAP is now sourcing apparel from India at an accelerated rate. In addition to these companies a number of other brands, including Gucci and Giorgio Armani, are slated to open their first stores by 2008, as the Indian government has now removed restrictions for retailers with single-brand products.

The Indian fashion apparel had its first awakening with the opening of the first National Institute of Fashion Technology (NIFT) in India in 1986 under the Ministry of Textiles. Many believe that the Indian fashion industry became an industry only after the institute was incorporated. There are seven NIFT centers in India now and the institution has produced some of India's most cherished fashion professionals. The government of India and the National Institute of Design (NID), an institution set up in 1961 as an autonomous national institution for research, service, and training in industrial design and visual communication, are working together on the National Design Policy. The policy intends to "prepare a platform for creative design development, design promotion and partnerships across many sectors, states, and regions integrating design and technological resources to stand out in the international arena."

Dr. Darlie O. Koshy, director of NID, is heading the project, which is slated to be ready by 2008.

Gaurav Gupta, a designer who graduated from NIFT Delhi, went on to graduate from the Chelsea College of Art & Design and spent time at the Parisian Atelier National d'Art Textile (ANAT), states the point directly: "Fashion education is a very important aspect to the growth of the Indian apparel industry. NIFT in India started in 1986 and with it fashion in India started." Indian fashion designers have woken up to realize the huge potential and popularity of their home-grown textiles in the international market as well, and intend to get the advantage of second mover in this market. Indian designers like Manish Arora, Ashish Soni, and Ashish Gupta are now showing at the London Fashion Week, the Paris Fashion Week, and the Olympus Fashion Week in New York. They now lobby and market their clothes like any fashion designer would. They have their own lines of clothing, fabrics, and embroidery techniques. And it's not only about apparel designing: The garment export industry is hot too, where designers generally work at their desks making new designs.

Domestically, the Fashion Design Council of India (FDCI) and IMG create a platform where designers are presented with a chance to showcase their talent. The rising middle class has meant an increased awareness of fashion, higher aspirations for branded products, and more affordability. Indian designers have now started to model their designs to reach the ever-growing India middle class, apart from catering to the upper class, who account for the majority of the annual US$14.4 billion expenditure on luxury goods. Fashion roots run very deep in India. Some of the most unique design patterns originating in India come from very primitive tribal areas. Gaurav Gupta explains: "The actual strength of the Indian design sector is crafts. The wonderful things they produce, I cannot imagine them in the wildest of my dreams. They are comparable to any big name in Indian fashion."

Assocham, an industry body, estimates that established as well as upcoming designers in India will grow in number and contribute close to US$500 million by 2012, up from US$50 million in 2007. "Overall, Indian fashion is growing exponentially. The industry would grow in size and there would be several stakeholders who would contribute to this growth. Both established and upcoming designers would be responsible for bringing about growth," Atul Chand, vice president, ITC Lifestyle, a leading Indian retail store, has stated. While the current contributions of upcoming designers is not much, their role is going to increase by leaps and bounds by 2012. As for the established ones—with Manish Arora being invited to participate in the Paris Fashion Week, the sky's the limit.

India's prime fashion events—Wills Lifestyle India Fashion Week in Delhi, by the Fashion Design Council of India (FDCI), and Lakme Fashion Week in Mumbai present an opportunity to the established as well as fledgling Indian designers to showcase their talent. They are a commercial exercise and it is at events like these that the designers meet their potential buyers. "While fashion is a business for us throughout the year, during these 5 to 6 days alone the business graphs of designers go up by over 15 to 20 percent," stated leading Indian designer Leena Singh on the utility of these fashion weeks. In 2006, the number of fashion weeks in India doubled to four from the traditional two. The buyers included Bloomingdales, Anthropologie, Zamzara, Maria Louisa, and Bon Marche, among others. Confidence in Indian fashion and its stakeholders was further substantiated when Luis Vuitton, designers of luxury leather goods, bought a 20 percent stake in Hidesign, a premium Indian leather garments and accessories firm.

Kamal Nath, Minister of Commerce, announced that the India Brand Equity Foundation (IBEF—an initiative by CII and the Ministry of Commerce) will now also be funding projects brought forth by Indian fashion designers. Gaurav Gupta says, "I am working for the past two years now. I am looking for funding, or venture capitalists, or business angels, who have faith in me and can take me one step forward. It's a creative industry. I cannot afford to be bogged down by scarcity of funds." Gaurav is keen on something similar to the Arts Councils in the United Kingdom, which promote different forms of art and also provide funding for a range of arts activities.

However, the opportunity in the Indian clothing market is far greater than what local apparel houses such as Madura Garments, Arvind Brands, Raymond/Park Avenue, Zodiac, and a few others can cater to. Some of the most interesting opportunities exist in product categories such as denim wear, Western-styled women's wear, men's formalwear (especially in tailored clothing such as suits and jackets), smart casual clothing, outdoor active lifestyle wear, and children's and young boys/girls clothing. All of these items would cater to leading retailers like GAP, Max Mara, Abercrombie & Fitch, The Limited, and many more. Pantaloon, a leading retailer, is investing US$450 million dollars to acquire consumer products companies. The company has stakes in fashion companies like Indus League and Planet Sports, among others. Indus League had earlier bought the women's wear denim brand Jealous. The company is looking to acquire 10 million square feet of retail space in India, and 40 percent of this will be for fashion apparel.

Seeing an opportunity in the kidswear segment, the Anil Dhirubhai Ambani Enterprise (ADAE) recently purchased a stake in leading kidswear brand Gini & Jony, and another Ambani group is reportedly also eyeing the retail segment. Leading corporate groups such as Raheja's, Bombay Dyeing, Piramals, and Tata have all expressed keen interest in investing in the Indian retail apparel market. One of the first clothing brands to have invested in a retail chain in India was the Zodiac group, which has a 2.93 percent stake in Shoppers' Stop and is now looking at picking up further stakes in more retail chains. "We are waiting for an opportunity to invest in domestic retail chains. If we get a good value we would definitely be interested," its managing director, Salman Noorani, has stated. Clothing and textiles constitute the largest block of organized retailing; if we were to consider all fashion and lifestyle markets, such as jewelery, accessories, health and beauty care services, and mobile handsets into one common group, then fashion as such would constitute about 60 percent of the organized retailing pie.

Additionally, the US$35 billion Bombay Rayon (BR) is in discussions with Credo Brands, makers of the apparel brand Mufti, for a strategic alliance. "We have known BR for almost nine years as their customer. We are still deciding on the business model. We take a long time to plan, but once we roll out, we will take the bull by the horns. We plan to get into retail very aggressively," states Kamal Khushlani of Mufti. Bombay Rayon managing director Prashant Agarwal reiterates Khushlani's words. Asked whether BR is looking to come out with its own brand, Agarwal answers in the negative: "We see a lot of retail growth coming in. It is still in a nascent stage, so we are focusing our energy on the developed markets. Post-quota, there has been an immediate jump in the export market, and we are exploiting that."

The Indian fashion apparel sector is going to play an important role in India's next wave of growth, with renowned fashion designers like Giorgio Armani believing that "The khadi [handspun fabric] made in India is among the most skin-friendly fabrics we know. In fact, the day isn't far when khadi-based designs will rule the world." Apart from Giorgio, Gucci and Donna Karan (DKNY) are also khadi fans; they source from the Sarvodaya Ashram in Delhi. Many Indian designers are now international icons, such as Rohit Bal, who designed outfits for Liz Hurley's wedding and has admirers in Naomi Campbell and Cindy Crawford. One of the most significant opportunities for global retailers will be in creating joint ventures with prominent Indian designers and fashion houses to develop private-label products for the domestic market as well as the international market. Luis Vuitton may have already caught the next wave with its recent investment in India.

MEDIA AND ENTERTAINMENT

Remember TV18? They have just won the Fox News franchise for India. The media and entertainment industry is one of the fastest-growing sectors in India, with a CAGR of 19 percent. Economic growth, rising disposable incomes, and increasing consumer spending, combined with technological advances and government policy initiatives, have all helped drive the rapid growth of this sector, which stood at US$9.71 billion in 2006 and is expected to reach more than US$50 billion by 2015.

In addition to economic drivers, a number of other factors are also likely to contribute to the growth of the Indian entertainment industry in the coming years. These include sparse media penetration in the lower socioeconomic class, which will offer immense potential—since the population is so large, a slight increase in penetration can result in a significant increase in base. And a liberalized foreign investment regime in India that allows 100 percent foreign direct investment (FDI) in film-related activities such as financing, production, and exhibition are factors that will drive the growth of the entertainment industry.

Today, India has the largest television market in the world. It accounts for the largest share in the overall entertainment industry, at 42 percent. In the past few years television has grown at an unprecedented rate. Television homes are growing at a staggering annual rate of 4 percent in India; this means that the number of television homes far exceeds the number of telephone-connected homes. India has 119 million television households, which account for around 60 percent of the total households in the country. Of these 119 million TV households, about 50 million receive cable television services, leading to a penetration ratio of about 42 percent cable TV households to total TV households and 25 percent cable TV households to total households in India. The television distribution market consists of revenues generated by distributors of television programming to viewers. This includes spending by consumers on subscriptions to basic and premium channels accessed from cable operators, satellite providers, or Internet protocol television (IPTV) services, as well as on video-on-demand (VOD). Remember Moser Baer, the company that manufactured DVD's? They're buying content for a DVD market that exceeds 1.5 billion units per year. This figure is expected to grow to 4.5 billion units per year by 2010. The explosive growth in DVD sales is also being attributed to the fact that most Indian households are currently single color TV (CTV) households. This is all set to change as rising incomes and a large pool of teenagers drive the development of multiple CTV households, commonly known as the "Teenager Affect."

The Indian film industry also plays a vital role, and contributes 19 percent to the entertainment industry. It is currently worth US$ 1.8 billion (2006) and is expected to grow at a CAGR of 16 percent for the next 5 years, reaching US$3.8 billion in 2011. It is the largest in the world, both with regard to the number of films produced and admissions. Every year it produces about 1,040 films and has more than three billion admissions. The film industry can be divided into three sections—production, distribution, and exhibition. Multiplexes constitute a large portion of exhibitions, and produce 65 percent of the revenue that comes from box-office collections.

Until the 1990s, most of the theaters in India were single screen, with low video quality. Companies such as PVR, Adlabs, and Shringaar took over such theaters and upgraded or converted them into multiplexes offering better picture quality and better services. The growth in such multiplexes has increased the average ticket price in India to US$1.7 from US$0.33 earlier. The average occupancy has also increased, as movie viewing has become a more pleasurable experience.

There are a total of 12,900 active screens in India; of those, about 550 screens are spread across 145 multiplexes, yet there are only 12 screens for every million citizens, as compared to 117 per million in the United States. PVR was the first to introduce the multiplex concept in India. It was incorporated in 1997 as a joint venture between Priya Exhibitors Private Limited and Village Roadshow Limited and opened its first multiplex, called PVR Anupam, in Saket, Delhi. However, in November 2002 Village Roadshow sold its entire shareholding to Priya Exhibitors Private Limited. In 2003, India Advantage Fund-I, a fund managed by ICICI Venture Funds Management Company Limited, invested Rs 380 million in the company.

PVR is the largest cinema exhibition player in the country and consists of 20 multiplexes with a total of about 80 screens. Its network is spread across Delhi, Gurgaon, Noida, Faridabad, Mumbai, Bangalore, Hyderabad, Lucknow, and Indore. In March 2006 PVR completed an initial public offering (IPO) of 7,700,000 equity shares for setting up new theatres. After gaining a foothold in most of India's metropolitan cities, PVR is now targeting Tier II and Tier III categories by opening no-frill multiplexes under the brand name PVR Talkies. The first two projects are being established in Aurangabad and Latur, with a seating capacity of 1,151 and 1,148, respectively.

PVR plans to make an investment of about US$200 million by 2010 to add cinema screens in India. Investing in a multiplex costs around US$600,000 per screen, while an average investment for the no-frills PVR Talkies is around US$350,000. It plans to spread across 13 states and 70 cities, with the target of having 500 screens by 2010, of which 200 will be PVR Talkies. The company recorded an income of US$23.7 million in 2006. Box office revenue and food and beverages revenue contributed 68.4 percent and 20.6 percent of the unconsolidated net operating income, respectively. Advertising and royalty income constituted 8.2 percent and 1.8 percent, respectively.

PVR had 14 million admissions in 2006 and aims to have 20 million in 2007. Besides film exhibition, PVR—under its subsidiary,

PVR Pictures—is also into production and distribution. The subsidiary is now venturing into production and has signed Bollywood star Aamir Khan for two movies, to be released in 2007 and 2008. An investment of about US$4.8 million will be made in these films, with the plan of producing two movies every year. This backward integration helps PVR become an integrated player with a presence in all three stages—production, distribution, and exhibition.

The company is also foraying into holistic approaches to entertainment and has changed its tagline from "movies first" to "bringing smiles." The company will set up food courts, video parlors, bowling centers, and fitness and youth centers. It will also provide consumers with a complete range of entertainment, thereby creating a comprehensive, wholesome brand experience. The food courts will operate under the brand name PVR Food Union and will work with franchises such as Domino's, Street Food of India, Nirula's, Salad Chef, and Masala Twist, among others. An investment of about US$24 million will be made to develop food courts in 30 to 35 multiplexes. Saatchi and Saatchi has been hired as PVR's new advertising agency.

Multiplexes form just 5 percent of the total cinema screens in the country. India needs a total of 20,000 screens to cater to the increasing cinema population. The burgeoning economy and India's favorable demographics will all contribute to the growth of multiplexes in the coming years, with PVR playing a vital role in the development of the film and entertainment industry.

One of the most significant opportunities in the media and entertainment industry in India, however, may exist in the radio market. This sector, which has seen a declining market share in many developed countries' markets, is experiencing a 22 percent growth rate in India. With the normalization of India's licensing mechanism, it is expected to triple in size and reach about US$145.9 billion by 2009. The key growth factor that will drive the radio industry is reaching local audiences that have until now been served largely by print media. This audience will grow at least four-fold in the next 5 years.

Today, radio reaches out to 99 percent of the Indian population. It is currently the most cost effective mass communication media in the country. The revenues in this sector are from advertising on radio stations, radio networks, and satellite radio subscriptions. The radio market size is attaining a growth at a CAGR of 22 percent in the coming years. The overall spending for advertising in India is about 3 percent, compared to the worldwide average of 8.7 percent. The percentage of advertising that radio receives depends on how much privatization there is in a country and how aggressively its players are able to promote themselves. Technology has influenced the way consumers listen to the radio. Radio has reinvented itself by finding a presence in portable devices such as phones, Ipods, and personal digital assistants (PDAs), triggering multiplatform development.

The radio industry has become a major sector for investment in the entertainment and media (E&M) space due to the availability of as many as 338 FM radio licenses up for bidding. These cover 91 cities, most of which until now were being serviced only by the state broadcaster, *11*. The private FM radio sector is expected to get foreign investments of US$111 million in the next 12 to 18 months, and that is just the beginning of this growth.

Another unique opportunity for investing in India's E&M industry is the print media, with a CAGR of 12 percent. A rise in literacy levels in both urban and rural areas, a booming economy, a growing need for content, and government incentives to encourage foreign investments in this industry have triggered the growth of this sector. With more foreign investment happening in this sector, the demand for Indian content is on the rise. The print media industry revenues (including newspaper and magazines) consists of spending by advertisers and readers of daily print newspapers (both newsstand purchases and subscriptions). Weekly papers constitute a separate and distinct market in terms of content, advertising base, and subscriber interests.

What does all of this mean for you? Consider the fact that on average, advertising spending as a percentage of Indian GDP is 0.34 percent, as compared to other developed and developing countries, where the average is 0.98 percent. While low ad budgets are one of the major challenges faced by the E&M industry, it opens up an immense potential for growth. Consider the fact that in India, radio is presently estimated to garner a share of about 2 percent of overall advertising spending, as compared to the Australian outlays for radio ads at 9 percent. This will present significant opportunities for ad agencies, media conglomerates, and publishers.

HOSPITALITY AND LEISURE

With a current shortage of an estimated 200,000 hotel rooms and a rapidly growing middle class, India's hospitality and leisure industry is poised for dramatic growth. That's not hard to believe, considering the fact that New York City has more hotel rooms than currently exist in the entire country of India. Travel to India in 2006 exceeded 4.3 million individuals, with a growth rate that will exceed 17 percent per year until 2020. As importantly, there is a huge domestic tourism and hospitality market in India, with more than 300 million Indians traveling within the country in 2006 for business, social, and religious purposes. The dramatic growth in travel will have a direct impact on hotels, restaurants, and leisure parks.

Reduced travel costs, improved relations with Pakistan, and a focus on bringing about improvement in infrastructure has put India on the world tourist map. As the domestic market continues to expand, the growing economy will provide the rising middle class with increased disposable income. The arrival of low-cost airlines and associated price wars has also given domestic tourists more options. The "Incredible India" tourist campaign has also helped the growth of many domestic markets, including religious tourism. As a next step, the government has recently launched the "Atithi Devo Bhavah" ("guest is God") campaign, aimed at increasing the awareness of tourism in India. What's more, the players in the hospitality industry have taken aggressive steps in the direction of accommodating more guests, and in various categories, also. For instance, companies like Choice and Best Western plan to increase their portfolio significantly over the next 2 years, by 100 percent and 50 percent, respectively. Other hotel companies have also taken steps to ensure that they benefit; the Intercontinental Hotels Group is introducing their economy brand, Holiday Inn Express: They have 10 properties planned, starting later this year. Marriott has also announced plans to introduce its Courtyard brand in India. MGM Entertainment is developing a 600 room, five-star hotel in Chennai, and Ambuja Realty Development is planning four high-end luxury hotels, with a combined capacity of 1,000 rooms, in West Bengal over the next 3 years.

India's appeal to international travelers has been previously marred by the political situation in Kashmir as well as by the global events of the past few years. However, this has now improved, due to relative geopolitical stability and international economic growth. Tourism in India is also benefiting from the stronger economies of India's two major source markets, the United Kingdom and the United States. While corporate business will naturally continue to expand as the economy grows, there is an enormous untapped potential in the country's leisure market. "Incredible India" has focused not only on promoting traditional holiday attractions and cultural experiences, but on defining specific individual markets, from medically related manufacturing to religious tourism. In fact, India has already seen increasing numbers of Japanese tourists due to the promotion of Buddhist travel. But India still faces many challenges in attracting the international traveler. This will continue as the government addresses the quality of India's infrastructure, as it improves the poor roads, overstretched railways, and old airports that discourage international travelers.

Hotels in India receive twice as many domestic as international guests. With the most familiar brands in India occupying the top tier of the market, expensewise, the hotel industry is currently very top heavy. While many companies are beginning to address the needs of the growing domestic market for more economical hotels, most projects are still in development. The future growth of the hotel industry will not be helped by archaic land laws that make construction of new hotels time consuming and expensive. While an opportunity exists to develop the hotel industry to meet this growing demand, India experiences large seasonal shifts in demand for hotel rooms, and corporate travelers currently represent the bulk of guests. Due to the lack of a widely distributed business mix, annual occupancies and average room rates in India did not rank very high in the 2004 Hotel Benchmark Global Ranking Index.

The opening up of India's aviation industry in India will bring significant opportunities for hotels, as they rely on airlines to transport 80 percent of international arrivals. Increased airline activity has stimulated demand and has helped to improve India's troubled airport infrastructure. Increased competition will lead to the development of new and improved services. In addition to new aviation brands, many existing companies have ordered new planes. This is long overdue, considering that state-owned Indian Airlines has not purchased a new plane in 16 years. The open skies policy has benefited both international and domestic travel. On the international front, the capacity and availability of destinations serving India continues to grow. The increasing competition in the domestic airline industry will continue to drive the growth of India's domestic market. The government has expanded the scope of airline liberalization with its approval in January 2007 for private airlines to fly all international routes (excluding the Gulf). The growing aviation industry in India will drive future tourism growth, with the continued increase of flights and greater travel options.

According to the estimates of the World Tourism Organization (WTO), international tourist inflow in India by 2020 will be 10 million. Today, India is one of the most exciting emerging markets in the world. According to recent estimates of the World Travel and Tourism Council (WTTC), Indian tourism demand will grow at 8.8 percent (CAGR) over the 10 years from 2005 to 2015. That would place India as the second-most rapidly growing tourism market in the world. Inbound tourism will reach new levels, fueled by low-cost airlines, a growing infrastructure thrust by the government, and India's emergence as a global outsourcing hub. With an estimated 26,000 rooms in the name-brand hotel segment, the current size of the hotel industry continues to present an abysmal figure for India's size and growth prospects. Based on the forecasted growth in demand, we expect that another 175,000 to 200,000 rooms will be needed in the next 5 years. Occupancies and average room rates (ARRs) have continued to remain strong, not only in the metro areas, but also in the secondary cities like Pune and Noida, where, due to the lower costs of land in these areas, many new foreign companies and private entrepreneurs are setting up shop. This strength has been witnessed in the first half of fiscal 2006 and is expected to be higher during the second half of the financial year, as this period is considered to be the peak seasonal time for the hospitality industry. Not only have the numbers of international travelers to the country increased, but according to the Indian government, domestic travelers have also increased substantially. From US$200 million in the fiscal year 2003, the number has more than doubled during 2006 and is expected to further increase in the current calendar year (2008). Many international hotel chains either already have or are on the lookout for setting up shop in the country. Companies like the Hilton and Hyatt groups have already joined with local giants East

India Hotels and Asian Hotels. Others, like the Four Seasons, are on the lookout for a partner or would be setting up their own hotels, government permitting. Hence, measures such as speeding up the infrastructure development programs like the Golden Quadrilateral, better rail and sea linkages, and providing stable administration to increase investor confidence, like further increasing the FDI limit, will take India's hotel industry to great heights.

Despite the dramatic increase in upgrading hotel services, only a quarter of these rooms are in the name-brand segment. HVS International, a global hospitality consultancy firm, expects another 100,000 to 125,000 hotel rooms to be added in the next 5 to 7 years, with ARRs rising by 20 to 25 percent over the next 2 or 3 years. According to its preliminary estimates, there are about 55,000 to 60,000 rooms presently under construction. Bearing in mind the growth prospects, domestic hotel players have already started ramping up their existing capacities. Hotel Leela is adding to its existing inventory in Bangalore and Mumbai. Hyderabad-based Taj GVK Hotels & Resorts is increasing its capacities in Hyderabad. Royal Orchid Hotels, which offloaded its equity beginning in 2006, is making over all three of its hotels at a capital expenditure of US$7.5 million. Bharat Hotels is adding a new block to its properties in Bangalore, and renovating its property in New Delhi. Viceroy Hotels, which is affiliated with JW Marriott, is refurbishing its existing hotel in Bangalore. Along with expanding existing capacities, industry players are also adding new properties to tap the growing demand-supply gap. Chennai is expected to be the most active city, with a new IT corridor to house IT-ITES companies being developed along the old Mahabalipuram Road. Many players have chalked out expansion plans for Chennai, as it could develop into an IT hub like Hyderabad. Hyderabad is also experiencing huge activity, with the presence of Hitec City, Hitex, Genome Valley, and ICICI Knowledge Park, along with Asia's biggest convention center, built by Emaar-MGF in collaboration with the

Andhra Pradesh government. Taj GVK Hotels & Resorts is putting up a new hotel in Begumpet on leased land. Hotel Leela's 325-room luxury hotel is under construction in Banjara Hills, the hotel hub of Hyderabad. Acquiring land in the metro areas is a challenge, so hotel majors and other investors are turning to Tier II and III cities. Pune is turning into a new IT hub due to its proximity to Mumbai. The city is expected to add 11 new hotels, serviced apartments, and mixed-use developments, with approximately 1,600 rooms in various categories over the next 3 to 4 years. The addition to supply, although quite high, is likely to be successfully absorbed, taking into account Pune's low room base of approximately 800 rooms and the amazing growth in the city's IT, ITES, BPO, and manufacturing industries. Hotel Leela is building a 350-room hotel near the airport. The ITC Welcomgroup is also planning a hotel in Pune. The Bangalore-based Royal Orchid Hotels will lease a hotel by October 2008.

To ride the boom fueled by the combination of increased business tourism, declines in air fares, and greater investment in infrastructure, big realty players, too, are foraying into the hotel business. North Indian-based realty major DLF is planning to develop hotels in the four- and five-star and deluxe segments as well as to develop tourism and leisure-related assets such as serviced apartments, clubs, and golf courses. It will use its existing real estate capabilities as well as go into joint ventures with hotel players to build these assets close to other developments such as commercial centers, IT parks, and shopping malls. DLF has identified 21 sites for their hotels. Unitech, another Delhi-based realty developer, is making a foray into the hospitality sector with a joint venture with hotel major Marriott to launch its Courtyard brand of business hotels in Gurgaon, Noida, and Kolkata. Traditionally, Indian hotel majors follow the ownership model, while international hotel chains typically adhere to the lease/license model. This allows international hotels to manage more rooms. While Indian players remain restricted by balance-sheet constraints, they are now seeking to leverage their many years of expertise in managing their own hotels to manage other hotels not owned by them.

Another source of fast-growing revenue in the coming years will be the meeting, incentive, convention, and exhibition (MICE) segment. Hotel majors are not only exploring Tier II and III cities as pilgrimage centers for MICE activities, but are also examining the feasibility of building budget hotels, with room rates ranging from US$22 to US$35. These hotels primarily target the domestic tourist as well as the economy-seeking foreign traveler. Indian Hotels has a 100-room budget hotel under the brand name, Ginger, in Bangalore and Haridwar, and is planning another 10 hotels, to be operational by March 2008 in various Tier II and III cities, with a capital expenditure per hotel of Rs 120 million. Indian Railways has also shown interest in using its land to set up 40 budget hotels across the country. Many hotel companies have evinced interest in this project.

Hotel Leela runs three hotels, one each in Bangalore, Mumbai, and Goa. The Leela Palace in Bangalore is the most profitable, with occupancy rates above 85 percent. Bangalore's status as an IT hub creates a big business travel market, less prone to the vagaries of tourism. Leela commands high average room rates here, from Rs 9,000 a day in August 2006 to over Rs 13,000 a day today, the highest in the country. The hotel has huge operating margins of 60 percent and accounts for 50 percent of Leela's revenues. The city has attracted nine new hotel projects, typically with construction periods of 3 to 4 years; Leela has time to milk the market before competition steps up. Leela Palace will have added 110 new rooms by April 2006, but costs will be marginal since the existing infrastructure can easily be leveraged. The property's revenues are expected to go up by another 15 percent in the next fiscal year. The 423-room Leela Kempinski in North Mumbai is also in a commercial zone. With businesses shifting from congested south Mumbai to the northern area, closer to the airport, hotels here are seeing occupancy rates above 80 percent. Leela Kempinski expects ARRs above US$125 per day in the year ahead. Leela Goa is the smallest, with 152 rooms. Leela has launched a campaign to promote Goa to European travelers, particularly Germans. The Leela Group has just relaunched its beach resort in Kovalam, with 194 guest rooms and suites, and plans a capital outlay of about US$250 million for expansion in Chennai Udaipur and Hyderabad. In addition to this, another 120 guest rooms will be added to the Bangalore property.

Numerous hotel and restaurant chains are making forays into the market. The Bird Group, a leading hospitality chain, has entered into a joint venture with Dusit Hotels & Resorts, Thailand's leading premier hotel company, to develop six four- and five-star hotels in India. The first three properties, projected to open by 2010, are in Delhi, Goa, and Rishikesh, and the next three, which will open by 2013, will be in Pune, Amritsar, and Jaipur, with a total investment of approximately US$200 million.

Of special note is the Taj Hotels Resorts and Palaces group, which was founded in 1902 by Jamsetji N. Tata, founder of the Tata Group. In 1903 the group opened its first hotel, the Taj Mahal Palace Hotel in Mumbai. It's been over a hundred years since the Taj Hotels Resorts and Palaces group has been serving guests in India and abroad, and it's one of the largest hotel chains in south Asia. The Indian Hotels Company Limited (IHCL) is the Taj Hotels Resorts and Palaces' parent company. Its hotels have more than 9,000 rooms and over 200 food and beverage outlets. It added 583 rooms to its arsenal during the fiscal year ended March 31, 2006. News is that the group will be swelling its room count to 13,000 in India in the next 5 years, at an estimated cost of US$250 million.

The group is now spread across 40 locations and 59 hotels in India, with 17 other hotels in foreign locations. "We have taken a view that in the international market we don't want to be a me-too player," Anil Goel, chief financial officer of IHCL, has stated. The group is very aggressive about creating a name for itself in the international market and is selling off its not-so-exclusive properties to generate surplus cash for luxury purchases. San Francisco's Campton Place purchase in April 2000, for US$60 million, is the latest such purchase.

There are clear signs of Taj being aggressive about becoming a truly global brand. In late 2006, the group purchased Boston's Ritz-Carlton Hotel for US$170 million. The purchase of the W Sydney hotel, for US$27.1 million, marked Taj's entry into the Australian hospitality market. In 2005, the group entered into a lease agreement to operate and manage The Pierre, a landmark hotel in New York. The group also has London, Paris, Frankfurt, South Africa, China, and Abu Dhabi on its mind. It also held talks with the realty major Sino Group of Singapore for a proposed joint venture to tap into the huge opportunities in the Far East market.

The hotel chain operates in the luxury, leisure, and business hotels segments. The group's properties in Mumbai, New Delhi, Kolkata, Bangalore, and Chennai are among the members of the Leading Hotels of the World, Ltd. Its properties in Udaipur, Jaipur, and Maldives are part of the Leading Small Hotels of the World, Ltd. It manages exclusive stores carrying hard-to-find brands; even the country's most vocal critics find its services warm and caring.

The growing mobility of the new middle-class Indian has meant more business and leisure travel. Gauging the new trend, IHCL has collaborated with renowned corporate strategist Dr. C. K. Prahalad to develop the concept of budget hotels in India. In 2004, it launched a chain of hotels designed to meet the basic needs of a daily traveler. This was a one-of-a-kind offering in India. These hotels were affordable yet provided the basic necessities and concomitant luxury and style.

The first hotel in this segment, now run by the Ginger Hotels group, was launched in Bangalore. The chain has also partnered with a popular coffee shop, Café Coffee Day, to expand its array of offerings for guests. Starting in June 2008, IHCL will be investing

US$50 million to increase the number of Ginger Hotels from eight to 25 within 12 months in Indian Tier II cities. Ginger Hotels is operated by Roots Corporation Limited (RCL), a wholly owned subsidiary of IHCL.

Next on Taj's target list will be catering to the millions of entrepreneurs, businessmen, and executives visiting the upcoming special economic zones (SEZs) in India, which in themselves offer a huge business opportunity. "With a number of SEZs being established across the country, there would be a great need for residential arrangements in these zones. Taj is exploring opportunities in the same," states Raymond N. Bickson, MD and CEO of Indian Hotels Company. The cities of Gurgaon, Hyderabad, Bangalore, and Nagpur can soon witness Taj hotels, resorts, or apartments popping up. The group has held talks with property developers in these SEZs and has also signed management contracts for properties in the cities of Vijayawada, Chennai, and Surat. The group also won the contract for renovating and running the Rail Yatri Niwas, owned by Indian Railways, on a 15-year lease.

The Taj group is also venturing into the wildlife tourism business. The group has entered into a joint venture with an African tourism company, Conservation Corporation Africa (CC Africa), and Cigen Corporation, from Nepal. This association will operate through a new entity, Taj Wilderness Lodges. "This safari experience will be a fascinating alternative to Africa. We are making a concentrated effort to improve the quality of safari management in India, while promoting wildlife and ecotourism," Raymond Bickson has stated. The heretofore uninvestigated tiger reserves in the Indian states of Madhya Pradesh and Uttaranchal have attracted Taj. It plans to build lodges in Bandhavgarh Tiger Reserve and Pench National Park in Madhya Pradesh. "There is huge potential for these lodges, as India is a great wildlife destination—totally undersold." CC Africa's marketing director, Nicky Fitzgerald has said. Taj Wilderness Lodges (TWL) plans to invest about US$4 million in a total of five lodges.

Apart from hospitality services, the group also operates Taj Air. It is a luxury private jet operation fitted out with state-of-the-art Falcon 2000 aircraft, and covers 114 destinations. The aircraft have been customized to seat 8 people instead of the original 16. Apart from this, the group offers its guests in Mumbai and Kochi two three-bedroom luxury yachts. In 1993 the group established the Indian Institute of Hotel Management in Aurangabad, which offers a 3-year diploma in hotel management and is affiliated with several American and European programs. The group has also partnered with Singapore Airlines to provide in-flight catering and manage Airport lounges.

For the fiscal year ended 31 March, 2006, The Indian Hotels Company Limited's revenues increased 40 percent, to US$490 million. Net income increased 94 percent, to US$65 million. Employing approximately 8,500 people, its market value hovers around US$2 billion. The increase in foreign tourist arrivals, the efforts of the Indian government (i.e., the Incredible India and Atithi Devo Bhavah campaigns), and the general boom in international tourism has led to an increase in occupancy rates and average room rates, which has benefited Taj hotels. The group recently won the "Outstanding Exporter of the Year in the Travel, Tourism and Hospitality Category" from CNBC Universe for 2006–2007. If you are involved in the hospitality and leisure industry, India must be a priority for you.

PRIVATE HEALTH CARE

Demand outstrips supply in India's highly fragmented health care market, which is valued at US$23 billion. The two extreme parallels of India's health care industry can be seen in the facilities offered by public health care facilities and those provided by private hospitals and health care centers. While on the one hand the public health care system lacks even the basic facilities for conducting many medical treatments, medical tourism and organized health care, on the other hand, are progressing in the country to offer sophisticated medical care to consumers.

Surging income levels, as well as the spread of medical insurance, have improved India's access to premium and quality medical care. This has led to the burgeoning of private health care institutions in order to cater to the growing demand. The newly affluent middle class has also been accompanied by various "lifestyle" diseases, such as diabetes, asthma, obesity, and cardiovascular ailments. Most of the expansion in the private health care sector is being fueled by the increasing expectations for better health care services from this segment of society. In the coming years, the pace of privatization of the Indian health care segment is expected to shift into high gear. It has already surpassed the commitment levels that India had made to the World Trade Organization (WTO) under the General Agreement on Trade in Services (GATS).

Revenues and growth in the sector are expected to be enhanced by health care's increasing privatization and by legislation to harmonize private health care standards in private health care delivery. Private health care in India is also being backed by several international investors. Warburg Pincus, for example, has invested over US$30 million in MaxHealthcare, in which it holds a 23 percent stake, and about US$43 million in the parent, Max India.

In early 2007, established private health care groups announced extensive investments for the coming 5 years in India. Existing players are looking to strengthen their presence through greenfield projects, capacity expansions, and acquisitions of mid-sized and large hospitals. It is believed that each corporate group is attempting to create niche areas of operations by identifying their core strength. Wockhardt Hospitals will spend nearly US$54 million to set up two specialty hospitals in the cities of Surat and Rajkot in West India. MaxHealthcare plans to enlarge its domestic coverage of hospitals with a US$201 million expansion program. It aims to more than double the number of its seven specialty hospitals and also branch out into other areas, including hospital management and acquisitions. In fact, private health care groups such as MaxHealthcare are also venturing into the health insurance industry. The company has sold over one million policies through a joint venture with New York Life Insurance. MaxHealthcare's operations are mainly restricted to the national capital region (NCR), due to which it currently lags behind industry leaders Apollo and Fortis. But the company plans to go beyond the NCR in 2007 following the completion of its 100-bed hospital in Gurgaon.

Fortis Healthcare Ltd. (FHL), a Ranbaxy Group company, will invest about US$224 million. FHL, which was formed in 1996 (although operations commenced only in 2001), will establish a medical center with specialty hospitals and research centers devoted to specific therapy areas such as oncology. Fortis has a network of 12 hospitals across India and a heart center in Afghanistan. An important milestone for FHL was in 2005, when it acquired Escorts, a Delhi-based hospital specializing in heart treatment. FHL has established its presence across North India in cities such as New Delhi, Faridabad, Noida, Amritsar, Raipur, and Srinagar. It recently forayed into West India by acquiring a stake in the Mumbai-based Hiranandani Healthcare.

FHL plans to concentrate on select super-specialties such as cardiac care, orthopedics, neuroscience, oncology, renal care, gastroenterology, and mother-and-child care. The company further plans to undertake greenfield projects in Jaipur, Delhi, and Gurgaon to expand the current bed capacity of 1,800 by another 750 over the next 2 years.

India's largest private hospital group, Apollo Hospitals, is to invest US$69 million in the present fiscal year toward its expansion plans at home and abroad. Apart from setting up four specialty hospitals in India, which will increase bed capacity to over 8,200, the group will also establish 57 cardiac care units. Apollo is, in fact, an established player in the industry. In June 2007, the Apollo

Group launched the first functional health city in Asia in the city of Hyderabad. The health city comprises a 300-bed multispecialty hospital with more than 50 specialties and super-specialties, with an additional 10 centers of excellence. One of Asia's largest health care groups, Apollo runs 41 hospitals in India and abroad. The group is further expanding overseas through joint ventures as well as mergers and acquisitions in the United States and Europe.

New legislation is currently being drafted for streamlining operations and increasing monitoring in the private health care sector. Mandatory registration of all hospitals with the central and state health authorities has been proposed; bills for licensing and registration requirements have also been introduced by individual state authorities. It is hoped this will allow for the provision of a centralized database of the number of private hospitals and health care units. A new accreditation system is also in the pipeline. The Quality Council of India (QCI) and National Accreditation Board for Hospitals and Healthcare providers (NABH) entered into an agreement with the Australian Council on Healthcare Standards International (ACHSI) around mid-2006 to facilitate the upgrade of India's hospital accreditation system and standards.

Medical tourism is another important factor that is expected to drive private health care demand. India is a leading name in the medical tourism industry. Due to rising health care expenditures, costly medical procedures, increasing health insurance premiums, and a long waiting time for treatment in the West, India is becoming a preferred choice. India is also attracting medical tourists from countries in Africa and Asia that do not possess adequate health care infrastructure. The Indian government, interestingly, has been advertising internationally for several years that people can enjoy "First World treatment at Third World prices." In 2004, about 180,000 patients from around the globe traveled to India for medical treatment. Estimated to be a US$333 million industry in 2004, medical tourism is projected to be worth US$2 billion by 2012.

A more corporate arrangement is likely, with the growing interest in the sector from newer players. Novel players from the pharmaceutical industry and the leading Indian industrial houses such as Reliance and Birla are also looking to capture a piece of the growing market. Currently, small operators with less than five hospitals primarily dominate the market dynamics (in volume terms) of private health care. A culture of integrated chains, however, can be expected with bigger groups such as Apollo, Fortis, and MaxHealthcare.

6

LOOK BEFORE YOU LEAP

Jaipur-Kishengarh Highway. India is Building Thousands of Miles of New Roads, Which Will Help Drive Economic Growth.

In preparing for battle I have always found that plans are useless, but planning is indispensable.

Dwight D. Eisenhower

India is akin to a manic-depressive state of mind. The typical businessman, fund manager, investment banker, or entrepreneur departs from Chicago, Los Angeles, New York, Frankfurt, or London with a sense of optimism. After all, you're a pioneer and you're flying to the world's oldest living civilization, now one of its biggest emerging markets. This is one of the new economies of the twenty-first century, and opportunities abound if you have the skill, vision, and confidence required to unlock the vast wealth that is percolating just below the surface. You board the plane and settle into your comfortable business class seat, surrounded by that ever-present optimism, your competitive advantage. A glass of wine, a good meal and some light conversation with a fellow passenger, and before you know it you are landing in Bangalore, home to India's Silicon Valley. The airport terminal lowers your confidence just a notch—it is dingy, and difficult to find any hint of India's economic boom on the faces of the airport staff, who are there to accommodate weary travelers. As you wait for your luggage you swat at mosquitoes, which you hope are not malaria-laden, and you begin to wonder—why can't they do something about simple insects. You greet your driver with a hearty hello but quickly get the sense that his English is not what you were expecting. The ride to the hotel does little to buoy your optimism; upon checking into what is clearly an over-priced accommodation, you unpack and turn in for the night.

FIGURE 6.1 *A Technology Driven Economy Will Require Significant Investments in Education*

The next morning you arise from a good night's sleep, and with it a renewed sense of optimism. Today you're meeting with a variety of India's movers and shakers, men with the same sense of optimism that you have, and the same shared vision. Their success is what the American dream is about—only it is now happening in India (Figure 6.1). Often starting with nothing more than a plan, some money borrowed from family or friends, and a gritty determination, they have built world-class companies. The conversations prove to be lively, and at times you feel animated—these people have got what it takes to succeed and they have proved it. A land of a billion entrepreneurs—the possibilities are endless, and you're experiencing a new high!

You get into your car for the drive back to the hotel. It's hard to contain your enthusiasm, and it probably shows in the form of a smile on your face. That smile instantly disappears when your car stops at an intersection and you are surrounded by hungry children clutching their malnourished babies. They press their faces against the window and you look straight ahead, not daring to make eye contact. Your rebounded optimism has been replaced by stark, cold reality, and you just want to get the hell out of there—quick! Reaching the hotel, you head straight for the bar and order a stiff drink. The bartender looks at you, not certain as to what you mean—after all, a regular drink costs more than many people earn in a day. You go up to your room, call your wife, and try to not let her know the anxiety and doubt that you're feeling. Right now, the only thing you want is to be home, so you can hold your kids tight and tell them that all's okay!

Welcome to India—a rollercoaster ride of emotions, experiences, and an extremely complex market that is home to a population that has eighteen official languages, hundreds of different dialects, at least four separate ethnic groups, and every religion known to man. It is true that India shares many values common to North America and Europe; democratic principles, religious tolerance, free enterprise, and the rule of law. But just below that common exterior is a unique market that often defies explanation, and a people who refuse to wear a common label. For instance, begging in India is in many cases an organized business with a citywide command-and-control structure. Many of the people living in apparent squalor, like the "Potters of Bombay," are actually part of a trade group that has proudly inhabited that area of the city for three generations, and for them it is home. None of these facts may give you solace—nor should they—but understanding the complexities of the market are critical if you wish to succeed here.

Take the case of Frito-Lay, the subsidiary of the American soft drink giant PepsiCo. PepsiCo began operations in India in 1989, several years before the concerted economic liberalization of the country had begun. For the first 5 years, the company tried to force an American business model and American products on the exacting tastes of the Indian consumer. Cheetos with Cheese was a hit with the American consumer, so why shouldn't it do equally well in this market? For one, Indian consumers are used to local cheeses, which have a nondistinct flavor. The taste of the cheddar cheese on PepsiCo's Cheetos was strong and was often perceived as being stale or rancid. Indians are also value conscious, and food is food—consumers are aware of global brands, but that's not enough reason to buy them—and certainly not reason enough to pay a premium.

By 1994 PepsiCo had failed to achieve scale, and the Indian operation was nearly terminated. By now, however, governmental economic reforms had begun to kick in, and the elimination of the license Raj had created a more level playing field for all competitors. In 1995 PepsiCo decided to regroup, with a new strategy that was centered on understanding the Indian market. They had some solid assets on the ground, including a factory that was already in operation in Punjab. PepsiCo focused on their strengths, the Frito-Lay franchise and the potato chip market. The key was to develop a distribution model that gave them scale—not an easy task in a market dominated by mom-and-pop stores, completely devoid of big-box retailers like Wal-Mart.

Potato chips were popular in India long before Frito-Lay developed their brand. They were typically manufactured in the kitchens of local stores or homes, almost always served fresh—with a cost overhead that was hard to even measure. Frito-Lay decided to pursue a three-pronged approach to its strategy. First, they would develop a dependable product that would maintain the highest quality standards. Second, they would create a distinct brand—and third, they would be constant innovators.

Realizing the first goal was more difficult than one might think. India's agricultural sector is dominated by small farmers who have minimal access to modern planting and harvesting techniques, and because most farms were typically ten acres or less, mechanized farming practices were seldom employed. Frito-Lay decided to develop a contract farming model, beginning initially in Punjab with 200 farmers. The model quickly took hold. Frito-Lay provided the farmers with seed, technical advice, fertilizer, and long-term contracts, which created predictability for the farmers—something that was unheard of at the time. And by negotiating long-term contracts, the middleman was removed, creating increased value for the farmer. Within several years over 13,000 farmers were involved in the program, and the scope of related benefits has broadened as well. Now, farmers participating in the program have access to low-interest bank loans and crop insurance, leveraging the buying and brand power of PepsiCo. The use of crop insurance was to prove fortuitous—in 2006, torrential rains wiped out the potato crop—this time, the farmers suffered no financial loss.

The second part of this equation was to create local brand appeal. Working with local manufacturers, the Frito-Lay developed products based on local tastes and local flavors. Using a lentil-based product, Frito-Lay created a distinctly Indian version of their internationally recognized Cheetos. The company used the same approach with local manufacturers that they had used with farmers. They provided advice, technical support, and quality control processes, which gave Frito-Lay a low-cost manufacturing base with adequate scale.

The final piece of this equation is distribution. In a mature market like the United States, with well-established retail distribution models and large chain stores, this would be a straightforward task. But in India, the retail sector has been informal, dominated by millions of mom-and-pop stores. Frito-Lay calculated that they would need to have a presence in one million of these small retailers in order to achieve the scale required for a successful market presence. Adding to this challenge, there were no large retail exchanges in the country—Frito-Lay was faced with the fact that the majority of India's retail outlets were spread across thousands of rural villages, each with minimal infrastructure.

Frito-Lay devised a new concept, the "Shop within a Shop" approach. Historically, the small retailers of India gave very little thought to shelf space, often actually stacking various types of products up to ceiling level, with little or no thought given to brand positioning. Many of the products that they carried were staples—rice, cooking oil, and flour, for example—and in a small store shelf, space is limited. Frito-Lay designed a simple, moveable presentation rack that all of their product would hang from, creating both a dedicated display front and a practical storage space. This model gave the consumer an interactive experience and maximized the use of floor space, creating a win-win situation for the retailer and Frito-Lay. The company then began working with thousands of small distributors who typically service anywhere from 500 to 2,000 retailers. Frito-Lay provided training for the sales representatives in merchandising, stocking, and up-selling, as well as advertising support. Today Frito-Lay is a market leader in India—with well-established brands and with a steady increase in domestic income levels, new opportunities abound.

Frito-Lay adopted what we like to call *the market approach strategy,* which has been used with varying degrees of success and value by a wide range of companies. The driving factor behind the development of this approach is based on the classic push-pull argument. Simply stated, planners recognize that with a special emphasis on emerging markets you can only push so much of a product developed for affluent developed markets to emerging economies. Also, by not creating market-specific products one misses a significant amount of the potential market. Indians have rich cultural roots and are proud of local products and traditions. Like many other emerging markets, India also has a very low per capita GDP; even though incomes are increasing rapidly, it will be many years before they approach the per capita income levels of mature markets. For a company that produces high-cost products—such as cardiovascular medical devices—a decision has to be made. Do you try to force your existing products into a market where only a small fraction of the population could afford them, or do you design and manufacture a new suite of products locally, so that you can gain access to a much larger customer base while maintaining strong margins?

The challenges of emerging markets, however, go much further than simply creating a better mousetrap.

My father-in-law, Luís, once told me a joke that aptly describes the challenges facing companies and investors that have an interest in doing business in emerging markets. The story goes like this: A Brazilian engineer and a Japanese engineer are working on a project together; during the course of the project, they become good friends and vow to stay in touch with each other. When the project ends each returns to his respective country.

A year later, the Brazilian engineer decides to visit his new friend in Tokyo. He arrives in the heart of the financial district. His friend's office is located on the top floor of a beautiful building. Upon entering such a grand office the Brazilian engineer asks his friend, "How have you achieved so much in such little time?" The engineer takes his friend to the window and points in the direction of a newly completed office tower. "You see that building?" he asks his friend, "We built that building, and 15 percent of the profits went to us."

Six months later the Japanese engineer has a chance to visit his friend in Sao Paulo. He arrives at a most opulent building, in the heart of the financial district. His friend's office takes up the entirety of the top floor of the building and is resplendent with antiques, art, and handmade rugs. The engineer is dumbfounded, and still recovering from his amazement, but still manages to ask his friend, "How have you achieved so much in such little time?" His Brazilian friend walks him over to a picture window that overlooks the bay beyond. The Brazilian points toward the bay and asks "Do you see that bridge over the bay?" The Japanese man scans the entire bay and finally exclaims, "No!" "Exactly," his friend replies, "100 percent of the profits went to us!"

Emerging markets are complex, and India is probably the most complex of all. With varying amounts of corruption, ethnic and religious tension, and complex social interactions, developing a sound understanding of India's markets is a fundamental first step if you plan to succeed. Investing in a sound emerging-market entry strategy is similar to investing in a life insurance policy. You invest in the policy and you're secured for life. You invest in an entry strategy and you're secured for business. The modern-day customer offers no trial-and-error periods. First impressions are often the last impression.

It is often said that "An intelligent businessman is one who learns from his own mistakes, an astute businessman is one who learns from other's mistakes," and India is rife with examples of mistakes made in market-entry strategies which, in best-case scenarios, have cost the unlucky entity millions of dollars and lost market share—and in worst-case scenarios, have caused physical harm to employees and/or property.

Consider the case of Peugeot, the French car manufacturer. In June 1993 the Indian government deregulated the automobile industry. Entry to foreign automakers was no longer restricted, which was a good thing for everyone—especially Indian consumers, who had been forced to buy the Indian equivalent of a Lada for many years. In many ways the Indian market seemed like an automaker's dream, with a huge population to cater to, open economy, no entry barriers, and a superior product—when compared to domestic competition, it was the classic slow, fat rabbit.

A number of foreign car manufacturers smelled blood and quickly moved to enter the Indian market. Fiat in 1993, Daewoo in 1994, Honda Siel in 1995, Ford in 1995—the list kept growing. Among them was the French automobile manufacturer Peugeot. Peugeot came to India in 1994 via a joint venture Pal Peugeot Ltd. (PPL) with Premier Automobiles Ltd., owned by the Doshi family, one of India's few established automakers. The partnership intended to manufacture and market the Peugeot 309 in India, but it never bore fruition.

The famed Peugeot 309 was to be manufactured at the JV's Kalyan unit in the state of Maharashtra. Peugeot controlled a 31.96 percent stake in the JV. It had initially invested close to US$75 million. However, Peugeot's 309 assembly plant was hit by strikes throughout 1996, which disrupted production, and from thereon it was always a downward journey.

It took only 3 years after the formation of the joint venture for Vincent Adenis-Lamarre, area manager for South Asia, to comment that "I'm not in a position to say whether we will stay in India or not." It was a clear case of overestimating the market size and underestimating the competition. The fact that Peugeot made its debut in India with a model that had already been phased out framed their view of the Indian market. And the fact that Peugeot's management did not anticipate that its competitors would be entering the market with better and more contemporary models is even more amazing. Most Indians in Peugeot's target market were aware that the Peugeot 309 was old news in Europe, which created a "residual market" feeling among potential buyers. Hormazd Sorabjee of Auto India magazine commented in 1997 that "Peugeot took a colonial approach: They figured that after driving old cars for so long, Indians wouldn't mind driving a discontinued model. But today in India, a car is an icon of what you are and how well you are doing."

In 1997, most of Peugeot's international competitors were not making money in India. But Peugeot's initial basic errors meant that declining sales hit it harder than any of its peers. The company had entered India 1 year before other automakers, but it did not prepare for the ensuing competition. To make matters worse, there was a growing belief among Peugeot's executives that its Indian partner was walking a financial tightrope, and that liberalization had cost the family-run business dearly.

A series of strikes at Premier's plant exacerbated the Doshi family's financial struggles and Peugeot's rapidly deteriorating situation. Repeated proposals by Peugeot to Premier to invest money were turned down by the family-run company. Peugeot wanted a real partner in the venture—one that was willing to share risk. Instead, Premier offered to sell out entirely to Peugeot. Peugeot countered by offering to acquire a majority stake, but the Doshi family declined.

Tension between Peugeot and the Doshi family continued to grow when Peugeot took Premier Automobiles Limited to court in an endeavor to stall that company's planned joint venture with Fiat.

Peugeot continued to struggle: By September 1997, it had producd only 3,000 Peugeot 309s. The low production levels essentially stemmed from intermittent strikes. Sales remained dismal: In February 1999 Peugeot's JV failed to sell a single unit. This was at a time when its competitors were selling almost 25,000 units monthly. The company had sold only 162 Peugeot 309s in February 1998, and by Q1 of 1999, Peugeot sales had completely eroded.

Observing Fiat and Peugeot's initial outlook toward the Indian market makes for an interesting contrast. Fiat entered the automotive market with the intention of investing US$1 billion over 5 years across businesses in India, while Peugeot minimized its investment in India from the outset. Paolo Cantarella, CEO of Fiat, made multiple trips to India, meeting with various government officials, potential partners, and dealerships. His repeated trips to India reflected the importance of the Indian market to Fiat. On the other hand, Jacques Calvet, the chairman of Peugeot, never bothered to visit India, even when the JV was being set up.

Low sales, a crippled partner, and mounting competition spelled defeat for Peugeot. In August 1999, it gave up its entire stake in the joint venture to the Doshi family, thereby giving Premier its consent to sell its holding in the venture. Paul Alvarez, Peugeot's global spokesman, commented that India is a "forgotten and buried market as far as Peugeot cars are concerned. We had a failed adventure in India and do not intend to venture back to the market, having burnt our fingers there," Peugeot also did not claim any of its dues from the JV. Alvarez's distress was clear. "India and the Indian venture is history for us now and we do not want to have any association with the venture whatsoever. The matter is now being handled by PAL," he said. The Doshi family's efforts in selling the plant to Mahindra & Mahindra or Skoda of Czechoslovakia failed as well. The joint venture left investment bank ICICI, which had a significant interest in the company, high and dry. The financial institution later petitioned the Bombay high court for relief.

Newspapers have since alluded to Peugeot's reentry, sometimes in the two-wheeler sector; It has reportedly had talks with Hero Scooters and Monto Motors and has reputedly collaborated on a new car with the TATA group. But nothing significant has developed. From the manner in which Peugeot handled its partners, creditors, and customers, it is evident it could not manage risk, assess the market, and develop a successful entry strategy.

Peugeot had attempted to enter the Indian market using what is referred to as the colonial approach. This approach is based on the premise that emerging markets are truly the tail on the dog. The colonial strategy is actually notable only in the sense that there really is no strategy. Investments in emerging markets are often made ad hoc, typically driven by emotional and/or relationship considerations.

The use of distributors is commonplace, with a belief that any type of revenue contribution is sufficient. The primary focus in this approach is to minimize investment and assets in these markets. While the use of distributors is a viable and often-recommended entry strategy for a company's first foray into emerging markets, it must be built on a sound strategic plan. The colonial approach is often driven by a complete lack of strategic planning and is often dominated by one individual within the organization. This individual may have the title of Vice President of International Markets and is often distinguished by his continuous and often mysterious global jaunts. The successful colonialist will have created such high levels of mystique and confusion among senior management that they are unwilling or unable to accurately define country-specific contributions, growth rates, local relationships, and their overall competitive position in emerging markets. But even when a market entry strategy has been well thought out it can still go terribly wrong.

Take the case of Kerry Packer, the media tycoon from Australia, famous for the way he changed the game of cricket from a low-key sport to a global competition. And in India, where everyone follows cricket like a religion, that's important! Kerry Packer had big plans for India "We have looked at Asia closely and have decided that our major play in Asia will be India and not China. India is the place to be and will be the growth area of the future," Packer declared. Packer's entry in India was nothing short of carpet bombing.

He moved aggressively into just about every sector—information technology, software, e-commerce, telecom, media, entertainment, biotechnology, and more. In March 2000, he launched a US$250 million venture capital fund, KVP Ventures, so as to invest in these sectors and route all his investments in India through this fund. Packer's partners were Himachal Futuristic Communications Ltd. (HFCL), chairman Vinay Maloo, and stockbroker Ketan Parekh; the stakeholdings of all three were equal. "My company has no intention to control or have a majority stake," Packer stated. The purpose was to support the budding Indian entrepreneurial culture financially, intellectually, and managerially.

Packer started by acquiring a 10 percent stake in Himachal Futuristic Communication Ltd. (HFCL); the profits went into enlarging the company's existing and new businesses. In September 2000, Packer's joint venture with HFCL-Nine Broadcasting India (HNBIL) secured a contract with Prasar Bharati, India's national public station, to host its television channel, Doordarshan Metro. Packer's earlier 2-hour show was moved to the prime-time slot of 7 P.M. to 10 P.M. At that time, DD Metro had an umbrella of over 30 million homes and 350 million viewers. E-corp, Packer's Internet investment company, made its first investment in monsterindia.com, a job portal launched in a joint venture with TMP Worldwide. "We will be seeking Indian companies for setting up ventures in the field of financial services, auctions, and reverse auctions and health care," stated E-corp COO Alison Deans.

The Indian market is changeable, however, and at the time it was still relatively unpredictable. In a matter of months the scenario had turned gloomy, and by March 2001 Packer's Indian investments had begun heading south. His investments in IT and media had already incurred a US$15 million loss, and his losses were increasing. The one-year contract with the national broadcaster, Prasar Bharti, showed no sign of being renewed, and by June 2001 his attempt at penetrating the Indian television market had run out of steam. "The venture has been shut down because it was not viable, since the national broadcaster did not give us the desired five-year extension after the current one-year period expires in September," Reuters quoted HFCL chairman Mahendra Nahata as saying. PBL chief executive officer, James McLachlan, stated that "We are not tendering (to renew the contract) because the terms of the tender don't represent a reasonable business proposition." The JV issued a separate statement, stating that money was not a factor in restraining it from extending the contract. The new tender apparently had "unrealistic non-financial terms," which Packer considered to be very surprising. HNBIL claimed that Doordarshan's Metro channel's viewership had increased from 15.6 million to 25.6 million during the partnership. If that were the case, why would the broadcaster terminate its alliance with HNBIL? One likely cause may have been the involvement of the stockbroker, Ketan Parekh, in Packer's ventures. During this period, charges were levied against Parekh, stating that he artificially inflated share prices.

It soon became evident that HFCL was controlled by Ketan Parekh and that Parekh, through various means, had driven up its share price. He was later arrested by the Central Bureau of Investigation on charges of bank fraud and stock manipulation. HFCL stocks began their decline by the end of 2001. The shares that Packer had purchased—approximately US$32 to US$34—were now worth about US$2! In September 2001, HFCL and Packer canceled their plans to start Exel Netcommerce, an e-commerce joint venture.

"As we are not keen to enter the business, the venture will not take off and the agreement does not exist now. Though the firm had prepared a detailed business plan after hiring one or two employees, we never invested in the venture," HFCL adviser C. K. Goushal said at the time of the annulment. It was Packer's and HFCL's joint failure in identifying a strategic partner that did not allow the JV to proceed. This was also a period when the software industry was witnessing a global downturn. By November 2001 Packer had reduced his stake in HFCL to 6 percent (from 10%). Packer is believed to have finally sold off his entire holdings at about US$1.50 a share, which meant a net loss of about US$225 million. Packer had correctly sensed that the Indian market could offer significant investment opportunities, but he failed to critically assess both the market and his local partners before jumping in.

Even Coca-Cola has had its share of challenges in India. The company had a well-established presence in the country, and was the leading soft drink brand, but in 1977 it chose to leave the country rather than share its formula with the government and reduce its equity stake, as required under the Foreign Exchange Regulation Act (FERA), which oversees the operations of foreign companies in India. Coca-Cola returned to India in 1993 after a 16-year absence, and moved aggressively to reestablish its presence by acquiring India's leading soft-drink brands and bottling network. With the acquisition of local popular Indian brands such as Thums Up, Limca, Maaza, Citra, and Gold Spot, Coke acquired their manufacturing, bottling, and distribution assets. More importantly, the brands Coke purchased were popular locally.

With a vibrant blend of local and international brands, Coke was able to reap the benefits of global branding and global trends in tastes and at the same time, tap into traditional domestic markets. The top Indian brands joined Coke's international family of brands, including Diet Coke, Sprite, and Fanta, as well as the Schweppes product range. The company launched the Kinley bottled water brand in 2000; the Shock energy drink and the powdered concentrate Sunfill were introduced in 2001. The company's manufacturing process held more than 400 tests during this period; Coca-Cola has a well-documented quality control and assurance program.

With investments of more than US$1 billion over a 10-year period, Coca-Cola became one of India's top international investors. In 2002, Coca-Cola India grew by 39 percent, while the industry grew 23 percent overall, and for the first time the company reached break-even profitability. Noting the market growth, Coca-Cola India then doubled its capacity, with an investment of US$125 million during the period September 2002—March 2003.

Next, Coca-Cola adopted the "think local, act local" mantra. Instead of a single, global campaign, the company resorted to locally relevant advertising. Both Coca-Cola and its individual local brands were undeveloped in the rural market; as such, the company had to focus on broadening its position. India's urban markets, on the other hand, had higher category and brand development. Therefore, Coke had to narrow the brand positioning there and concentrate on differentiation. The company realized that it needed separate marketing strategies for urban and rural India.

"India A" was the market segment comprising the large metro areas and towns, and constituted 4 percent of the country's population. This section responded well to ads that met their aspirations. Coke introduced the successful "Life ho to aisi" (life as it should be) tagline for this audience. "India B" is composed of small towns and rural areas, constituting the remaining 96 percent of the country's population. To make Coke more accessible, the company launched a new 200 ml bottle (smaller than the traditional 300 ml) and cut the price by half. "Thanda Matlab Coca-Cola" (A cold drink means Coca-Cola) was the company's highly successful tagline for India B. In 2003 Coca-Cola was named the Advertiser of the Year and Campaign of the Year. Coca-Cola attained significant success with the successful ruralization of its brand.

In India, however, you always have to be prepared for the unexpected, and that's what happened to Coca-Cola when, in 2003, the India-based Center for Science and Environment (CSE), an independent public interest group, alleged that tests conducted on soft drinks found dangerously high levels of pesticide residue. The report immediately made the front pages of every major newspaper in India, and Coca-Cola stumbled badly in responding to the allegations. They underestimated how quickly the allegations would turn into a nationwide scandal, they misjudged the speed with which local political parties would use an Indian environmental group's report to attack a powerful global brand, they did not respond swiftly to consumer anxieties, and they failed to comprehend how fast news travels in modern India.

While Coke formed investigative committees in the United States and India and worked simultaneously on legal as well as public relations issues, it also commissioned a group of scientists to conduct tests in its own laboratories. The company chose to wait for their results before commenting in detail. That decision proved to be disastrous! The delays merely aggravated the suspicions of consumers. Within days, partial bans were issued on Coke (and Pepsi) products in one state after the other. Kerala, a South Indian state, issued a total ban, and public agitation reached a fevered pitch.

In 2006 allegations of pesticides were raised again, but this time Coca-Cola opted for a somewhat more aggressive marketing response. The company launched three rounds of advertisements in leading dailies refuting the claims. Based on its research, Coke also launched a television advertising campaign featuring testimonials by influential celebrities. The campaign also included an ad showing popular Bollywood actor Aamir Khan touring a Coke plant. After looking at the available research himself, he said he was convinced the beverages were safe.

Following the 2003 pesticide controversy, Coca-Cola had changed its management approach to address a number of vital problems—most importantly, how to handle the next public relations crisis. Tests conducted in three government labs in India showed that the products contained little to no pesticide residue; the levels were well within statutory limits. A prominent government lab in the United Kingdom also reported that it found none of the pesticides claimed by the public interest group.

Coke has been closely tracking consumer preferences and beliefs since the renewal of pesticide allegations in August 2006. Research shows that there has been a dramatic fall in the number of people who believe the pesticide allegations and a rise in the number of people who have gone back to drinking Coke. This episode reflects the fact that in developing countries such as India, political sensitivity to foreign influences can be catastrophic—often driven by perception and not reality. Some companies, however, have effectively developed and deployed an optimal entry strategy for the Indian market, and their approach is worth noting.

Take McDonald's, a leading global food service retailer with more than 30,000 local restaurants, serving nearly 50 million people in more than 119 countries every day.

McDonald's entered the Indian market as a 50-50 joint venture partnership between McDonald's Corporation (USA) and two Indian businessmen—Amit Jatia and Vikram Bakshi. Jatia's company, Hardcastle Restaurants Pvt. Ltd., owns and operates McDonald's restaurants in west and south India. The Connaught Plaza Restaurants Pvt. Ltd., headed by Vikram Bakshi, owns and handles the northern and eastern operations.

After consummating the joint venture agreements with McDonald's, in April 1995, Amit Jatia and Vikram Bakshi trained extensively, along with their management team, in McDonald's restaurants in Indonesia and the United States before opening the first McDonald's restaurant in India. The first Indian restaurants were opened in Delhi and Mumbai in October 1996. The partners realized right from the beginning that they could not succeed in India if they offered their standard fare. They were fortunate to have access to 5 years of intensive market research analysis that McDonald's had conducted on the Indian market. When they opened their first stores, in 1996, more than 70 percent of the products on the menu were developed to specifically suit the Indian consumer.

McDonald's approached the localization of their business by addressing three key issues. First, they focused on understanding the local culture. The Indian culture is deeply religious, and a majority of the Indian population do not eat beef, as the cow is considered to be a sacred animal. Many Indians will not eat pork, either, and as a result India became the first country in the world where McDonald's does not serve beef or pork items. There are also a large number of vegetarians in the country, and as a result, special vegetarian dishes are offered (prepared with special care, to ensure that at no point would vegetarian and non-vegetarian dishes be processed together). This distinction is carried throughout the stages of procurement, cooking, and serving, with dedicated utensils and equipment for vegetarian products at every stage.

The second aspect of the localization strategy was to understand the local palate. Special vegetarian dishes were developed, using Indian spices. Some of these, like "McAloo Tikki" burger, have also become popular overseas. In fact, India is now used as a hub for sourcing vegetarian dishes for McDonald's restaurants in other parts of the world. Care is taken to ensure that even the sauces and mayonnaise were specially developed to be eggless. The company uses dedicated equipment for preparing its vegetable as well as non-vegetarian products, and maintains separation of the vegetarian and non-vegetarian items throughout.

The third part of its strategy focused on pricing. While in the United States McDonald's stands for convenience, in India it is still, to a large extent, a luxury. To counter this, and to generate more customers, the company has had to price its products very competitively—to overcome the perception of being expensive, the brand started focusing on affordability. It thus introduced its "Happy Price Menu" at $US.50. The company also recognized that there were an increasing number of motorists, and their need for convenience, so it launched Drive-Thru outlets. The company has also deployed aggressive marketing strategies, such as offering discount coupons and the "I'm loving it" campaign, which was heavily promoted in India so as to appeal to India's current transition to more Western trends.

A very important reason behind McDonald's success in India is that complete flexibility was given to the domestic partners to run the business. The India team brought local knowledge into the joint venture. The Indian team also brought in the entrepreneurial drive necessary to make the business a success, given the unique challenges the country presented. To be able to competitively price its products, the company had to source from local suppliers; at the same time, it had to ensure that these suppliers were able to meet their high standards of quality and on-time delivery. In this regard the company has invested a large amount of time and money in building up a supply infrastructure and in supplier training and development. At present, more than 96 percent of McDonald's supplies are sourced from local suppliers.

McDonald's India's entire supply-chain operations are handled by Radhakrishna Foodland Pvt. Ltd., which is a part of the Radhakrishna Group, which is engaged in food and related services. This activity is a challenge, since the Indian infrastructure is so inefficient that nearly 30 percent of India's food production is lost due to spoilage in the supply chain. Through supplier development and training, not only has McDonald's succeeded, but the suppliers themselves have been able to build larger and more profitable businesses.

The company met with scientists in potato research institutes to source a particular variety of potato for producing their world-famous french fries. Since the right variety was not available in India, they had to bring in the seeds and work with the farmers of Gujarat to improve their agriculture practices, from irrigation system to harvest storage methods. In the case of hamburger buns, McDonald's worked with Cargill in identifying wheat varieties with higher protein content. It began by using the existing facilities of the bakery supplier in Ludhiana, and later it invested in a greenfield plant near Delhi.

Even though the poultry supply base in India was relatively better developed, McDonald's has still managed to bring about improvement in the average size of the birds, from 1.2 kg at the launch of McDonald's in India to 1.6 kg now, with a bone-to-meat ratio that is on par with international benchmarks. In India, the company has also succeeded in implementing its famous QSC&V philosophy (Quality, Service, Cleanliness, and Value), that makes it a benchmark for quality in the industry. How is McDonald's India doing today? The company presently operates 108 restaurants, and that's just the beginning.

McDonald's India had successfully implemented the product/market approach strategy, which is driven by the belief that product mangers should individually tailor their approach based on the local characteristics of the market and their product. This approach has attributes that can maximize growth in emerging markets. Specifically, products are localized based on the results of the emerging market assessment, utilizing such factors as size of market, market fragmentation, competition at the product level, marketing requirements, barriers to entry, and investment requirements.

The product/market approach allows a manager to maximize the revenue contribution of his or her product by taking a global product and localizing it to fit the vagaries of the local market. By empowering the product manager, the corporation achieves a highly efficient and targeted use of finite assets and resources. The product manager is interested in one thing only—the maximum profit for the product under his or her charge. The primary limiting factor to this approach is the potential lack of coordination among the various managers, thus inhibiting the overall strategic plan.

What you should take away from this, first and foremost, is that the Indian market is extremely complex. That complexity reaches across every aspect of the country and the people, and can be seen in a broad range of religious, cultural, ethnic, and political differences. In order to understand India's complexity and how that complexity might impact your product, service, or investment, you need to do your homework. And that should include a rigorous assessment of the specific market that is conducted using a disciplined approach. While there are many potential reputable local partners there are plenty of disreputable ones as well. Like the market assessment, potential partners need to be vetted using the same disciplined approach.

There are many top-tier professional services firms that have a strong presence in India, and a number of them are well suited for conducting strategic assessments and market entry strategies. The firm you decide to use should be willing to commit senior partners and staff to the project and their project methodology should heavily weight the use of human intelligence-gathering techniques (HUMIT). The problem with most market analysis is that it relies too heavily on the use of third-party data and other published reports. In emerging markets, all data should be considered suspect; even if it is proven to be accurate, it will most likely not be current. In order for a market assessment to be actionable it must include first-party data and insights that would include the use of targeted interviews and surveys. Additionally, the firm you decide to use should have a well-established first-tier network of local relationships that can be leveraged in identifying potential partners and other strategic relationships.

What can happen when you don't do your homework? Consider the case of Posco Steel, the South Korean company that plans to make the single largest direct foreign investment in India to date, at more than US$12 billion! Posco plans to build a steel mill in the mineral-rich state of Orissa, taking advantage of favorable financial terms offered through the state's special economic zones. The company had conducted detailed economic feasibility studies, but they failed to assess public opinion and the impact that various political groups might have on the project.

The problem for Posco is that in order to build the steel mill and roads and other infrastructure needed, 4,000 tribal families that live in the area will need to be relocated. Adding to the tension is the fact that Posco plans to ship iron ore from the region to Korea for processing there, which, of course, further intensified nationalist sentiments. The fact that the project will mean direct employment for more than 13,000 people and indirect employment for another 20,000 has done little to calm the waters. In May 2007, three executives from Posco went to the village of Gobindapur to meet with farmers about acquiring land for the proposed project. They were kidnapped and held hostage by the local residents for 3 days before finally being released. They weren't harmed, but the incident highlights the fact that if local government actions are not aligned with public sentiment big problems can result. The lesson learned? Do your homework. It could save more than time or money.

7

Understanding the Indian Business Culture

The New India

And the end of the fight is a tombstone white with the name of the late deceased, And the epitaph drear: "A Fool lies here who tried to hustle the East."

Rudyard Kipling

Like the economy itself, present-day Indian business culture is in a dynamic state of evolution. India's pre-1990s attitude to foreign investment could be characterized as somewhat ambiguous at best, with an almost schizophrenic approach—like an open/closed view that found companies like Coca-Cola wondering what the hell had just happened. India has come a long way since an earlier, more insular regime practically severed all connections with the rest of the world. Today, the *World Values Survey* points out that India is among the most competitive of nations. In fact, India overtook the United States in 2005 to 2006 to become the second-most attractive global FDI destination. Various surveys of executives at leading global corporations now rank India second only to China in this regard. This is a story about corporate India's radical makeover: It is a story of a transition in the making, and of the attempts to showcase certain key facets of contemporary Indian culture, even as its economy opens up. In doing so, it also prescribes certain cultural axioms for foreign players pursuing business interests in the Indian marketplace.

Let me share with you a first hand, word-of-mouth narrative of a series of experiences that may shed light on the evolving Indian business culture. I happened to be a witness to one of the first joint ventures in India, during the early years of my professional career. This joint venture was composed of a leading IT hardware manufacturing company from India, and a globally celebrated IT company from Silicon Valley. The joint venture between the Indian and American firms was initiated in 1991. The Indian firm later bought back a 26 percent stake in the joint venture in August 1997. It was at this joint venture that I began my work life, and I was very excited to begin work at one of the high-tech icons of the 1990s.

In retrospect, the joint venture between the two firms was a marriage of complementarities during the early days of India's new economy. There was the Indian firm—aggressive and sales-focused—and there was the American powerhouse, a globally acknowledged product/service innovator. Back then, each needed one another. The Indian firm needed access to R&D, process know-how, and a strong product pipeline. On the other hand, the American firm needed a sales and distribution network, access to manufacturing units, and logistics, as the import of finished goods was accompanied by a prohibitively high duty of 110 percent. Since importing individual components involved a duty of only 40 percent, it made sense to bring in the components and then produce the final product at the Indian firm's nationwide facilities. Notwithstanding the economic synergies of the time, the joint venture was a classic case of cultural mismatch.

Much of the initial synergy was subsequently enhanced when the duty gap between imported finished goods and components was reduced by the government. The American firm could now import finished products. Likewise, the Indian player could import other brands. But clearly, there were other reasons for the breakup. "Call it whatever, the stark reality is that the American firm has outlived its usefulness as far as its Indian partner is concerned," said a Mumbai-based computer industry analyst. "This is the first time an Indian company has used a foreign alliance to grow in the marketplace and then ditched the partnership when it became too restrictive."

The joint venture had also begun to restrict the overseas ambitions of the Indian firm. Under the terms of the joint venture, the Indian firm could not bid for overseas contracts in cases where the American partner was also in the running. There were other, less overt issues. The American firm had a true service orientation, and their service expectations from the JV were much higher than the Indian firm's, where the focus was primarily centered on the sales target: Numbers mattered, and thus customers were often over-promised. There were instances where after-sales would take a hit because of an over-commitment on initial sales. Moreover, the Indian player was very keen to get into the high-margin services business, where it could directly compete with the American firm.

On the face of it, these may all sound like strategic issues, but there were pronounced cultural overtones. Contrast the aggressive sales culture of the Indian firm with the more product-innovation/service-oriented culture of the American. The American player, a proconsumer, professional outfit, was not used to manipulating customers, something its JV partner was adept at. It was a typical American firm, with non-negotiable values and principles. Quality never took a back seat. The American firm was like a family working on the floor—managers supporting their associates, team lunches, pats on the back, friendly banter. The Indian firm, on the other hand, was a fledgling firm, coursing through the tides of a constantly changing economy. The necessity of dealing with government officials, politicians, and policemen—satisfying them was essential—had, however, made it a very unorganized organization. It was awkward for management to accomodate guests at five-star hotels at nights and then talk about organizational culture the next morning. The management had developed rough edges during this time, and clearly its way of doing things was to just "get them done." One could sense the impersonal, impolite air. In this case, the Indian and American ways of running a business starkly contrasted. Later, a lack of trust between the joint venture partners ensued, and there was only one way to end this relationship—divorce.

Moral of the Story: Entering a new territory is a high-risk, high-benefit proposition. Aligning with a partner that identifies with your ethics and values is of utmost importance. Understanding your partner's corporate culture may help you be aware of differences in cultural wavelengths. Sometimes the normal internal practices of a partner, if not identified at the beginning, can cause so much friction later on that the relationship starts to drift apart.

That being said, joint ventures have been a widely utilized and successful route of entry for foreign players in India. In 1999, Morgan Stanley made its entrance into India via two joint ventures, with JM Financial—the brokerage house of JM Morgan Stanley Securities—and JM Morgan Stanley, which was essentially into investment advising. In early 2007, Morgan Stanley decided to quit the relationship so it could pursue its own goals. It bought complete control of the brokerage and research business while it sold the investment advisory stake to JM. Note that it was important for Morgan Stanley to partner with an Indian firm in 1999, when the market was more regulated, but with the easing of rules and regulations, Morgan Stanley decided to go solo. JM Financial's director, Vishal Kampani, told Forbes.com: "We would have preferred a joint venture but they wanted a divorce, so we accepted it." Meanwhile, the U.S.-based investment services major is expected to kick-start its investment banking, capital markets, fixed income, and private wealth management platforms in India.

Moral of the Story: Morgan Stanley very intelligently entered the Indian market. Get a foot in the door, then rule the house. Partnering with a domestic firm can help a foreign business understand the rules of the game. The domestic partner often tends to share knowledge as rapidly as possible in order to grow as quickly as possible. A thorough indoctrination—followed by a successful implementation of that learning, via a joint venture, and you are all set to dominate the market—singlehandedly.

There are many well-hyped instances of successful JVs. Superficially, strategic reasons are always claimed to be responsible for break-ups, when they do happen. Although cultural differences are not usually cited as the reason for the success or failure of cross-border joint ventures, it is our firm belief that it does play a key role—its manifestations range from ego clashes between the Indian promoter and the overseas entrant to the ways in which two players who are culturally different work together.

After working in India during the early period of my life, I then spent time in the United States. It was there that I had a first-hand introduction to what was then referred to as the "Western mindset," Upon my return to India, I was positioned to appreciate the contrasts as well as the changes that had slowly but surely crept into the Indian workplace. Many Indian companies are reforming, but if there is one comprehensive change that must take root, it will have to be that of management being more direct, rather than going round and round in circles, and taking forever to formulate policy. Quite often in such cases, reaching an agreement is elusive.

One of the biggest fallouts of not being able to assert—or say "no"—is what is called the "over-promise and under-deliver" syndrome. This is sometimes evident at some of the Indian BPOs, where a Western client says that he needs a solution in 2 days (and the local firm thinks it will take 5), they will still commit to the client's expectations. There is an inclination to be nice and not push back. End result? Delivery of average/below-average work to a client, after setting high expectations. Having said that, currently there is a movement toward being more assertive and direct without being offensive. I have heard work teams tell clients: "You know, I will deliver seriously bad work if you make me deliver in 2 days. You don't want that, do you? But I can give you something by way of work-in-progress in the next 2 days . . . and give you the rest in another 2 to 3 days."

I remember asking someone to work on pivot tables for a large data analysis study I was doing for a big logistics and transportation firm. I was told that I would certainly get something within a day.

When nothing came my way, I checked, only to discover that the person responsible did not know how to conduct pivot table exercises and was desperately trying to figure them out. Indians sometimes don't want to share weaknesses—they sometimes forget that it's not necessarily "bad" to say that one does not know the answer, and then work out a solution—whether it's identifying someone with the right skill set or saying that "I need more than a day, since I need to figure out how to do it." There have been positive changes, however. Most people are now more open about what they know and what they don't. Recently I interviewed someone and asked if he knew how to use Lexis Nexis and Factiva for business data trawling. He confidently told me that he did not, but then added that if someone could train him, he would quickly learn it and deliver high-quality output.

What about the issue of transparency within the Indian business culture? Corporate India, till the late 1980s, or even the early 1990s, was not as transparent as it is now. I still remember my boss's office from my first job. His room was in an exclusive area, barricaded by wall partitions on three sides and a window that overlooked the street. He had a large brass plate on his door that said Vice President. No one had a clue what he was doing in that room. There were two worlds in that office—employees and bosses.

Today, when I look at my firm's India office and the offices of other leading organizations, I see almost everyone in the management team working in 100 percent glass-enclosed rooms. This symbolizes a spirit of openness. At my first assignment in India, I remember a lot of folks addressing the senior management as "Sir." Today, there is still formality, but more and more the workers now address the senior management by their first names. At our operation in India, which is a knowledge services and research outfit, we are introducing a "Create the Company Values" exercise where we ask all of our employees to tell us what they believe the values of the company should be. This was inconceivable in India just 10 to 15 years ago . . . some grey-haired men behind closed doors would redefine your value system for you!

The concept of time in the Indian business culture is often referred to as *IST*: Indian Stretched Time. Indian businesses need to respect other people's time. I recall chasing invoices in the early 1990s. I had to meet a client who was just not paying up. His office was about 50 kilometers from the city, so I had to make special plans for transportation. I was asked to be at the client's office by 10 A.M. sharp. The person I was to meet came in an hour late. He then said that I should go to another person in Finance who could help. I again waited for the finance person. To add insult to injury, I was then told to come after lunch. Eventually, I was told to come again the next day! A whole day wasted—that attitude led to a lot of inefficiencies in those days.

It still exists, even today, in the habit of employees' walking over to someone's desk and spending time talking about nonwork issues while that person is trying hard to focus on something important. In America, people tend to make appointments and then stick to them. Such basic professional etiquette, however, is a more recent realization for most Indians.

On the positive side, Indian workers have also started thinking big. This, I feel, is a function of the confidence engendered by strong economic growth, better opportunities, and reliable infrastructure. Look at the new-found confidence of Indian corporations doing large international M&As, such as Hindalco-Novelis. which, in 2006, completed what was the largest-ever deal by any Indian pharmaceutical player when it bought one of Germany's largest generic drugmakers, Betapharm Arzneimittel, for a reported US$572 million. That new sense of confidence is now being seen at the individual level. I recently interviewed someone for a junior analyst position at our India office, and I asked him what he wanted to be doing in 5 years. "My job!" he answered politely. Fifteen years ago, one just did not think like this. We were afraid to dream; we did not know our latent potential. In effect, dreams were only for the Western world. Today, there's a generation of Indian entrepreneurs who want to take on the world. People are clearly more ambitious. I have seen this at our firm, though there is the inevitable downside—considerable impatience and a desire to quit if one does not get promoted, even when one has not deserved it!

At the end of the day, the average Indian employee is still a very sensitive person. Say something that has even an iota of insult, and you can be pretty confident that the person will pick up the "not intended offence" and take it to heart. I still remember answering a phone call from a junior employee's wife after I came back from my U.S. stint. She had a pleasant phone voice and a lovely accent—quite unlike the junior. I told him all this, but I don't think I communicated it correctly. Come evaluation time, I discovered that this employee was truly pissed at me—he thought I was indirectly hitting on his wife! With the passage of time, there has been some modernization of the Indian business psyche, which allows one to be more liberal in expression, though one still has to be very careful. The concepts of appraisals and feedback were not really a formalized exercise at most corporations till as recently as a decade ago—you most likely got shouted at if you made a mistake. Nowadays, it's more about communicating in a nonthreatening way and trying to generate solutions that prevent repetition of mistakes or disruptive behavior.

On the whole, things were definitely more chaotic just a few years ago in India. One would be put into sales and simply told what the audience should be. Nowadays, when sales organizations train new employees, they bring out well-structured selling techniques, demographic profiles, and competitor information. In a like manner, communication methods have changed. Until the late 1980s, business correspondence was bulky, long-winded, arcane, and potentially confusing. After coming back to India and working with McKinsey in the early 2000s, I learned elegant frameworks about how to communicate more powerfully—SCR (situation-complication-resolution) was one such framework that I strongly endorse. In business communication, one needs to set the context (situation), then bring out the issue (complication), and finally state what can be done to solve that situation (resolution).

Above all, I'm proud to be part of a generation that espouses a customer-centric mindset, as opposed to the traditional bureaucratic outlook. Not very long ago, most Indians were satisfied with delivering average quality. There was even a special catch phrase for this: *Chalta hai* (anything goes). This is still the case in some Indian companies. Long lasting acclimatization to Western standards, however, has introduced a considerable degree of quality consciousness. Over time, we have introduced many best-practice methodologies to stimulate the workplace culture. And just as in our company, there are a growing number of executives at various other forward-looking companies who have ushered in changes at the workplace based on their exposure and their learning.

The fundamentals of retaining and inspiring people at the Indian workplace are not very different from those in the Western world: Interesting and challenging roles and responsibilities, good compensation, inspiring leadership, and recognition. It is these drivers that will make the Indian business world competitive, forward looking, and innovative.

India is now acknowledged as a worldwide hot spot for the outsourcing of technology and business service functions. Its value potential is based on its vast pool of knowledgeable workers with English-speaking and relevant domain skills, as well as its low-cost, high-quality scalability model. The success of India's information technology industry has created a new global image for India. It has come to be regarded by many business leaders and international institutions as a model for India's development. From a past when the ability of any Indian industry to gain a global stature was a distant dream, it is to the Indian IT industry's credit that a newfound confidence has been generated within the nation. Some business leaders believe that the growth in Indian IT is responsible for the ongoing boom in the Indian economy.

There's much more to India and the Indian economy, however. Foreign direct investment (FDI), joint ventures, exports, and outsourcing all comprise the economic manifestations of the winds of change ushered in by the liberalization of the early 1990s. And such manifestations have not been the exclusive preserve of IT. Things weren't always like this. Independent India's pre-1990s attitude toward foreign investment can be thought of as somewhat ambiguous at best. And cautiousness on this front has been an on-and-off characteristic, at least until the turn of the millennium.

What were the reasons for such cautiousness, which some would call paranoia? In what has been attributed as a throwback to an era of colonial resource drain, there has been a pronounced degree of caution regarding the types of foreign firms that can operate in India. In all fairness, however, there is a sea of a difference between a colonial master and modern-day multinationals. Much of the difference can summed up in one word—competition. Again, in the Indian case there is no concrete evidence that the multinationals have acted any worse than their similarly placed Indian peers.

Perhaps a simple explanation would be that a legacy of protection against domestic and foreign entrants makes its beneficiaries lazy and inefficient. The resulting lack of competition bred corporate indifference to the efficient provision of factors of production, while the resulting inefficiency reinforced resistance to liberalization. Then again, Indian politicians of various hues have stymied foreign initiatives in the past. Nothing unique about this, though—even American politicians complain about outsourcing! But politicians are only effective when they cater to strong constituencies. Indian farmers form a powerful political constituency against competition.

But things are now changing, as the recent *World Values Survey* pointed out. Granted that the older generation in India is still rooted in its socialist past, but as more and more of India's young reach working and voting age, unencumbered by the baggage of the past, they are sending out more and more of their kind of representatives to form the government. Moreover, attitudes in India have gradually shifted in the direction of tolerance toward competition and openness with the spread of education and professional skills. Today the nation offers a compelling study of contrasts in culture. This is more so for a foreign business player contemplating forays into the Indian marketplace. Such a study assumes fresh relevance as India both readies and steadies itself in its bid to become a globalization hub.

For a foreign player contemplating business in India, it is important to be sensitive to the diversity of Indian business culture. Large portions of Indian business are owned by members of different social communities. Though many of these business houses are quite modern in their operations, it is useful to understand their specific community culture. There is also a distinct difference in the cultures of government and nongovernment business organizations. Government-owned public sector companies are more often bureaucratic and hierarchical, compared to many of their private sector counterparts. On the other hand, the "new economy" service sector companies are more egalitarian and flexible than the traditional manufacturing sector firms.

It is said that the Indian nation is endowed with a rich cultural heritage that dates back at least 6,000 years. Contemporary India, however, is a surprisingly young country, with around 38 percent of its population falling into the 20 to 44 age group. Compared to older generations, this generation has more liberal values and is also more ambitious. This, in turn, produces a culture in transition.

India is also a land of many contrasts. To start with, there's a wide urban-rural divide: Close to 65 percent of India's population lives in villages and subsists on agriculture. However, agriculture contributes only slightly over 26 percent to India's GDP. Then again, India has one of the largest populations of technically qualified manpower, comprising around 15 million doctors, engineers, and scientists. But the overall literacy rate in the country is just over 50 percent. India hosts a large linguistic diversity. It has 18 constitutionally recognized major languages in addition to myriad minor languages and dialects. Hindi is the official national language, but less than 40 percent of Indians speak or understand Hindi. English—replete with its accents, inflexions, and tonal nuances—is the lingua franca of Indian business.

Religion is a way of life and must be respected in India. However, in spite of the elimination of the traditional caste system, which was a direct outcome of Hinduism, attitudes still remain embedded, and both aspects of Indian culture still influence the hierarchical structure of business in India today. Program evaluation and review technique (PERT) charts—a project management tool—notwithstanding, one obvious outgrowth of religion is the notion of *karma*, wherein everything happens for a reason. Such shades of fatalism find an echo in the decision making of many Indians.

Moral of the Story: One needs to ensure that the workplace population is not heavily tilted toward a particular group of people. People of the same caste, religion, or region bond very well with each other and tend to work in their own closed groups. This does not ensure a healthy atmosphere.

Changing times have ushered in a marked shift in career aspirations among India's youth. This shift can be explained in terms of an increasing awareness and endorsement of nontraditional career paths. Until just a couple of decades ago, most new entrants into the workforce actually aspired for government jobs, while out-of-the-box career paths were a strict no-no. Such risk averseness on the career front is now being steadily replaced with an appetite for professional adventure and self-actualization.

Meanwhile, from real estate, retail, hotel management, media, and telecom, to life sciences, biotechnology, paramedicine, or even fashion design and entertainment—the career options are growing widely. Contrast this with a young Indian in the 1980s, who was rather one-dimensional in his or her approach to education and profession. Parents, peers, and Indian society put a lot of pressure on performing brilliantly at school and becoming a doctor, engineer, or a chartered accountant. Back then, the crème de la crème would vie to join the civil services, the hottest career option. All this represented the rather limited career horizon of the older generation. Until the late 1980s, the private sector was, at best, a second-rung alternative for the young and educated. Today, in the most competitive of Indian markets—the Indian joint venture market—a multinational appointment is seen as a definite plus, almost at par with the elite Indian Administrative Services of the socialist era. In a way, this tells its own story about changing mindsets.

Case in point: In 2005, more than 191,000 students took the nationwide Common Admission Test for a postgraduate management diploma at the prestigious Indian Institutes of Management. This was almost double the number that appeared at the turn of the millennium. An opening economy has translated into a rising awareness that, in turn, has multiplied options for the young Indian who has professional aspirations. Thanks to advances in technology and the resulting proliferation of new and refined communication channels, we are now a part of a world that is more connected and aware.

Take the case of news dissemination. Today, Indian news coverage is richer, more broad based, and easier to access and comprehend. Not very long ago, there was just state-owned television, for only a few hours a day. Contrast the vibrant, present-day coverage of the budget, M&As, product launches, FDI, and stock market movements with the abstruse and dull fare dished out by the print and visual media of the 1980s.

Then again, a 16- to 22-year-old Indian in the 1980s figuring out his first job did not have much to look forward to in the private sector. Back then, there weren't very many role models in Indian business. Times have changed, however. Today, from Sabeer Bhatia of the Hotmail fame to Infosys' Narayana Murthy—there is a growing list of entrepreneurs and business leaders who serve as potent sources of inspiration for the young.

There are other accompanying changes that are complementing the development of the new Indian workforce. The United States is now increasingly becoming a destination for managerial rather than technical education. In 2005, India was placed sixth on the list of the top 10 countries, based on the number of GMAT applicants. Aspirations are now veering more and more toward Harvard, Wharton, Chicago, or Stanford compared to MIT. In a way, this is a replication of the larger trend in India itself, where there's a cooling off in the number of technical aspirants compared to those seeking higher education in areas such as management and economics. In effect, aspiring professionals now attach more value to management skills in their career game plans.

Since the onset of liberalization, in the early 1990s, business schools (B-schools) have been sprouting up all over the country. Today, there are more than 1,200 recognized B-schools in India. Dual degree programs such as BTech–MBA are also becoming popular. Moreover, many professionals who have worked in health care, computer, or engineering firms have gone on to pursue an MBA to improve their prospects. Until very recently, getting a second degree was compulsory in India. Now, many aspirants are comfortable with a single degree, getting jobs in domains such as ITES and retail.

Although there have been many comparative analyses between the United States' system of higher professional education and its Indian counterpart, quality has been one irrefutable differentiator. American B-schools offer a heady mix of theory and practice, something that has only lately been emulated by the Indian B-schools. Now we see more and more collaboration with Western institutions, and there is a pronounced emphasis on the case study approach and on teamwork. Practices such as "push-back," constructive criticism, and assertiveness, which we now take as givens, were alien to the Indian curricula not so very long ago.

Collaborations, associations, synergies, and affiliations are bywords in India's bid to create a globalized workforce. Today, the

Indian School of Business at Hyderabad has formed associations with the Kellogg School of Management, at Wharton, and the London Business School. The Indian Institute of Management (Ahmedabad) has partnered with Duke University's Fuqua School of Business to introduce Indian MBA students to international best practices.

Interestingly, many young Indians are now beginning to spend time working before going on to further studies. The entrenched culture has always been about finishing education before thinking about working. But it is increasingly now more about young people logging 4 to 5 years of work before entering a B-School or going back to do a MA/PhD. Also, Indians have previously been known to be very brand minded when it comes to work. Earlier, most of those who opted for the private sector preferred a large, established corporation. This, too, is changing. Aspirants now look at smaller companies offering steeper learning curves and multifaceted opportunities, and say: "I'd rather be a big fish in a small pond than a small fish in the ocean." Moreover, young aspirants are today more keen to understand role-responsibility, career paths, and corporate expectations before they jump into the fray.

Taking it further, many have also set up their own entrepreneurial ventures. There are many instances that reflect a growing appetite for risk. Take the case of Sarath Babu. After graduating from the Indian Institute of Management, Ahmedabad, he said no to an assured future and started his own food catering services. Another IIM-A grad, Gaurav Dagaonkar, chose to follow his passion for music. More than a quarter of the engineering and technology companies launched in the United States between 1995 and 2005 had at least one foreign-born founder. And Indians set up more immigrant-founded firms (26%) compared to newcomers from China, Taiwan, the United Kingdom, and Japan combined. Interestingly, industry domains where the Indian immigrants established start-ups included: software (46%); innovation/manufacturing-related (44%); computers/communications (5%), and semiconductors and bioscience (2% each).

No discussion on charting new career horizons is complete without discussing reverse brain drain. Many established Indian professionals, who have tasted success overseas, are returning to India to set up businesses. And there are quite a few cases of "alternative" entrepreneurs who have defied the stereotyped options.

Vikram Akula, the founder of SKS Microfinance, got his BA from Tufts, his MA from Yale, and topped it off with a PhD from the University of Chicago, where his dissertation focused on poverty alleviation strategies. Before launching SKS, Akula was a Fulbright scholar in India and coordinated the government-funded *Jawahar Rozgar Yojana* (a nationwide income-generation scheme covering public works). He also worked as a community organizer with the Deccan Development Society in Andhra Pradesh and as a researcher with the Worldwatch Institute. Today, SKS Microfinance is one of the world's fastest-growing microfinance institutions. As its founder/CEO, Akula has been named by TIME magazine as one of "The People Who Shape Our World" in 2006. In May 2007 SKS and Citi announced a US$40 million rural microfinance program.

Moving from the world of microfinance to the heady world of wine, Stanford alumnus Rajeev Samant was one of the youngest finance managers at U.S.-based Oracle. He chose to quit and return home with an idea—growing grapes and making wine. Evidently, San Francisco, where he was based, had something to do with this. Samant developed a family plot of 30 acres in India's key grape region of Nashik. He teamed up with Kerry Damskey, a leading winemaker from California, and started his first plantings in 1997. Samant's Sula Vineyards received US$3.5 million in private equity in 2005.

In effect, there has been a sea change in the Indian attitude and approach to education and career building. And the change is ongoing. Today's youth constitute tomorrow's vanguard in India's development odyssey. Not surprisingly, amid all this there is now also an evolved understanding of the dignity of labor. Consider this: In India, a hotel management position at a five-star property was considered "socially unbecoming" just a decade and a half ago. Today, the Pizza Hut and McDonald's outlets are staffed with bright and upbeat youngsters. Students who work part time are also appreciated. And classmates warmly greeting each other across the counters at burger joints is now an everyday sight.

Alternative career paths. New definitions for success. A brand new lifestyle. The winds of liberalization have spurred a radical transformation in the middle class culture in India, one that defies cultural stereotyping. Epitomized and hyped by popular media as essentially an "information technology" phenomenon, it is now spreading beyond purely urban enclaves. However, many of the observations on the lifestyle and cultural orientation of IT professionals also apply to other sectors of the upwardly mobile Indian middle classe. This is because many such changes in consumption patterns are broad trends that have swept across India in the wake of liberalization.

Working in a globalized industry environment—one that involves frequent interaction with foreign clients, overseas travel, and exposure to different working norms—has led to significant shifts in lifestyles, family structure, and identity. Interestingly, it seems to have given rise to a certain genre of cosmopolitanism, while at the same time reinforcing traditional identities and cultural values in a sort of reflex action. Such a divergent trend is an inevitable outcome of the complexities of the process of globalization, which produces both a transformation as well as a reassertion of cultural mores.

Take the IT hub of Bangalore, for instance. The current high demand for software engineers, with the entry of more and more companies in this south Indian metropolis, has pushed salaries sky high. As a result, striking cultural shifts have been observed in consumption patterns over the last several years. Today there are close to 240,000 IT professionals living in Bangalore. Most of them possess many of the consumer goods that have become symbolic of a new, middle-class lifestyle—a car, top-end cell phone, elaborate music and home entertainment systems, and so on. They also tend to shop at the new malls and brand stores that have sprung up in the city. Many wear expensive, branded apparel, and eat out at fancy and expensive restaurants. Most importantly, many have been able to purchase their own spacious homes at a relatively young age.

So far, so good—but even while many software professionals outwardly appear to have adopted the new consumerist lifestyle, their reactions to consumption and materialism carry marked connotations of a different story. Their reactions actually border on a direct critique of the new consumer culture and cosmopolitan lifestyle. This is articulated through a distinction between money and material comfort and social and spiritual wellbeing. The postindependence middle class had its roots in the Nehruvian "engines of growth" regime, which, through the rapid expansion of the higher education system, created a large contingent of technical and managerial experts as well as a bureaucratic class. This middle class was force fed on the ideologies of nationalism and state-led development, and had to make do with lifestyles that were relatively austere, even spartan, by today's standards. With the opening up of the economy, television and advertising catalyzed significant shifts in the middle class mindset. Consumption now became synonymous with development, and overt signs of wealth became emblematic of national progress. The Nehruvian ideals of "progress with austerity" were jettisoned somewhere along the line.

Today, many IT professionals define their economic status in terms of their ability to consume more than the previous generation. In effect, this style of consumption is a key differentiator between the traditional and the new middle class. However, despite obvious changes in consumption patterns and visible changes in lifestyle, most among the new middle class have not fully bought into the ideology of consumerism. Despite their apparently opulent lifestyles, they tend to be relatively conservative and use their money to pursue what have essentially been traditional middle class goals.

This, for instance, is reflected in their investment in property. It is important to note that the goals themselves have not changed, even though timelines have been compressed.

Time is premium. The new Indian economy also exhibits a marked blurring of the line between work and personal time, between office and home. Extended and flexible working hours are coupled with the fact that everyone is wired through cell phones and wi-fi laptops.

Cities such as Bangalore, Hyderabad, and New Delhi's satellite township of Gurgaon host large populations of upwardly mobile new economy professionals. Residential patterns in these cities reinforce lifestyles that are now geared toward minimizing the time needed for family responsibilities. Most neo-middle class professionals prefer to buy flats in large, upscale, self-contained complexes that have been built in and around these cities. Here, basic needs—such as security, maintenance, and recreation—are readily available in situ. Within these gated ghettos, an army of support staff looks after family needs and domestic work, freeing professional couples from the demands of housekeeping.

There is also a sharp cultural contrast between home life and life at work. Though many incumbents come from urban, middle class backgrounds, the culture of this class is still very different from that found in the globalized corporate culture of the modern-day, new-economy industry. Until recently, any contrast between home and work life had been managed through the process of compartmentalization. But compartmentalization as a strategy is becoming less viable as the world of work penetrates increasingly into personal lives. The links with family and community are becoming elusive. And as work overwhelms their lives, the new professionals are unable to find the time or energy to sustain social relationships.

At the end of the day, cultural identity within this group of upwardly mobile global IT professionals is molded by several cultural spiels: Indian society as a happy mixture of tradition and modernity, India as an ancient land with a long tradition of science and math, and India as a rising economic power that will soon overtake China, once it is freed from its remaining shackles. For now, the new economy has had a multiplier effect that is largely responsible for the recent boom in the Indian economy. And there is no doubt that the IT industry has played a substantial role in the current rapid expansion of the urban economy, due to its links with the real estate, consumer goods, automobile, and telecom sectors.

To some extent, the cultural domain of Indian business is marked by a constant pull and push between strongly held traditional values and modern business practices. While this may sometimes cause frustration among foreigners doing business in India, it is also the means by which India has been defining itself in the global marketplace. Capping our discussion on Indian business culture, it would be fruitful to learn what works for a foreign player in the Indian business setting. More pointedly, what are those elements of business culture, or culture per se, that have contributed to the business success of foreign players in India?

Emerging markets are today a lucrative proposition for foreign players. Real GDP growth is currently estimated at close to 10 percent in the case of China and 9 percent for India. Again, China and India are together expected to grow from the current 8 percent of global output to around 21 percent by 2025. It might seem natural to describe community-based initiatives as a form of corporate social responsibility. Yet, in most cases, such local initiatives are actually sound business sense. In short, addressing social issues is not an accompaniment to strategy, but central to it.

Coca-Cola has succeeded despite well-entrenched Indian beverage consumption habits—*chai* (tea), *lassi* (whey-yoghurt), and *nimbu paani* (lemonade). It actively leverages regional Indian festivals through below-the-line activity. Today, the company has an extensive rural distribution network, and rural India now accounts for almost 30 percent of Coca-Cola's country sales volume.

Using a nontraditional distribution network, the consumer-goods major, Unilever, through its Indian subsidiary, Hindustan Lever Ltd., is working with community groups of women to sell its products in villages with a population of less than 1,500.

When Kellogg entered India, the per capita consumption of breakfast cereals was a low 4 gram per annum, compared to a global 5 kilogram per annum. The budding Indian ready-to-eat cereal market posed several challenges: A population not used to processed foods, easy availability of traditional breakfast options, and a low awareness of caloric requirements. Kellogg India has taken various initiatives to enhance awareness about breakfast cereals. Apart from advertising, it conducts school contact programs, and also develops interfaces with opinion leaders such as India's Central Food Technology Research Institute. But Kellogg's entry into India was not smooth sailing at the beginning.

The Kellogg Company introduced its first products in India in 1994 under its fully owned subsidiary, Kellogg's India Pvt. Limited. The company was hoping to take advantage of the 950 million inhabitants of the country, 250 million of whom were considered middle class. It was estimated that if Kellogg's managed to capture even 2 percent of the market, it would be selling more volume than in the United States.

With an investment of US$20 million, Kellogg set up its 30th manufacturing facility in India. The Indian market was considered important for the company, as it was experiencing stagnating sales in the United States, and only regular price increases had helped boost the revenues in the 1990s. However, within a year, the company realized that it was not going to be smooth sailing, though it would not be correct to call Kellogg's a failure in India. A Centre for Monitoring Indian Economy (CMIE) report suggested that breakfast cereal consumption in the country had increased to 4,380 tons in 1999 to 2000, from 1,090 tons in 1994–1995. And Kellogg's enjoyed a substantial 65 percent share of the market. In fact, Kellogg's advertising and promotional activities have been touted as the primary reasons for the extraordinary growth rate of this market.

The company managed to capture a 60 percent share (or US$2.2 million) in its very first year of operation (this on an investment of US$18 million at its Taloja plant). But this performance could not be termed a resounding success, as the market size remained abysmally small, at an annual 1,000-odd tons. Further, growth in volumes reported a sharp fall, from 50 to 70 percent, since launch (admittedly on a small base) to just 6 percent in 1999 to 2000.

In 2001, the annual losses of the company were estimated to be about US$2.6 million, and the Taloja plant was running at just 15 percent capacity. To make matters worse, the company faced a global slowdown, and they could no longer give its Indian subsidiary time to break even. So what really went wrong?

Kellogg's was faced with the tough task of changing the ingrained eating habits of Indians. However, in its effort toward this end, executives at the company overlooked the importance of taking into account the values and culture of the country before formulating a strategy for its products. Some of the key reasons for the company's poor perfromance included the fact that there was a basic difference between the way corn flakes were consumed in the West and in India. Whereas in the West people preferred to have corn flakes with cold milk, in India people preferred to have it with warm milk. The company had failed to take account of this and thus, the product was not changed accordingly. On mixing with hot milk, the cornflakes lost their crispiness and turned soggy, just like the cheaper varieties.

Price was another key element that the company failed to get right. When its products were launched, in 1994, Kellogg's cost nearly twice the price of its sole domestic rival: Mohan Meakin's Mohun brand of cereals. While a 450-gram pack of Kellogg's cost US$1.58, a 500-gram pack of Mohun's cost US$.83. The 500-gram pack of Kellogg's, introduced in 1996, carried a sticker price of US$2.00. If a family of four had the cornflakes for breakfast every day, one pack would not last for more than a few days.

However, Kellogg's explained that the premium was the price of providing an international quality product—as compared to the local competition, the cornflakes were thicker and crisper. The cornflakes also came in expensive packaging, which, according to Kellogg's, kept its flakes extra crisp. Packaging constituted 45 percent of the product cost in the early days.

Another issue was that the taste of the flakes was not changed to be better suited to the Indian palate. To cut the blandness caused by the fortification with iron and other minerals, Kellogg's cereal required some sugar. However, most Indians prefer a savory rather than a sweet breakfast. Apart from the taste, Indian's breakfast habit was a big hurdle. While in most countries where Kellogg's was present, eating habits were largely uniform, in India, they varied with almost every region. For instance, breakfast dishes in south India are very different from those preferred in the northern part of the country. Further, these dishes were considered more filling compared to the crispy cereals. Indians typically treat breakfast as a lunchlike meal.

Most of its early customers were first-time experimenters; the proportion of regular customers was very low. Failing to realize this, the company accelerated its roll-out plans to 60 cities. Again, the company took a long time to realize that its advertisements should be focused on kids rather than housewives. However, even then, there was nothing really exciting about the product, so as to attract children. Kellogg's managed to generate some interest among this segment only when the Chocos range of chocolate flakes and biscuits were introduced.

Further, the company's attempt to localize its products seemed rather forced rather than well researched. For instance, in 1998, the company launched its Mazza line of cornflakes, in three flavors—mango-elaichi, coconut-kesar, and rose. However, the company discontinued this range, as the flavors seemed very outlandish for breakfast cereals. Unfortunately for Kellogg's, Mohan Meakins took advantage of its efforts by exploiting the market created by Kellogg's. Mohan Meakins spruced up its brands packaging and increased its availability on the retail shelves. As it was cheaper, consumers converting to cornflakes tended to buy Mohun's instead of Kellogg's.

Kellogg's serves as a good example of managers mistaking globalization for homogenization. The company felt it had no reason to change a product that had become so popular in the West. They also overlooked some basic customs and observations regarding Indian consumers and their habits. The company turned to other avenues with the stagnation of the corn flakes market. They ventured into snacks with their Cheez-Its brand, and also launched the Chocos brand of biscuits. However, both measures failed to achieve the desired results. Chocos started out being very popular among children, but eventually it faded out, and in 2003 the company decided to discontinue it. Kellogg's also tried to overcome the price barrier by introducing smaller packets.

In its promotional efforts, the company started incorporating more of the local language in its communication. The "Dimaag Chalega Nahin Daudega" (for enhanced mental capabilities) campaign did meet with some success. They also started referring to the product as having "Iron Shakti" in order to reiterate that it was fortified with iron.

Kellogg's Indian story is still far from being termed a success. The company has realized its past mistakes and is looking to rectify them. After all, Kellogg's has been in difficult situations earlier; it took over two decades to break even in countries like France and Mexico, both of which had very different breakfast habits from cornflakes and milk, as in India.

But not everybody can rectify mistakes. It really is difficult matching Indian tastes. Ask Blue Bunny, Wells' Dairy's ice-cream brand that came to India in 1999. After a test launch in Delhi, it launched outlets in Chandigarh, Ludhiana, Mumbai, Surat, and Ahmedabad. Sno Shack Frozen Foods imported and marketed the ice cream.

The company was interested in a long-term presence. Within the first year the firm had 50 outlets in Delhi. From April 1999 to July 1999 it had sales of INR 5,000,000. The pricing premium its products carried meant Blue Bunny could open outlets only at selected locations. Sixty-nine percent of its cost price was duties. It still targeted a turnover of US$1 million by the end of the 2000, and targeted a market-share of 3 to 4 percent by the same period. "This is our long term plan and we do not intend having more than two parlors in each metro" G. S. Malik, CEO, Sno Shack Holdings Ltd., stated.

"India will be our largest export market. We have the right product and right people in place and a market which is ready for us," stated Dan Duran, international sales manager, Wells Dairy. But Blue Bunny prices were almost 30 to 40 percent more than most brands. The firm dismissed manufacturing in India as an option, saying that maintaining the same quality would mean importing many of the ingredients, which would bring little change in prices. The firm even opened an exclusive chain for its "imported" American ice creams to cash in on the Diwali season in India.

But 4 years after its test launch, Blue Bunny had to exit the country. From 2001 to 2002, it recorded a turnover of US$350,000. The company had had enough of costs that did not budge and a limited market of six to seven metro areas. The marketing initiatives of Sno Shack Frozen Foods were also limited. Labeling problems, regulatory issues, and steep excise duties were thought to be the reasons behind its departure. In July 2002, it closed its shop.

McDonald's India is a joint venture that is managed by Indians with complete operational flexibility. The India team has brought local knowledge into the fold. Many products from McDonald's global menu have been adapted for India; it does not offer any beef and pork items in the country. In effect, it has reengineered its operations to address the special requirements of a vegetarian menu. Interestingly, vegetarian product development for India has become a source for vegetarian items for McDonald's worldwide.

Moral of the Story: Matching Indian tastes and preferences is of utmost importance. This is the reason why Hyundai, McDonald's, and Domino's are household names now. If you are an FTV, chances are you will be barred from broadcasting in India. Don't sell rugby balls in India—Indans are not intrinsically motivated to play physically hard—give them chess—match their tastes! If you are a restaurant owner, remember: You need to have a couple of super spicy dishes. If you are a Pizza Hut, don't forget adding a couple of cottage cheese pizzas to your menu.

While the challenges in various emerging markets are many, the business opportunities are undeniable. Consumers in emerging markets are becoming more sophisticated and demanding. The competition to develop products and services that meet those needs, by manufacturers from the developed as well as emerging economies, is now fierce. In competing for the Indian market, the auto manufacturer, Hyundai Motor Company of South Korea, adjusted its design so that women wearing traditional Indian dresses could get in and out of the car more easily. Procter & Gamble now spends 30 percent of its US$2.15 billion R&D budget on developing products for low-income consumers, with laboratories that recreate the temperature and humidity conditions in Mexico, India, and China.

At the dawn of 1994, Germany's Bayerische Motoren-Werke (BMW) entered into an agreement with leading Indian motorcycle and bicycle manufacturer Hero group. According to the JV, Hero group was responsible for assembling BMW's single-cylinder motorcycle F650, or Funduro, in India and will roll out 600 such bikes a year. The motorcycle used to be the third-highest-selling motorcycle in Germany. In one year of its introduction, BMW had produced 11,000 units of the bike. "We are convinced that by working together we shall be able to open a new and promising market in India for larger-engined motorcycles," W. Hasselkus, then president of BMW's motorcycle division, stated at the signing of the memorandum of understanding with Hero. The bike was believed to add US$9.5 million worth of sales.

Motorcycles were a burgeoning market in India at that time. Sales had literally doubled, from 1 million in the 1980s to 2 million in 1994. The automobile market had recently been deregulated. But not all opportunities lead to success; it would have been very difficult for such heavy bikes, with a naturally higher price tag, to find buyers in India then.

Hero started converting semiknocked-down (SKD) kits in September 1995. BMW's entry into India was now complete. The bikes were introduced to India in the same year in November. BMW supplied all of the bikes' parts, and Hero assembled them. The arrangement helped BMW to also assess the quality of auto parts supplied by Indian suppliers. If the quality happened to be good, BMW would not only use India-made components, but might have also used India as a sourcing hub for production in Europe.

Later in 1995, the Hero-BMW relationship went to a different level. They now started developing a blueprint for jointly producing cars for India. Manufacturing plans for 5,000 luxury cars in 1996 and 1997 and 10,000 in 1998 were also in the pipeline. In April 1996, they announced that the new JV was all set to make cars and would involve an INR 2.7 billion investment. BMW was slated to control 51 percent in the venture and the balance by the Munjal family-owned Hero group. BMW and Hero identified a plant site and set the initial capacity of the plant at 10,000 cars. The "Five" series of BMW was lined up to be the first model. This was at a time when Fiat, Peugeot, Opel, and Mercedes Benz had already entered India. The JV also had intentions to make Britain's Rover range. In July 1996 the Indian government's Foreign Investment Promotion Board (FIPB) approved 84 foreign investments with a total value of US$600 million. Among the investments approved was BMW's joint venture with Hero to manufacture their cars.

But after a slight economic downturn in 1998, BMW got restless. At the beginning of the year, BMW reduced its equity exposure in the auto joint venture from 51 percent to 50 percent. For many, this step killed doubts that the JV was in danger, but for many, the joint venture's death seemed imminent. BMW had earlier decided to debut with the less-costly 3-series range instead of the 5-series. In 1998 newspapers disclosed BMW's decision to put off the car-manufacturing JV. It wanted the economy to recover first. "The joint venture with BMW for manufacture of premium cars is pending at present. However, the proposal will be taken up once the economy recovers and the market for premium cars opens up," Munjal group chairman Brijhmohan Lall Munjal said.

What accompanied this shutdown was the annulment of the BMW-Hero bike revival plan. The Munjal family had earlier exhibited all the interest necessary to keep the Indian media from asking about the future of the bike joint venture. Low sales figures and logistic issues were dismissed as causes by the Munjal family for a possible break-up of the arrangement. Failure to assess the market intelligently (both in car and power bike segment) and an inability to create a contingency plan in case of economic problems cost BMW dearly.

China-based consumer electronics enterprise Konka entered the Indian market in 1999. Konka Electronics India Co Ltd. (KEIL) was jointly established by Konka Group, Hong Kong, and Indian firm Hotline. It was among the first holding companies that Konka Group had established abroad. In its total investment of US$9 million, Konka Group held 51 percent, with the rest coming from Indian television components manufacturer Hotline and Hong Kong-based Wittis. It planned to produce and sell Konka color TVs, refrigerators, VCDs, DVDs and other communication products. It started off optimistically, targeting a production of 300,000 color TV sets in the calendar year 2000 to 2001.

The company relied on aggressive marketing of its low-cost, Chinese-made products to tap the large Indian demand. From June

1999 to June 2000, Konka targeted a turnover of US$52.37 million. "We hope to break even with a US$52.37 million sales turnover within the first year of operations in India," Konka India's chief Rajeev Puri, had said. Konka believed that Korean brands LG and Samsung and Japanese major Sony and European brands like Thomson would not pose a threat because of Konka's distinctive cost advantages. Konka wanted India to be their export hub for west Asia, and because of this it was willing to dish out US$125 million. US$125,000 was earmarked for promotional activities. US$34.5 million were set aside to set up a television manufacturing plant in Greater Noida, near New Delhi.

Konka wanted to be listed on Indian stock exchanges. But it received a surprise when it split with its Indian partner, Hotline. Hotline withdrew from the joint venture on allegations of not being given enough power in the relationship. This meant it had to get approvals from FIPB all over again. "After Hotline withdrew from the JV we had to apply for a fresh FIPB nod and this took over two months, delaying both our product launches as well as further investment plans," stated managing director of Konka India Ronald Zhang. "The joint venture was short lived because of the differences with the partners, as Konka wanted majority control," *Business Standard* quoted an employee. The color TVs that were slated to reach the market by December 1999 were delayed to June 2000. Konka started working as a completely owned subsidiary in September 1999.

The Chinese-made TVs, which were supposed to woo Indians because of their cost advantages, could not. High import duties meant they could not price the products lower. Konka could only sell 60,000 color television (CTV) sets during the financial year 2000–2001. Its market share hovered around 1 percent in a market whose size was pegged at 5 million. "We have not been aggressive in implementing a proper marketing strategy," KEIL's MD had said. Konka had tested three different suppliers for marketing in the last 2 years. The broken engagement with Hotline, which supplied picture tubes, had also affected the supply chain. Huge investments—coupled with extremely low returns left Konka with no other option but to say bye-bye to India.

In fact, the Indian Hotline group might just be jinxed. Its joint venture with China-based kitchen appliance-maker major Haier also met a similar fate. The Hotline group entered the joint venture with Haier in the latter half of 1999. As per the arrangement, Hotline held 70 percent of the US$10 million initial paid-up capital. Hotline Haier Appliances Ltd. (HHAL) planned to manufacture kitchen appliances first and then gradually shift to CTVs. FIPB approved HHAL's move to manufacture home appliances. Haier brought an FDI of US$3 million. But within a year the JV ran into rough waters, as arguments started over Hotline's insistence on setting up a manufacturing base in India. Hotline had outlined this as a stipulation for entering the JV. Haier wanted Hotline to import its products from China and market them in India. The resultant import duty charges would have severely affected Hotline's revenues. "Contentious issues need to be sorted out before any further progress is made in the businesses of the joint venture," Hotline chairman Anil Gupta remarked. By the time this issue cropped up, HHAL had already acquired land in Greater Noida, near Delhi.

In September 2000, Hotline decided it had had enough. Allegedly, Haier did not invest even a penny of the US$30 million funds promised. Haier accepted Hotline's decision not to continue the relationship. Interestingly, when Haier reentered the Indian market in 2004, it could not evade Hotline. Haier awarded a contract to Dixon to produce CTVs, which Dixon promptly subcontracted to Hotline! "I am a businessman. I have to look out for business. I do not mind if they come with a clean deal. In this case anyway, they have not come to us directly," Gupta said.

But amid all the hype, it is pertinent to ask whether India is really ready to play a pivotal role in the global economy. Instead of going through a proverbial list of strengths and weaknesses, it is useful to pose the question a little differently: Does India have the mindset it needs to be a player in a globally integrated economy? A national mindset is, at best, an amorphous concept. But it does seem that there are times when a nation feels confident that it can take on the world. It is this very spirit that built the Pudong city at Shanghai. And it is the same spirit that is instrumental for the development of the world-class, on-time New Delhi Metro.

Moral of the Story: Changes will happen, although gradually. Firms will need to persist, as both the Indian government and Indian consumers are not rigid. FDI regulations, entry norms, minimum investment limits: the stranglehold will gradually be eased. A case in point is the retail sector, where initial opposition to any FDI has now changed to open entry for all single-branded products.

While Indians can be inductive in their approach to understanding things—something that might irk their friends from the West, who follow a deductive approach—in the Indian psyche, reality can be understood only in its overall context. One needs to be prepared for questions and enquiries that may not seem to be directly related to the subject. Knowing the personal and social contexts of people and ideas is a precondition set by Indians for comprehending people accurately. In general, Indians are very thorough in accepting a new idea or proposal. Openness to a new idea depends not only on its quality, but also on its source and endorsement. That is, information about whom else has implemented it and who has proposed it has a major influence on the decision-making process. This is not only because of the bureaucratic nature of many Indian organizations, but also because a decision may have to be ratified by people who may not be present at the negotiations. Thus, decision making in Indian organizations may become a long, drawn-out process, but with so many heads slicing, dicing, and dissecting, the head often finds the nail.

In some ways, India is well prepared to be a global hub. It has a multicultural society with a vibrant democracy and a free press, and this reflects a willingness to assimilate and to work with foreign influences, in the broadest sense of the term. Some of India's corporations also demonstrate this readiness. The global expansion of the Ispat Group reflects the emergence of Indian multinationals. But it isn't just large corporations that are spanning borders—technology has made it possible for small firms to do so as well.

I would like to leave the readers with a simple tip: To really blend into Indian culture, one must learn to live with shades of grey (not white and black), accept the foibles and inadequacies of the general population, which is moving in the right direction, understand and empathize with the complexity and sensitivity of the Indian psyche, and empathize with a fast-changing yet young mindset, which could once in a while stumble!

CONCLUSION

THE TIGER BEGINS TO ROAR

A friend of mine once asked me if I thought emerging-market countries would ever truly emerge. It was a good question and one that I continue to give a lot of thought to, and basically my answer is *yes*. Emerging-market countries *can* become mature economies if the right conditions are met. Many of the large emerging-market countries, like China, Brazil, and Russia—and of course, India—have undergone dramatic transformations in a relatively short period of time. Brazil was ruled by a military dictatorship until the late 1980s, and had a closed economy. China began to open up its economy around the same time, and Russia was ruled by a communist dictatorship with a command economy until only a few years after that. Today the Chinese economy is the second largest in the world, Brazil has a vibrant democracy with open markets, and Russia is experiencing robust economic growth. However, I continue to believe that for a country to reach the full measure of its economic and social potential it must have a transparent political system that encourages debate and dissent.

That political system must be beholden to the will of the people, with full protection of the people's rights and liberty.

If, as in the case of China, a country attempts to enact free-market reforms while at the same time maintaining an authoritarian regime that is not transparent and that does not guarantee full protection of the people's rights and liberty, economic and social distortions are bound to occur. At the economic level, these distortions can be seen in a number of ways. Private companies are forced to compete with state-owned companies or favored multinationals for capital and other resources, with the state being the final arbitrator. Capital tends to gravitate to those individuals who are connected to or favored by the state, not necessarily to those who are most capable (of the 20,000 richest men in China, over 95 percent are directly related to Communist Party officials). And the government tends to protect inefficient state-owned companies—in some cases, dangerous ones, like the Chinese mining industry—as a direct result of corruption. Chinese mines are considered to be some of the most dangerous in the world, with hundreds of workplace deaths being reported annually.

At the economic policy level, the Chinese government, using its unchallenged control over the economy, can manipulate investments, capital markets, and the currency. Free from debate, economic viability, the rule of law, or even a sense of fair play, the Chinese government can build airports that have no passenger traffic, office buildings without tenants, and roads that have no cars. Having control over their capital markets, with no credible independent oversight, allows the government to pick and choose which companies will become public, often using its capital markets to salvage mismanaged state-owned companies. However, the economic policy that is having the greatest negative impact on other economies is China's use of currency manipulation to bolster its exports. It is true that other countries like South Korea, Taiwan, and Japan are also benefiting from the undervalued Chinese currency by moving their manufacturing bases to that country. However, it is the other developing countries, like India and Brazil, that are paying the true price. India and Brazil, like most democratic countries, both maintain transparent free markets and both have seen their respective currencies appreciate significantly over the past year, often to the detriment of their own domestic manufacturers and trade balances. When I recently spoke with the chairman of a leading Indian pharmaceutical company, he voiced his amazement and frustration at what he called a completely unrealistic pricing strategy by Chinese pharmaceutical companies, coupled with an undervalued currency. The economic distortions in the Chinese economy are beginning to become evident, with more than US$1 trillion in foreign currency reserves, a currency that is 40 percent undervalued, domestic manufacturers operating on razor-thin margins, and an extremely volatile stock market.

The distortions in Chinese society are also becoming evident. Each year thousands of farmers are forced from their land by corrupt local officials, with little or no compensation. Journalists who dig too deep in exposing corruption or malfeasance are either jailed or censored. Intellectual property rights and patent protection laws continue to be ignored by the government, causing billions of dollars in losses for legitimate companies. Pollution and environmental degradation continue to grow, with no real legal recourse by the populace. And the income gap is continuing to widen between 750 million landless peasants and a growing upper class that is concentrated along China's coast. Democracy on its own will not ensure transparency within the government, or for that matter, the elimination of corruption. However, it does tend to bring important issues into the light of day, and over time the key attributes that are critical in creating a more equitable society do tend to blossom.

The value of democracy may have been best articulated by Professor Ashu Varshney. He stated that, "We really do not know what is going to happen to China. The Soviet Union imploded,

Korea and Taiwan went from authoritarian regimes to democracies, but they always had strong opposition parties, even when they were authoritarian regimes. What will happen in China when the rising expectations of 800 to 900 million people, who have not benefited from the economic boom, outpace what the government is willing to give up?"

That is why I believe that the real success story will be India—a country that, like other big emerging markets, only recently began to dismantle a disastrous command economy that was virtually closed to the outside world less than 20 years ago. When you think about India, imagine a boulder. When you first attempt to move a boulder it will not budge. Then, after some time, you begin to rock it back and forth, slowly gaining some forward momentum. At a certain point the boulder will begin to roll—slowly at first, but continuously gaining speed. Before you know it it's not possible to stop the boulder, and the path it takes can no longer be influenced by external forces. India is like a boulder: For many years the economy remained stagnant and resistant to change, stifled under the misguided direction of a socialist government and a command economy—but now it's starting to move.

In the early 1990s a new class of Indian entrepreneurs, many of whom had honed their skills in Silicon Valley, began to push the boulder. At first the change was difficult to gauge, with many entrenched interests within the government fiercely resisting a new direction for the economy and the country. But India's entrepreneurs continued to push, and they were soon joined by a new breed of forward-thinking politicians. By the year 2000 India had entered a new phase of economic development, with companies like Infosys, Ranbaxy, and many others developing global leadership positions. The boulder had begun to roll, and as it did, many Indian professionals who had developed successful careers abroad decided to return home.

The tipping point may have come sometime in 2005, when the media began to pick up on the Indian economy. That media coverage began to increase, and the international business community began to take notice as well. At first, much of the press coverage was negative, often focusing on India's dilapidated infrastructure or Hindu nationalism. Other writers focused on the "strange rise of India," questioning how India could develop world-class IT and BPO sectors without first developing the more basic manufacturing sectors.

I believe that many of these writers missed the point by looking to the past and not to the future. There was nothing strange about the development of India's IT and BPO sector. Those sectors developed first because they were not beholden to the legacy of the license Raj and they had the dual benefits of a large U.S. customer base and the cross-pollination of entrepreneurs from Silicon Valley. It is also important to note that economic development and the transitioning of a country from an agrarian-based society to an industrial based society is quite different now than it was one hundred years ago. One obvious difference is technology. In many instances it takes far less manpower to produce the equivalent product today than it did even 30 years ago. A perfect example is the U.S. steel industry, which produces more steel now than it did 30 years ago with approximately half the workforce. A second key difference is information technology, which will tend to mitigate the large-scale migration to urban centers by the rural population that was a hallmark of the old industrial era.

The poor infrastructure that is so often highlighted by the press is now being modernized at an incredible pace. The Indian government, unlike the government of China, which does not have to deal with environmental lawsuits or the rights of individuals who might be affected by this change, is driving this modernization in a democratic manner. In many cases this democratic process will slow the completion of certain infrastructure projects, and in others it will force modifications. In the long term, however, India's entrenched democracy will help create a more equitable society. Evidence of that is already being seen with the recent state elections in Uttar Pradesh (UP).

An unprecedented coalition of rich and poor came together to win the election. They had a shared common interest in wanting to see economic prosperity for their families and society, and that trumped any type of caste or other ethnic differences.

India is now at the beginning of what may be the most amazing transformation of a free market economy in modern history. Resistance to free markets and economic development has disappeared, and Indian citizens who were openly pessimistic about the virtues of free markets have now embraced them. It wasn't so long ago that Indians weren't willing to pay for parking, and certainly not for a toll road—both of which are now a permanent part of the Indian landscape. And even the most ardent socialists within the government now talk glowingly about new infrastructure projects.

While the Indian economy is projected to grow at 9 percent over the coming years, that may in fact be a conservative estimate. Very little analysis has been done on the impact that the sale of private property will have in India. Private property rights, especially in the rural areas of the country, will give India a distinct edge over China, and when that untapped wealth is unleashed the results will be amazing. The value of those holdings could exceed US$3 trillion, and that doesn't even take into account the multiplier effect that capital could have on the Indian economy.

India is a country of entrepreneurs, often called a country of shopkeepers, but that spirit is not limited to the IT and BPO sectors. There can be no doubt that the development of other sectors, like high-tech manufacturing and pharmaceuticals, will create significant benefits for the Indian economy and society in the form of jobs and economic growth. But what will really give the Indian economy and society a strategic boost is the fact that such a large portion of the populace are natural entrepreneurs. The key component to unleashing this vast entrepreneurial potential will be education. Without a massive investment in education, by both the public and private sector, India will fail to realize its true potential as a global economic power with a concurrently high standard of living for the populace. If India's citizens have access to high-quality education that encompasses the full spectrum of professions and trades, the true capabilities of India will be unleashed. Providing the quality education required to a population that currently has a literacy rate that is less than 60 percent will not be an easy task. However, the partnership that has been created between the Indian government and private enterprise for infrastructure development could be replicated for education.

Education is highly valued in Indian society, and with access to quality education that includes skilled vocational trades such as electricians, auto mechanics, plumbers, welders, and others, a much larger percentage of the Indian population will be able to have a productive and meaningful livelihood. An educated and informed populace also tends to ensure that public institutions and officials deliver more than rhetoric. Investments in education by both the private and public sector have already begun in earnest in India, and my expectation is that this process will accelerate as both groups realize the benefits of partnering.

An educated and entrepreneurial populace combined with an entrenched democracy will create the foundation for what may be the greatest economic and social success story of modern history. The boulder is rolling, and the story of New India is already being written. Do we really believe that democracy and free markets are a fundamental part of the human condition, or do we believe that democracy is for a privileged few? The conclusion to the story of New India may ultimately decide that verdict.

ACKNOWLEDGMENTS

Writing a book about the New India is a difficult task at best. India is an incredibly complex country, and the changes taking place at all levels of the society and economy are so dynamic that it is impossible to capture all of it in a single book. We were fortunate to have the support and guidance of many individuals who are at the forefront of the New India, and perhaps more importantly, are at the forefront of a more equitable global society. A few individuals must be singled out for special thanks; among them is our good friend and mentor Dr. Marvin Zonis, without whose help and guidance this book would have never been written. There are thousands, if not millions, of leaders in the New India, among them Luis Miranda, the president and founder of the IDFC Private Equity. He was gracious enough to give us unparalleled access to his organization, and in doing so we were able to develop a clearer understanding of the radical transformation that is occurring within India's infrastructure, which impelled us to write a whole chapter—"The Road Less Traveled." Our conversations with Jerry Rao, the president and founder of Mphasis, were equally enlightening; with his passion for history and the Indian people, Jerry is far more than just a successful Indian entrepreneur. On a similar note, G. M. Rao, the chairman and founder of the GMR Group, gave us insights into the subtleties of Indian humor and the team-oriented nature of successful Indian corporations. Many others, such as K. K. Agarwal of Delhi Assam Roadways, were gracious enough to invite us to meet their families, and in doing so we gained an understanding of the strengths of the Indian family-owned business. Time and time again we were able to witness the unique nature of the Indian entrepreneur, which exists at all levels of the Indian economy. Raghav Bahl, the founder of TV18, helped us capture the full magnitude of that entrepreneurial spirit and what it will mean for the Indian economy going forward.

So many other people shared with us their valuable time and commented on different parts of the book. We want to thank in particular Haresh Chawla, Sucheta Dalal, Nandan Nilekani, C. K. Prahalad, PhD, Gurcharan Das, Suresh Prabhu, Ashutosh Varshney, PhD, Susan Rudolph, PhD, Lloyd I. Rudolph, PhD, Mathew Rudolph, PhD, Ashu Varshney, PhD, Abhirup Sarkar, PhD, Saurabh Gupta, Ankit Sarwahi, Zhang Xiaobo, Che Jia Hua, Yingyi Qian, Kaavya Kasturirangan, Ratul Puri, Vijay Anand, A. Ramakrishna, Puneet Agarwal, Dipesh Garg, Vijay Vancheswar, S. K. Kulkarni, Ravi Shankar, Vinod Giri, Haresh Chawla, Maj. Gen. Anil Sawhny, Manu Anand, Ajit Kapadia, Pramit Jhaeri, Ravi Narain, G. V. Prasad, Nasra Roy, Shivani Bhasin, Ved Mani Tiwari, Shravan Tripathi, and Gaurav Gupta. No project can be completed without a good team, and we were fortunate enough to have the best team of researchers in the business. They have treaded through long nights, conducting rigorous data analysis, and have provided a solid platform for us to build our story on. Thanks go out to Ruminder Dhillon, project manager; Harminder Singh, for his thoughtful leadership; Ankit Sarwahi, chief research analyst; Bhanu Pratap Sharma and Tanushree Chatterjee, for their editorial support; and Anubha Suri, for identifying the fine examples of India's next wave.

A personal note of love goes to my wife Carla (Rio), who is my true partner in life: She is my constant source of inspiration, perseverance, and happiness. And to my son Devon, who always spent time with me in my office, cheering me on and reminding me what is truly important in life. I consider myself blessed to have such a wonderful family.

William Nobrega

To my wife, Shubhra, for her immeasurable patience, and my sons, Kayvan and Kyran, for giving me a purpose in life.

Ashish Sinha

INDEX